THE
UNIDENTIFIED

ALSO BY COLIN DICKEY

GHOSTLAND

THE
UNIDENTIFIED

MYTHICAL MONSTERS,
ALIEN ENCOUNTERS,
AND OUR OBSESSION WITH
THE UNEXPLAINED

COLIN DICKEY

VIKING

VIKING
An imprint of Penguin Random House LLC
penguinrandomhouse.com

LIBRARY OF CONGRESS CATALOGING-IN-PUBLICATION DATA

Names: Dickey, Colin, author.
Title: The unidentified : mythical monsters, alien encounters,
and our obsession with the unexplained / Colin Dickey.
Description: New York: Viking, 2020. | Includes bibliographical references.
Identifiers: LCCN 2019043380 (print) | LCCN 2019043381 (ebook) |
ISBN 9780525557562 (hardcover) | ISBN 9780525557579 (ebook) |
Subjects: LCSH: Occultism. | Parapsychology.
Classification: LCC BF1411 .D525 2020 (print) | LCC BF1411 (ebook) |
DDC 130—dc23
LC record available at https://lccn.loc.gov/2019043380
LC ebook record available at https://lccn.loc.gov/2019043381

Printed in the United States of America
1   3   5   7   9   10   8   6   4   2

BOOK DESIGN BY LUCIA BERNARD

In Memory of Audrey F. Dickey

It is simple enough to apply reason to what
is reasonable, but it is much more difficult to
argue logically about the illogical.

—JOHN NAPIER,
Bigfoot: The Yeti and Sasquatch in Myth and Reality

●   ●   ●

If a man will begin with certainties, he shall
end in doubts; but if he will be content to begin
with doubts, he shall end in certainties.

—FRANCIS BACON,
The Advancement of Learning

CONTENTS

INTRODUCTION: THE FIRE

History operates behind our backs.

—STEPHEN ERIC BRONNER

June 1996, and the United States was on edge. A year after Timothy McVeigh had bombed the Alfred P. Murrah Building in Oklahoma City, the country watched anxiously as a standoff between the FBI and a militia group unfolded in Jordan, Montana. The Montana Freemen had declared themselves a sovereign township outside the reach of US law, had stopped paying taxes, and had embarked on a massive scheme of counterfeiting and bank fraud. When the FBI attempted to arrest them in March, they grabbed their weapons, and the Feds, eager to avoid the bloodshed that ended similar standoffs at Ruby Ridge, Idaho, and Waco, Texas, settled in for a long siege. During the second month, news broke that another Montanan—Ted Kaczynski, the Unabomber—had been caught and charged with a series of bombings he'd carried out over the course of seventeen years. Then on June 14, the same day that the last of the Montana Freemen surrendered peacefully to authorities, police in Long Island, New York, arrested yet another group of dangerous men, revealing a plot far stranger than anything the country had yet seen.

Martin Thompson, the head of Rackets for the Suffolk County's District Attorney's office, had been leading an investigation into illegal gun sales when he first learned of the plan. Listening to a wiretap of two suspects, John J. Ford and Joe Mazzuchelli, he suddenly found them talking about something very different than guns.

"Once they find this stuff on, let's say in Tony's car, front seat," Ford is heard saying on the tape, only to be cut off by Mazzuchelli, who chimes in, "Nasty bastard glowing in the dark." Ford adds, "With this isotope, he'll start glowing in twenty-four hours." Thompson and his team had stumbled on a deeply bizarre assassination plot, one involving stolen radium, a forest fire, and a UFO cover-up.

In addition to stockpiling a large cache of weapons, John J. Ford was the president of the Long Island branch of the Mutual UFO Network, or MUFON, a collection of UFO enthusiasts who investigated sightings in an attempt to finally prove that extraterrestrials existed and had visited Earth. MUFON members are not, by nature, violent: most see their job as simply gathering evidence, as objectively and dispassionately as possible, in hopes that eventually there'll be a documented, undeniable sighting of some kind.

But Ford was not like the typical UFO researcher. He claimed he had been recruited by the CIA when he was eighteen, and had routinely participated in clandestine operations against the Soviet Union. The KGB, he claimed, had tried and failed five times to kill him, and they'd given him the nickname "the Fox," due to his wily nature. But by the mid-1990s, things had taken a turn for Ford: he injured himself on the job and had to retire, and his mother died, an event that, friends said, affected him deeply. And then there was the forest fire.

The blaze that swept through Long Island's Pine Barrens in 1995 was large enough that the smoke was visible from Manhattan, some seventy-five miles away, ultimately scorching seven thousand acres. Over time, Ford became convinced that the fire was, in fact, caused by a UFO crash, and that the Suffolk County Board was involved in a large-scale cover-up. He felt that the only way to get answers was by taking control of the government himself, and he began conspiring with Mazzuchelli and another man, Edward Zabo, to kill three county officials using stolen radium. Zabo, deeply in debt, agreed to provide the radium that Mazzuchelli, himself an ex-con, would plant in the men's homes. At a press conference the day of the arrest, Suffolk County district attorney James M. Catterson stood before Ford's extensive collection of weapons spread out before the podium and explained that when he'd first heard of the plot, "the idea that someone would attempt to introduce radioactive material into someone's food or someone's living area at first seemed so bizarre that there's a human tendency to discount it. It didn't take very long to realize that this was some of our worst nightmares come true."

•   •   •

The past few years have revealed to us that such fringe beliefs and conspiracy theories are becoming more prevalent, and they're becoming more consequential. Belief in fringe topics like Atlantis, or cryptids (Bigfoot, the Loch Ness Monster, and other associated "hidden" animals), or UFOs, or ancient aliens has risen drastically in the last few years. For several years Chapman University has surveyed Americans' fears and irrational beliefs, including beliefs about aliens, cryptids, and lost civilizations. In some cases, the numbers have been steadily creeping upward: belief in Bigfoot has moved from 11 percent in 2015 to 21 percent in 2018. The belief that aliens have visited Earth during modern times went from 18 percent to 26 percent in 2016 and then rose to 35 percent in 2018; the belief that aliens have visited Earth in the distant past, meanwhile, has more than doubled from 20 percent in 2015 to 41 percent in 2018. And the belief that "Ancient Civilizations Such as Atlantis Existed" likewise shot up from 39 percent in 2016 to 57 percent in 2018.

We are, in other words, experiencing a time of resurgence of fringe beliefs, when ideas mostly dismissed by science are being embraced and are spreading throughout popular culture. Alongside a rise in conspiracy theories about vaccines, water fluoridation, and chemtrails, and political conspiracies from the Illuminati to *The Protocols of the Elders of Zion*, we are more and more ignoring "experts" and embracing the kinds of beliefs that were once relegated to cults.

As for Ford's little cult: both Mazzuchelli and Zabo turned on Ford in exchange for lesser sentences, and were sentenced to three years and one year in prison, respectively. Ford was pronounced unfit to stand trial and involuntarily committed to the Mid-Hudson Psychiatric Center in New Hampton, New York.

"Yes, this all sounds way out," District Attorney Catterson said of Ford's plot. "But when I read the Unabomber manifesto, some of his ideas were just as bizarre. That's why I take this and the imminent threat to the individuals concerned here very seriously." Recalling the World Trade Center bombings and Oklahoma City, Catterson commented, "This all convinces me that there is a side to humanity that defies definition."

Murder plots like Ford's are clearly the aberration in the world of UFO and cryptid enthusiasts, most of whom are normal, law-abiding folks. But there are shades of overlap between these searchers and the darker strands of conspiracy theory that have come to dominate the landscape of late. They share a similar distrust of established voices, be they scientific or governmental—a distrust that encompasses a spectrum from healthy skepticism to paranoia.

By themselves, these ideas don't necessarily breed paranoia or violent ideas. Much of what attracts people to these fringe beliefs is a belief in a world of wonder and marvel, a world outside the ken of humanity, a world just out of reach. But our fascination with things unexplained, our obsession with things hidden from view, our need to believe in monsters at the margin—these drives, through the decades, have contributed to a rising sentiment of distrust in science, in academic institutions, and in government. The toxic mélange of anti-vaxxers, school-shooting truthers, and right-wing militia groups didn't appear overnight; as long as there has been a scientific establishment, there's been distrust of that establishment, and as long as there have been democratic governments, there's been suspicion about what's really going on. The rise in our fascination with things like cryptids and UFOs offers one vector for explaining how we got to where we are today.

Why? How do such beliefs take root? Often, their genesis and evolution follows a fairly standard, almost predictable, pattern. Something genuinely anomalous or difficult to explain happens, and it's followed by increasingly elaborate explanations—explanations that are designed, ultimately, to resist positive or negative confirmation. The curious case of Erich von Däniken and his wildly successful "ancient alien" hypothesis offers a particularly paradigmatic example of how a fringe belief is structured.

It begins, as often as not, with legitimate science, and with a legitimate, unsolved question—in this case, the Fermi Paradox (named after nuclear physicist Enrico Fermi), which posited that, based on what we know about the size of the universe, the likely number of planets conducive to supporting life, and the statistical probability that a civilization like our own would develop, it seems inconceivable that we are the only advanced civilization in the universe. In 1950, at Los Alamos National Laboratory, Fermi was discussing extraterrestrials with a few other scientists when he asked, "Where is everybody?"

Since then, other scientists have worked to better understand this paradox; various mathematicians and astrophysicists have attempted to better understand the probability involved, the likelihood of another race capable of interstellar travel, and other aspects of the science involved. Then in 1963, a young assistant professor at Harvard named Carl Sagan authored a paper entitled "Direct Contact Among Galactic Civilizations by Relativistic Interstellar Spaceflight," which offered a highly provisional hypothesis that perhaps "Earth was visited by an advanced extraterrestrial civilization at least once during historical times." Sagan never did much to follow up on this article, or test this hypothesis, and gradually moved on to other questions of astronomy and physics.

But there were others who were less willing to let this idea go, among them, a hotel clerk and convicted fraud Erich von Däniken. Von Däniken had no formal science training, but he liked the idea that aliens had visited Earth in the distant past and that they may have left behind tangible clues and evidence. His 1968 book, *Chariots of the Gods?*, suggested that the Egyptian pyramids, the Moai statues of Easter Island, and

Stonehenge in England were all artifacts of previous contact between humanity and alien civilization. An instant bestseller, *Chariots of the Gods* (the book's title long ago lost its question mark) has spawned a seemingly endless series of follow-ups by von Däniken, who turned his idea into such an industry that he opened a theme park in Switzerland devoted to it.

Von Däniken's success came in part from his ability to start with legitimate gaps in our knowledge—the Fermi Paradox, as well as aspects of ancient culture that were still poorly understood by archaeologists and historians. Science, a fringe theorist argues, is too hidebound and self-satisfied to admit what it doesn't know and to entertain viable theories that may explain those gaps in scientific knowledge.

Accusing the scientific establishment of failing to address counter-evidence, the fringe theorist quickly begins to ignore any evidence that contradicts their own claim. From there, they magnify the supposed ignorance of science, arguing, for example, that Egyptologists don't know how or why the pyramids were built.

In fact, we have detailed records from the Egyptians themselves as to how they built the pyramids and what their function was. But this counterevidence is immaterial, as the main hypothesis grows exponentially to incorporate more and more evidence. Much of this is driven by what's sometimes called apophenia, the tendency to see shapes and patterns where none exist. This apophenic perception lies at the heart of many fringe beliefs and conspiracy theories—it is the idea that everything is, one way or another, connected.

A fringe belief like von Däniken's is an endless work in progress, constantly assembling new bits and pieces into an ever-expanding grand scheme. An associative process of connecting the dots, the belief spirals out: everything becomes further proof of a central, simplified claim. Stonehenge, Easter Island, the Nazca lines, Mayan iconography—all are the result of aliens, and all are mysteries "solved" by a single thesis that encompasses all of ancient religion, art, architecture, and mythology. It is a theory seductive in its simplicity, but lying behind it is a fair amount of cultural chauvinism: von Däniken and his adherents, it would seem, refuse to believe that ancient civilizations were intellectually sophisticated, that they could have created wondrous buildings or understood complicated math and astronomy without the help of some superintelligent alien race.

Rather than following established scientific protocol, the fringe theorist fills those gaps with shoddy research, question-begging, and the selective presentation of data. A theory like von Däniken's ancient aliens belief starts from a legitimate and fast-moving scientific debate, and then short-circuits this process, offering a romantic oversimplification. It seizes on the initial paradox, but then quickly abandons the rest of the scientific method. In lieu of careful reasoning, falsifiable claims, and the scientific method, von Däniken proposes instead a solution that cuts through the debate; defying acceptable scientific proof, it can be applied to an ever-expanding list of places and ideas. Though its inspiration is scientific, its adherents must denounce and ignore science in order to propagate the theory, particularly when it comes to rebuttals and attempts to disprove the theory—all the while maintaining a thin veneer of the aesthetics of rigorous discourse.

When archaeologists and sociologists set out to study their students' belief in the ancient-astronaut theory in the late 1970s and early '80s, they found that as many as 28 percent of incoming college students believed in theories similar to von Däniken's; more dismaying, that number stayed consistent between first-year students and seniors, and between those who'd taken archaeology classes and those who hadn't. Simply debunking these beliefs, it seems, is not in and of itself enough. Believers have ample means to confront the evidence disproving von Däniken's theories, and yet the belief continues to rise.

When I talk to people who believe that Lemuria or Atlantis is real, that Bigfoot or the Loch Ness Monster exists, or that the government is covering up information about UFOs, it's easy to hit a wall very quickly. Trying to disprove any of these beliefs—or really, any conspiracy—is frustrating and foolhardy. A scientific fact will quickly be refuted by a flurry of data, often from a wide range of sources; topics will change, and if you debunk one belief, another will quickly be brought up. Soon enough, it becomes apparent that what matters is not *what* this person believes but *that* the person believes: the belief itself is the badge, the identity, and the details of it are of minor consequence. These beliefs seem to satisfy the believers in some deep and pleasing way, and that pleasure is more important than their truth or falsity.

Rather than simply debunking these theories, it may be more important to understand their genealogy: where they come from and how they came to take root in popular culture. While they appear to be ancient, drawing on a history dating back to the writings of Plato and ancient hieroglyphics, they are all (unlike, say, the belief in ghosts or haunted houses) relatively new phenomenon, and they all emerge as a result of two great shocks that shook the nineteenth century: the divorce of science and religion, and the disenchanting of the world.

For most of the history of the Western world, science and religion had been linked. The study of the natural world, for ancient Greeks and medieval Christians, only magnified one's understanding of God. But the Protestant Reformation and the scientific revolution of the Enlightenment set in motion a series of events that would, by the early nineteenth century, result in a complete rupture of these two ideas: science and religion were now opposed rather than complementary. On top of this, the world of science changed. No longer was inquiry carried out by talented amateurs or gentlemanly explorers; with the rise of the various disciplines of science as discrete fields came the professionalization of a discipline that concentrated itself in universities, museums, and professional organizations. By the twentieth century, the days of the splendid savant were more or less gone.

Many of these fringe beliefs contain various attempts to order the natural world—many of them, in their dubious and idiosyncratic ways, are trying to articulate a language that can once again reconcile that sense that science and religion are opposed to each other. The allure of pseudoscience is in its claim to bring scientific inquiry and mysticism back into harmony, and it is a powerful allure.

Conspiracy theories and fringe beliefs get their start in scientific and cultural revolutions like this, as a reaction to startling and sweeping changes in how we see the world. At the same time, the world was becoming, as Max Weber famously put it, "disenchanted." In a 1917 article titled "Science as a Vocation," Weber explained that "the increasing intellectualization and rationalization" of the nineteenth and twentieth centuries implied that we could, at any point, understand anything in the natural world if we simply set our minds to it. Which meant, in turn, "that principally there are no mysterious incalculable forces that come into play, but rather that one can, in principle, master all things by calculation."

Weber gave a name to a growing feeling among many in the industrialized world: that there was no more magic, nothing anymore that was inexplicable or mysterious; any unknown, we now understood, could be deciphered and made sense given enough attention. There has been a feeling among some segment of the population—one that's not small and is actively growing—that this scientific disenchanting has cost us something, and they turn to fringe beliefs because it is in Atlantis and Bigfoot and little green men from outer space that they find the world once again reenchanted.

Behind many of these beliefs, then, is what the writer Svetlana Boym once called the off-modern: a nostalgic reaction to the twentieth century's narrative of boldly going forward into the future, a reaction that was about exploring "sideshadows and back alleys rather than the straight road of progress." Even the most futuristic and far-fetched narratives about aliens and flying saucers, it turns out, are motivated as much by a fear over the future as anything else.

By the twentieth century, much of the world's borders had evaporated, its frontiers obliterated. As colonialism and capitalism stretched further and further across the globe, the sense in the West that there were vast "unknowns" out there began to vanish.

But the belief didn't go away entirely. There are still those who dream of the margins, the frontiers between a disenchanted modern world and an enchanted, distant place—be it sunken continents of past civilizations, the Yeti-infested Himalayas, or top-secret government black sites in the American wilderness where alien corpses are kept in cryogenic storage. So I set out in search of these places, beginning on the border of Oregon and California, at the Root of the World.

PART I

SUNKEN LANDS
AND FALLING MEAT

———◆———

Inspirational methods, indeed, will be found to be those
of the Archaeology of the Future. The Tape-Measure School,
dull and full of the credulity of incredulity, is doomed.

—LEWIS SPENCE, *THE HISTORY OF ATLANTIS*

And every formal design depends on blanks,
as much as upon occupied spaces.

—CHARLES FORT, *LO!*

FIELD NOTES:
MOUNT SHASTA, CALIFORNIA

Rising up from the Northern California wilds, the glaciered Mount Shasta is visible for hundreds of miles, a white beacon, beckoning. Its sister peaks in the Cascade Range—Mount Rainier in Washington, Mount Hood and Mount St. Helens near Portland, Oregon—have this peculiar quality: solitary, perpetually snowcapped, dominating their landscapes. But none quite have the pull of Shasta, the mountain of mystery.

Visitors come from all over in search of Shasta's cosmic powers. Like the human body, I'm told by the server in my hotel's restaurant, the Earth has seven chakras—Mount Shasta is the Root Chakra.

Is there a secret hidden in the mountain? Are there mysterious creatures living inside? Many of Shasta's visitors believe so. They will tell you they're here in search of elusive, powerful beings. Asking around town, I get differing reports. They are very tall or they are very short, depending on who you talk to. "Half the size of pine trees with heads bigger than boulders," according to one observer. Some claim they are entirely covered in hair. According to others, they all have blond hair and blue eyes. Or they're ten feet tall and hairless. Some maintain they're purple. The gift shop in the hotel where I'm staying sells key chains with more traditional green alien heads.

Whatever they look like, they have a name: the Lemurians. They're an ancient race from a lost continent—or they're extraterrestrials who came here on spaceships and made a home beneath the mountain. Either could be true, it seems. The only true consensus seems to be that wherever they came from, they are advanced and they are wise.

They live in a warren of caves dug under the mountain, known as the lost city of Telos. From here, the Lemurians control cigar-shaped silver airships with their minds. They seem to have the power to control the local ranchers' cattle, which respond to invisible signals sent by these strange figures. "I once saw a glowing spear above the mountain, with light pouring out of each end," an eyewitness named Dante tells me. Another person says he's seen three hundred UFOs since he moved here. "Blinkety-blinks," he calls them. At my hotel is a large mural of the mountain, and buried deep in the corner, like an alien in Where's Waldo, is a small UFO.

In the town of Mount Shasta, the crystal shops outnumber the bars, and in one, I find a display of "Lemurian Quartz," sold at a distinct markup compared to the other gems and stones. It looks like standard quartz but for a horizontal striation. "Supposedly," the gem dealer tells me, "the Lemurians encoded their wisdom on that quartz for us to decipher. They left this for us before they disappeared."

The guy selling me Lemurian quartz seems unimpressed by the whole thing. "I'm more interested in the science," he says, despite the fact that his livelihood depends on the mystical powers of rocks. He's not the only one. The locals in the service industry I talk to here will grumble about how rude the hippies can be. "One half of this town believes in Lemuria," a patron at the bar tells me, "and the other half wants to kill that first half."

At the bookstore, filled with Chinese herbal remedies, books on Heaven, and a large collection of books on Lemuria, the clerk downplays it all. "It's just some myth, some local legend. Probably handed down from the Natives."

Whatever these stories are, they did not come from the Native people who've lived here for centuries. The Lemurians and their secret mountain city are not the stories of the Winnemem Wintu, who see the spring at Panther Meadow, high on the mountain's slopes, as the place where "we first bubbled into the world at the time of creation." As such it is not only sacred, but threatened by the Anglo occultists who come to create makeshift shrines, leave crystals and other holy garbage, and dump ash into the fragile stream. The Winnemem Wintu have had to wage a PR campaign against this onslaught. Their warnings to New Age seekers ("Do not build anything in the meadows or leave anything behind," their website asks. "It's perfect as the Creator made it. You can't improve it.") makes clear a tension between the remaining indigenous population and these newcomers.

But neither group disputes that the mountain is sacred, and even the skeptics and those resentful of the hippies and their crystals agree that *something* is going on up on the mountain's slopes. Dante told me of hours lost on the mountain: "I was up there skiing one time, and just looked up at the clouds, and the next thing I knew an hour and a half had passed by. Where did that time go? I have no idea."

The bartender, Chris, tells me of one story he heard from a couple who were skiing on the mountain. The woman broke her ski at one point, so they had to hike their way out through the wilderness. A man appeared—tall, blond, blue-eyed, wearing a yellow rain slicker—and proceeded to guide them to the road. When they reached the road, they turned back to thank him, to find that he'd vanished: only two sets of footsteps were visible in the snow. "Craziest story I've ever heard," Chris says, then proceeds to tell me a crazier one. He was in town one night doing errands for his pregnant wife when he agreed to give a ride home to a tall man with a walking stick and a live raven in a box that was hung around his neck. Chris took the stranger up the side of the mountain, listening to his fascinating tales, and when they'd reached some remote distance, the stranger got out, barefoot, and walked into the pitch-black forest. "Did I give a ride to a Lemurian?" Chris asks, unsure of the answer.

Or is it military? When David, who works in construction, tells me he's seen some "weird stuff," I press him on what exactly, and he says, "Fences in the middle of nowhere, white vans on the north side of the mountain." Maybe, he conjectures, the Lemurian stuff is just a dodge to cover up military stuff. Chris and other patrons at the bar concur; they mention the Kingsley Field Air National Guard Base in nearby Klamath Falls, Oregon. It could be that the UFOs have something to do with that—or missile silos, someone mutters. "I think it's a conspiracy, just to keep you out. I think they're hiding government shit," David says.

But the more I press David, the more he seems to admit that he's not ready to dismiss the Lemurians. "I've seen weird shit on that mountain," he keeps repeating, hinting that he's not just talking about fences. "That mountain, it's like a magnet." He says he's seen Sasquatch up here—"a bunch of times." I think of the descriptions of the Lemurians as tall and hairy—is there a difference between Sasquatches and Lemurians? Are they the same thing? When I ask him what he thinks it all means, he holds his hands far apart: "There's what you can prove," he says, wiggling one hand, "and then what you can't," wiggling the other. He looks at me. "And then there's everything in between."

Okay, I press him, but what about the Lemurians? "Go up on the mountain," he says, "and you'll see some shit. You'll see some shit." Then he's quiet for a minute. Finally he says, "The Lemurians? They only let you see them when they want you to see them."

The next day I went up the mountain to see some shit.

After years of drought, California has had the wettest winter in years, and the snowpack on Shasta has turned almost the entire mountain a pure white. Most of the shit I saw was snow. Driving up the well-plowed route toward the mountain, patches of snow at 3,000 feet become walls of snow at 5,000 feet. At 7,900 feet the barriers of snow and ice are ten feet high on either side of the road, and rounding a corner the road abruptly ends—here, at Bunny Flats, is as far as the plows have made it. A handful of skiers and snowshoers are about on this late spring day, but the Lemurians are not ready for me to see them.

Who, or what, are they? An ancient civilization? Aliens? Bigfoot?

The government? And why are they living in Mount Shasta? If you ask the believers, they'll tell you these answers lie in the depths of the Pacific Ocean, thousands of years in the past—or in the stars, thousands of light-years away. But the real answer lies almost two thousand miles to the east, on the shores of the Mississippi River, in a place called Nininger, Minnesota, and it begins in the year 1856.

[1]

THE MAN WHO COULD NOT BE TURNED

L ater, Ignatius Donnelly would recall those heady days of 1856. Standing on the broad porch of his new mansion that overlooked the Mississippi River, he wondered to himself, "Here I am, but twenty-six years old, and I have already acquired a large fortune. What shall I do to occupy myself the rest of my life?"

He didn't have to worry; within a year everything would have changed, and the path of his life would take him through some of the most bizarre twists possible. Born in Philadelphia to two successful Irish immigrant parents, Donnelly had established himself as a lawyer in Philadelphia. But after his marriage in 1856, he'd decided the world held bigger things for him, so he'd come to Minnesota. He was part of a generation of young men who saw the West as the promised land, a place of wild speculation, where their fortunes would be made and their characters forged. The spirit of the age was embodied in a quote often attributed to Horace Greeley (though he likely popularized it rather than coined it): "Go West, young man, go West and grow up with the country." Donnelly took this to heart.

Donnelly, in concert with a few other investors, developed a bold plan to acquire a large parcel of undeveloped land just down the Mississippi River from Hastings, Minnesota. While Hastings was a thriving town, Donnelly was sure the site he'd chosen was better—a better steamship landing and a more entrancing view of the river—imagining it a future hub for the northern Mississippi. They'd bought the land for roughly six dollars a parcel, but were planning on selling those same parcels at one hundred to five hundred dollars each. The town was named for Donnelly's business partner, John Nininger, but it would be Donnelly who'd be the voice and the face of the project, and Donnelly who would in time earn the nickname the Sage of Nininger. He portrayed the West as a land of wealth and wonder, a place that "will yet play an important part in the great drama of human advancement." The West, he prophesized, would be the new Eden.

Such boosterism depended on the lie that the land was itself uninhabited, when in reality, of course, the indigenous peoples of North America were being pushed steadily westward. Manifest Destiny, as the policy came to be known, offered a mythological and seemingly predestined underpinning to a process of violent expropriation. Donnelly, like many, saw—and embraced—this, telling potential investors that the "embers of the Indian's fire will scarcely have disappeared from the heath where his wigwam stood, before the halls and palaces of the most elaborate social life will rise upon their site."

Initially things went well for Donnelly; plots sold, the money rolled in, and he put a down payment on a massive ferry that would serve Nininger and bring commerce to the town. But the tide quickly turned, and instead of a boomtown, Donnelly found ruin. In 1857 a panic swept the country's economy, constricting credit and drying up speculation. Nininger was just one of many casualties. He went bankrupt before the ferry could be delivered and defaulted on the balance.

Donnelly's dream of a utopia in the West had met with the harsh reality of capitalism. He entered politics, going on to serve as the lieutenant governor of Minnesota and later in the US House of Representatives, before getting pushed out of politics in the 1870s, leaving him to pursue another career. Ignatius Donnelly had been to the ends of the Earth, at least figuratively, and had met only financial ruin. Now he would re-create the history of a place that would never be touched by money, politics, or the imperfect hands of modern man: in 1882 he turned to publishing, producing an unexpected bestseller, *Atlantis: The Antediluvian World.*

●   ●   ●

When Max Weber argued that the modern world was becoming "disenchanted," he didn't just mean that it had lost religion. The physical world itself seemed to have lost its luster, its mystery and magic. As modernity, with its emphasis on transactions, calculations, rationality, and commerce, spread throughout the world, those places that had long been seen as "exotic" became ordinary.

In the United States, Weber's ideas took on a topographical dimension: the enchanted world was a place, a frontier, and that place was disappearing. In 1910, the historian Frederick Jackson Turner described how the American frontier was nothing less than a mythical place where the individual discovered and forged himself: "The first ideal of the pioneer," he wrote, "was that of conquest. It was his task to fight with nature for the chance to exist. Not as in older countries did this contest take place in a mythical past, told in folk lore and epic. It has been continuous to our own day. Facing each generation of colonists was the unmastered continent." Turner's was perhaps the most eloquent and influential voice of the self-serving story of Manifest Destiny. The frontier—wild and dangerous, composed of "vast forests," "barren oceans of rolling plains," and (significantly) "a fierce race of savages"—was where the American man became a man: where he faced danger, surmounted it, and established his civilizing dominion over the wilds. (In frontier romanticism, indigenous populations either exist as dangerous threats or they don't exist at all, as when destiny manifesters claim the wilderness is "empty.")

But this frontier, Turner lamented, was disappearing, this myth a victim of its own success. Rail lines had bound more and more of the earth into a tighter and tighter web, standardizing time zones and organizing the whole world into one interconnected network. Territories became states, and the continent's indigenous populations were forced into smaller and smaller reservations, leaving the rest for agriculture and mining pursuits. The enchanted frontier, with its danger and "primitive savages," was gone.

Donnelly is perhaps the best example of someone who resisted this disenchantment of the world by imagining a world beyond the reach of capitalism or the railroads, a place locked in a premodern time, a place of perpetual enchantment.

Atlantis was first mentioned in two dialogues of Plato, *Timaeus* and the unfinished *Critias*: as with his *Republic*, Plato uses the story of Atlantis to test out his theories about what does or doesn't make for a successful political framework. Socrates asks his interlocutors how an ideal state should operate, imagining a hypothetical situation, but Critias instead gives him a supposedly factual one: a "strange but true" story that he heard from his grandfather, who in turn heard it from a traveler named Solon, who in turn heard it from some Egyptians while he was traveling through the Nile Delta region. Atlantis would appear again as an allegory for an ideal place, akin to Thomas More's *Utopia*, as it did in Francis Bacon's unfinished 1627 novel, *The New Atlantis*; and as a fantastical civilization, appearing in Jules Verne's 1870 novel *Twenty Thousand Leagues Under the Sea*.

Donnelly was also likely inspired by Heinrich Schliemann, a German businessman with no formal training in archaeology, who'd used clues from Homer's *Iliad* to discover the ruins of the lost city of Troy. But Donnelly wasn't about to dive underwater in search of Atlantis; he wasn't leaving his library. Donnelly's book of armchair geology and anthropology argued it was a physical place, one irrevocably sunk under the ocean, taking Plato's *Critias* at an entirely new level of credulity. His book borrows freely from geology, climatology, anthropology, and literature (among other disciplines) in order to make a dramatic revision of the history of the ancient world.

Donnelly was well read, though he was not a trained scientist, historian, or anthropologist. But he was able to use familiar, if little understood, scientific principles to bolster his claims—that the Gulf Stream's circular motion, for example, could be accounted for by the lost continent. "When the barriers of Atlantis sunk sufficiently to permit the natural expansion of the heated water of the tropics to the north, the ice and snow which covered Europe gradually disappeared; the Gulf Stream flowed around Atlantis, and it still retains the circular motion first imparted to it by the presence of that island."

For Donnelly, Atlantis was an easy answer to a prevailing series of questions regarding geology, wind dynamics, and ocean currents, not to mention comparative mythology, archaeology, and evolution. Vague and all-purpose, it became a grand unifying theory bringing together all these strains of unknowns, a single geographic location marrying all the natural sciences, as well as the humanities. What's more, it offered new directions for all of these pursuits: "We are but beginning to understand the past," Donnelly explains, casting the potential discovery of Atlantis as of a piece with Pompeii, Herculaneum, pre-Columbian cultures, and hieroglyphics. "We are on the threshold. Scientific investigation is advancing with giant strides. Who shall say that one hundred years from now the great museums of the world may not be adorned with gems, statues, arms, and implements from Atlantis, while the libraries of the world shall contain translations of its inscriptions, throwing new light upon all the past history of the human race, and all the great problems which now perplex the thinkers of our day?"

What Donnelly offered was a style that *appeared* scientific while creating new frontiers, new borderlands, and liminal spaces, places not yet colonized—and in some fundamental sense, unable to be colonized. At a time when Western culture saw its borders filling in, Donnelly magicked up a mythical continent that could never be reached—and the public ate it up.

Atlantis: The Antediluvian World went through more than twenty editions in the United States and in Great Britain within the first decade of its publication. The prime minister of England, William E. Gladstone, wrote to Donnelly to say that "I may not be able to accept all your propositions, but I am much disposed to believe in an Atlantis." Charles Darwin wrote to Donnelly to report that he had read it with interest, though he remained skeptical. Even those unconvinced by his argument were appreciative of the sheer volume of scientific evidence Donnelly put forward. The mayor of Chicago told him he was "crazy as a loon," but he meant it as a compliment.

History has been harsher to Donnelly. A major problem with *Atlantis* is what anthropologists and archaeologists refer to as "diffusionism," and what archaeologist Kenneth Feder describes as the idea that "cultures are basically uninventive and that new ideas are developed in very few or single places. They then move out or 'diffuse' from their source areas." Rather than recognizing that the ancient civilizations like the Mayans and the Egyptians were fully capable (like the Greeks and Romans) of developing sophisticated literature, art, and architecture, diffusionists assume that they must have all gotten this from somewhere, a none-too-subtle racism that denies any non-European people their own culture. (This is almost a complete 180-degree revolution from frontier racism: these cultures aren't dangerous, and they aren't erased, but their cultural achievements are entirely subordinated to the diffusionist story.) Donnelly, never one to half-ass anything, took this so far that *Atlantis* is regularly accused of "hyperdiffusionism," so egregious was his error.

Like a conspiracy theorist, Donnelly's scholarship is a form of apophenia (the tendency to see patterns and connections where none exist), applied on a cultural level. Diffusionism looks for coincidences, similarities, and accidents that bear a superficial resemblance, and then constructs theories based on those false pattern recognitions. It is to take the messy soup of human history, its supreme varieties and differences, and find in them enough random correspondences that you can distill everything down to a simplistic creation myth.

Donnelly, meanwhile, went on to a series of increasingly more convoluted conspiracies and wild theories. He followed *Atlantis* with *Ragnarok: The Age of Fire and Gravel*, predicting the imminent end of the world;

and then with his magnum opus, a thousand-page book entitled *The Great Cryptogram*, which argued, as some had done before him, that Shakespeare was not the author of the plays attributed to him; and finally a series of novels in the 1890s.

But it was Donnelly's *Atlantis* that remains his legacy. In the years since its first publication, it has spawned dozens of imitators, including books by the founder of anthroposophy, Rudolf Steiner, and Lewis Spence, who published a flurry of books on Atlantis in the opening decades of the twentieth century. His 1924 *The History of Atlantis* (his third of five books on the continent) opens with a basic fact: "A history of Atlantis must differ from all other histories, for the fundamental reason that it seeks to record the chronicles of a country the soil of which is no longer available for examination to the archaeologist." Atlantis existed between these two poles: it was both the future of science and outside of its reach.

Donnelly's impact was not just in cementing a vision of a lost continent in the public; he also demonstrated firsthand a path toward minor success through a splendid amateurism, one that eschewed traditional academic research in favor of armchair theorizing—a theorizing that played to a deep-seated wish fulfillment on the part of his audience. What Donnelly demonstrated above all is that you don't have to take on the scientific establishment directly if you can convince the public instead.

There was a name for people like Donnelly. They were called cranks.

The term "crank" had been popularized by Oliver Wendell Holmes, who'd made a name for himself as the author of a series of pithy sketches originally published in *The Atlantic*, eventually gathered in a book called *The Autocrat of the Breakfast-Table*, a series of humorous tales of various occupants of a New England boardinghouse successful enough to span a number of sequels, including 1891's *Over the Teacups*. This last includes Holmes's narrator dismissing a "class of persons whom we call 'cranks,' in our familiar language," before he's interrupted by boarder "Number Seven" (everyone is identified solely by numbers), who rises to their defense: "A crank is a man who does his own thinking. . . . There never was a religion founded but its Messiah was called a crank. There never was an idea started that woke up men out of their stupid indifference but its originator was spoken of as a crank. Do you want to know why that name is given to the men who do most for the world's progress? I will tell you. It is because cranks make all the wheels in all the machinery of the world go round."

Unlike a snake oil salesman, a con artist, or a grifter, the crank is a true believer, convinced that they alone have seen through the myopia afflicting common society. The crank is always offering a version of the Perpetual Motion Engine: something that seems tantalizingly plausible, and utopian in its ramifications, but undercut by the stubborn reality of the laws of physics. To be a crank is to offer a Grand Unified Theory that explains everything, that reinvents the wheel or rediscovers fire. Holmes's Number Seven is not wrong that all messiahs are called cranks, because many cranks offer themselves up as messiahs.

In 1906, an anonymous writer in *Nature* magazine offered a further diagnosis of a crank. Signing his name (it was almost certainly a "he") only as "J. P.," he (reviewing a book on mathematics cranks) writes that "A *crank* is defined as a man who cannot be turned. These men are all cranks; at all events, we have never succeeded in convincing one of them that he was wrong." Clearly exasperated, J. P. was also slightly conflicted about the prevalence of these cranks: "It ought to be pleasant," he muses, "to think that there are so many men in the world who refuse to accept dogma." The entire methodology of scientific knowledge, after all, was built on refusing dogma, and the scientist ought to feel kinship with the crank—both have a similar aversion to received authority. And yet the problem with cranks is that they refused to accept *scientific* dogma: "The usually accepted axioms, definitions, and technical terms," J. P. continues, "are not for them." The problem was not that these cranks were unscientific; rather, "our real difficulty is with the men who are partly right, men who think they have a new idea and try to explain it in unscientific language, and, as they do so, denounce the orthodox beliefs which they have been unable to understand."

J. P.'s conflicted diagnosis is worth lingering over; the problem with cranks wasn't that they were wrong, but that they were half right. The history of the world has been filled with cranks, but a certain breed of crank began to emerge in the nineteenth century, one who borrowed from science when convenient and rejected it when it wasn't. They developed their theories during a time when science and religion were changing their relationships to each other, and these pseudoscientific cranks found increasingly receptive audiences.

What Donnelly proved was that if you could spin a wild tale with just the right mix of fact and fiction, it would burn itself indelibly in the public's minds, and it would prove almost impossible to disprove, regardless of how flimsy your evidence was. A little bit of scientific gloss, some specifics for garnish, nothing that could be factually verified one way or another, and something that played to people's sense of wonder and magic—these kinds of stories are remarkably durable. They infiltrate our pop culture, recur in our novels and films, inflect our scientific pursuits. There's a reason the name Atlantis appears on everything from all-inclusive Bahamas resorts to space shuttles, why a film set in Atlantis (2018's *Aquaman*) grossed more than a billion dollars—and it's not our love of Plato's dialogues. Donnelly's canny mixture of myth and science created a new borderland, a dreaming place beyond our borders.

To understand the twentieth century's obsession with UFOs, Bigfoot, the Loch Ness Monster, or the increasingly paranoid conspiracy theories of the twenty-first century, one must start with the cranks of the nineteenth century, who saw the world around them undergoing rapid change, creating anxiety and uncertainty at a time when there were far more questions than answers, and who attempted to carve out bizarre and outlandish theories and philosophies that might provide some of those answers.

Holmes's Number Seven, after all, was right about another thing: in their own way, cranks make the machinery of the world turn.

[2]

ABANDONED GEOGRAPHY

hilip Lutley Sclater was not a crank; he was a zoologist. In an article published in 1864, Sclater set out to try to solve a strange puzzle: Why were there so many different species of lemurs in Madagascar, yet so comparatively few in mainland Africa or India? How had they spread from this island to its neighboring continents? And did they have any connection to biologically similar monkeys in the Americas?

Sclater proposed a radical solution: a continent, he supposed, had once stretched from America to India, but at some point in Earth's prehistory, it was broken up, leaving behind relics in the form of Africa, parts of Asia, and Madagascar. Lemurs had once traveled freely throughout this vast, lost continent, but it had subsequently sunk beneath the waters, leaving only isolated pockets. Since he had conceived of this landmass's possibility while studying lemurs, he proposed to name it Lemuria.

The scientific debate over his theory would last for the next decade. Some fellow biologists embraced it immediately; Alfred Russel Wallace, in 1876, described the Lemuria hypothesis as "a legitimate and highly probably supposition, and it is an example of the way in which a study of the geographical distribution of animals may enable us to reconstruct the geography of a bygone age." Ernst Haeckel, the German biologist, dubbed it "the probable cradle of the human race, which in all likelihood here first developed out of anthropoid apes."

But almost as soon as Lemuria had been proposed, it fell from favor. By the 1870s, geologists had discovered the principle of isostasy, which proved that it was physically impossible for a landmass to "sink" to the ocean floor. Then in 1885, Eduard Suess proposed an alternative idea: instead of a connecting continent that had sunk, what if the existing continents had somehow been joined? Suess's idea quickly gained traction, and has since been expanded into the theory of continental drift.

The story of Lemuria, unlike Atlantis, began as an exemplar of how science is supposed to work: a hypothesis was proposed, it was tested against the facts, criticisms were proposed, alternate theories that fit the facts better superseded it, and it was discarded. That should have been the end of it.

But scientific mistakes are important for stigmatized knowledge and conspiracy theories, too, because a mistake proposes an alternate explanation for the world, and, once it's debunked and forgotten, it can exist in the minds of some as secret, dangerous knowledge that the institution is trying to suppress. Lemuria itself should have been discarded, too. Instead it would rise from the waves, thanks to Helena Petrovna Blavatsky.

◦ ◦ ◦

Helena Blavatsky's reputation precedes her. For Kurt Vonnegut, she was the "Founding Mother of the Occult in America." The spiritual organization she founded, the Theosophical Society, included in its ranks Thomas Edison, L. Frank Baum, and Mohandas Gandhi (who, while living in London in 1889, was introduced to the Theosophists, who urged him to study Hinduism and the Bhagavad Gita). Her work influenced the writing of poets like William Butler Yeats and Ezra Pound; her name appears in T. S. Eliot's poetry as well. The writer Christopher Bamford was not entirely wrong when he placed her along with Marx, Nietzsche, and Freud as one of the "creators of the twentieth century."

Blavatsky came from Russia to New York City in 1873, in her early forties. She had been born into an aristocratic family in 1831, the daughter of an Army officer who relocated frequently, instilling in her a sense of restlessness. The one place that seemed to anchor her when she was younger, though, was her great-grandfather's library, a collection filled with volumes on alchemy, magic, and Freemasonry.

It is difficult to say too much about her past, since her own account of her life is riddled with gaps, contradictions, and self-mythologizing. Much of it involves technically possible but highly implausible feats. Chief among them was her claim that she traveled to Tibet, at a time when the country was largely closed to foreigners and heavily policed by the Chinese, British, and Russian missions on the hunt for military spies. Did this woman, not known for her subtlety, manage to infiltrate such a foreboding place unseen? That for most of her life she was out of shape makes it more difficult to credit her claims of scaling Tibetan peaks unaided.

But the nineteenth century was a grand time for such self-aggrandizers, particularly for those offering new and unorthodox spiritual truths. The world had been moving gradually away from organized religion, particularly its doctrinaire attitude toward the world. But this didn't mean that people were abandoning spirituality—on the contrary, the hunger for something more than the material world was stronger than ever; everywhere you looked, cults, communes, and sects branched off in new directions, promising some kind of spiritual revelation without the fetters of hidebound traditional religion.

❋   ❋   ❋

There were numerous series of shifts—some cataclysmic—in the scientific and cultural thinking that would retroactively be grouped under the heading "the scientific revolution." There was an embrace of empiricism—no longer would knowledge be taken for granted; it was now subject to direct observation and experimentation. This was accompanied by a turn away from dogma, what Walter Charleton in 1654 called "the dishonourable tyranny of that Usurper, Authority."

Add to this Columbus's "discovery" of the Americas, which sparked an irrevocable change in how Europeans understood the fabric of the world. Early Christian theologians viewed the natural world as a "Book of Nature," a second book of God meant to complement the Bible. The natural world was an allegory for God's truth, and one could get closer to the divine by studying the habits of animals, the movement of the planets, and the patterns of the weather. For much of Christian Europe's history, animals, vegetables, and minerals had all developed a stable symbolic relationship to humanity and the divine: foxes represented cunning, snakes represented sin, ermines represented purity.

The sudden awareness of entirely new continents, entirely new animals, trees, fruits, peoples, and civilizations meant a whole host of natural specimens that had no ready meaning in this system. The Book of Nature now had hundreds of new chapters, all strangely illegible. By the seventeenth century, philosophers had begun to abandon the concept altogether. It is the opinion of a "heathen," Francis Bacon would argue in 1605, to assume that nature reflected the image of God: "The works of God," he argued, "show the omnipotency and wisdom of the Maker, but not His image."

Once the natural world was freed from the burden of perfectly reflecting God, it could be studied more accurately. By the eighteenth and early nineteenth centuries, any link between natural philosophy and religion was inessential. Since natural philosophy could no longer be seen as a means to understanding the divine, it gradually began to become an end unto itself. The term *"scientia,"* which had once meant both a mental disposition and a formal body of knowledge, gradually came to mean only the latter, a meaning that finally crystallized into the word "science." The natural world was just as fascinating as it had always been, but there was less and less enthusiasm in seeing it as the workings of the mind of God.

Fringe ideas, stigmatized knowledge, conspiracy theories—so many of them begin here, in times of major upheaval, in uncertainty and anxiety, and in fear of change. When there is a major cultural shift in how we understand the world, and when the vectors for acquiring and evaluating information undergo upheaval and change, it's only natural for some people to respond with a mixture of fear, resistance, and confusion. In this regard, Helena Blavatsky was simply a woman of her times.

◦ ◦ ◦

One of the main outlets for this desire for a spirituality free from organized religion in the nineteenth century was Spiritualism: a belief that the spirits of the dead lived on, in some vaguely defined, non-denominational realm known as the Summerland, and that the living could contact them. What began in 1848 with two young girls in Upstate New York claiming that they could communicate with the spirit of a man who'd been murdered in their house quickly exploded, consuming the country's imagination. Spiritualism offered the promise that there was life after death, and that one could still communicate with loved ones after their deaths; it offered, through séances and table sessions, a version of the communion and community traditional churches offered; through its reliance on female mediums, it offered an alternative to the male-dominated structures of patriarchal religion.

So Blavatsky began her career as a Spiritualist, intervening in a debate surrounding a house in Chittenden, Vermont: the two brothers who owned the house claimed it was haunted and had turned it into something of a tourist trap, eventually attracting skeptics. One such debunker, a doctor by the name of Beard, pronounced the brothers frauds in the journal *Graphic*. Blavatsky shot back; her first published article appeared in the same journal, attacking the debunker Beard. (Theosophy's co-founder, Colonel Henry Steel Olcott, met Blavatsky around this time, also at Chittenden, pushing back against skeptics.)

In the piece she referred to herself as "a Spiritualist of many years"; in her scrapbook, however, where she pasted a copy of the article, she crossed out the word "Spiritualist" and wrote "occultist." Blavatsky wasn't out to denounce spiritual communications. Instead, she argued, Spiritualists were wrong about *whom they were contacting*—these were not the voices of the dead, but something else entirely, and the truth behind this mystery would be the central idea of Theosophy.

The core of Theosophy involves a group of secret adepts centered in Tibet, who've learned extraordinary wisdom and seemingly supernatural powers; Blavatsky and Olcott began teaching that through study one can achieve spiritual emancipation and enlightenment. This is a far cry from Spiritualism, which offered reassurance that death wasn't the end but never offered a clear definition of what came next, and which didn't pretend to offer a consistent morality.

Theosophy would offer spirituality instead of Spiritualism, and the important voices would not be from the dead but from ancient figures from the East, communicating sacred principles honed over centuries. While supposedly in Tibet, Blavatsky had been shown some secret verses in an unknown language she called Senzar, which she memorized and later transcribed into the central tenets of her philosophy.

Blavatsky's cosmology, as laid out mainly in a pair of voluminous, byzantine texts (*Isis Unveiled* and *The Secret Doctrine*), was the antithesis of evolution. Humanity and civilization as we know it was simply the most degraded form of a former spiritual purity from a long-vanished age. Rather than a history of constantly evolving toward greater complexity, life on Earth had steadily degenerated. The goal of Theosophy was to reascend through those levels, to try to attain once more the spiritual purity that had long been lost.

Blavatsky found a niche in a world that was gradually being divvied up by two rival poles of influence. As religion and science grew slowly apart, a whole raft of human belief—magic, astrology, occultism, mysticism, and other esotericism—found itself without a home in either camp. People didn't necessarily abandon these beliefs, though, and increasingly looked for ways to preserve them so that they didn't come into conflict with either their religious beliefs or their understanding of science. Spiritualism, for example, grew in popularity as a semiorganized religion that was both in parallel with and somewhat in tension with religion and science. Occultism, including Blavatsky's Theosophy, occupied that same middle ground.

Though initial printings of *Isis Unveiled* sold out, the book did not lead to an influx of Theosophists; in fact, the movement withered. People wanted answers, but they did not necessarily want a guru or a replacement spiritual authority (unlike Spiritualism, Theosophy was top down; the truth was whatever Blavatsky or her inner circle said it was). The Theosophical Society's numbers would grow eventually, after Blavatsky moved to India, but they would never become a massive, worldwide movement. Rather, her ideas would steadily trickle into mainstream consciousness—often through writers and painters like Yeats and Wassily Kandinsky, who would interpret them as a mix of literal and figurative, turning them to their own poetic and artistic ends.

But for a devoted coterie of Theosophists, Blavatsky spoke the literal truth. Theosophy invited its followers to transcend debased existence and return to that ancient existence of purity and light, a process consisting of a series of stages to recover from the degradation of humanity. She organized this descent of man topographically, with a different continent for each successive degradation. In such a schema, the lost continents of Atlantis and Lemuria were perfect for her needs. She incorporated them into her prehistory, along with other, even more fantastical continents: the Imperishable Sacred Land and Hyperborea. Blavatsky's *The Secret Doctrine* suggests that each of these continents was home to a different race, beginning with divine mortals in the Imperishable Sacred Land, and down on through to Lemuria and Atlantis, until finally America and the current continents, home to a significantly degraded human race. In appropriating the name Lemuria, Blavatsky strove to root her ideas in the scientific, arguing that "Lemuria is half the creation of Modern Science, and has therefore to be believed in."

If the current age was messy, uncertain, and terrifying, Theosophy offered reassurance that we'd lost some earlier purity, but that it could be regained. Lost continents like Atlantis and Lemuria helped further bolster this picture of the universe, suggesting earlier civilizations that were more advanced and less degraded than our own. If we could find traces of these lost places, we might be able to cultivate our spiritual understanding of their inhabitants better, and reclaim some of their lost majesty.

Blavatsky accomplished more than Donnelly could have hoped, by taking his template of lost continents and embedding them in a larger, cohesive mystical cosmology. Above all, her success had to do with the fact that people wanted the world to be far more enchanted than Max Weber would have us believe. Industrialization and science had robbed the world of much of its magic, but people still craved mystery in their lives.

[3]

THE CREDULITY OF INCREDULITY

t's there in the heart of an ordinary suburban neighborhood in San
Jose, California, a beige stucco tomb rising out of the rows of identical
homes: an ancient Egyptian temple flanked by palm fronds and statues of squatting hippos, facing Herbert Hoover High School and a Star-
bucks. A massive trapezoidal temple flanked with sphinxes, obelisks,
and reflecting pools. The grounds are manicured meticulously, and the
walkways meander peacefully. But where did it come from? How did it
get here?

This is the Rosicrucian Egyptology Museum; it contains the largest
collection of Egyptian artifacts in the western United States, and is a
place of supreme weirdness. The museum was founded by Harvey
Spencer Lewis, founder of the Ancient Mystical Order Rosae Crucis
(AMORC). Lewis, born in 1883, had an early fascination with ghosts
and the paranormal, but was disillusioned by the number of frauds he
encountered. Looking for a mysticism divorced from Spiritualism, he
traveled to France in 1909 in search of Rosicrucians; there he was in-
ducted into the order and then returned to North America to establish a
branch there. As its First Imperator, Lewis established AMORC's headquarters in San Francisco, then Tampa, before returning to the Bay
Area and the order's current home in San Jose. As a devoted occultist, he

had a lifelong fascination for Egyptology, amassing a vast collection of Egyptian artifacts, which now make up the museum.

Nestled in among the grounds is the research library, a compact but inviting room that contains the remnants of Lewis's own library as well as various donations through the years. Decorated with the busts of Greek philosophers, Egyptian ankhs, and portraits of Lewis, it's a lovely and strange hidden treasure in a city that is often too forward-looking. The library contains a sizable collection of books on history, philosophy, and Egyptology, along with books on alchemy, mysticism, and the occult; and in its history section, a dozen or so books on the lost continents of Atlantis and Lemuria.

Among his other eccentric interests, Lewis, steeped in Theosophy, was a strong believer in lost continents. In 1931, under the pen name Wishar Spenle Cervé, he published *Lemuria: The Lost Continent of the Pacific*, a book "free from ponderous, scientific quotations," but nonetheless filled with "self-evident and indisputable facts." Lewis dedicated his *Lemuria* to Sir Francis Bacon, "in appreciation for the first researches into the history of the lost continents of Atlantis and Lemuria," a bold but calculated move. Bacon's unfinished utopian novel, *New Atlantis*, had proposed an ideal community in a yet-to-be-discovered island in the Pacific Ocean. But Bacon's New Atlantis was clearly meant to be an allegory. Lewis's dedication not only implies that Bacon was on the hunt for a real submerged continent, but that the father of the scientific method had an intellectual kinship with the mystic nonsense that Lewis was now proposing.

Lewis argued not only that the continent once existed, but that it stretched from the Philippines to North America, and that its remnants could still be seen in California. According to Lewis, the Great Salt Lake of Utah was evidence of a former ocean that divided North America to the east from Lemuria to the west, and the islands of the Pacific were all remaining tips of mountain ranges that had once stretched across the great continent.

Lewis's most noteworthy contribution was to conflate the concept of Lemuria, as handed down to him by Sclater and Blavatsky, with *Mu*, another lost continent. Mu had first been proposed by Augustus Le Plongeon in 1886, in which he synthesized what he knew about Mayan ruins in the Yucatan with Plato's Atlantis, claiming that refugees from the doomed civilization had fled west to the Americas, founding the Mayan civilization, and east to Egypt, founding its great ancient civilization. Mu was resurrected in the 1920s by James Churchward, who claimed he'd been shown some ancient clay tablets that established Mu as the place where humanity first appeared. Churchward placed Mu in the Pacific, rather than the Atlantic, so it was easy for Lewis to combine it with Lemuria (the lexical similarities also helped). By conflating the discarded geological concept of Lemuria with the antiquary tradition of Mu, Lewis yoked an entire mystical tradition to the thinnest of scientific veneers, moving even beyond Blavatsky. Now anything could be Lemuria, since anything could be Mu.

Including Mount Shasta. In suggesting Mount Shasta to be a fragment of Lemuria, Lewis was elaborating a theory first made by Frederick Spencer Oliver in his 1894 book *A Dweller on Two Planets*; and in 1908, Adelia Taffinder put California in Lemuria and thus at the origin of civilization. But it was Lewis who popularized it, using his wealth and fame within the occult community (Walt Disney and Gene Roddenberry were supposedly members of his secret society) to cement the connection between Lemuria and Shasta.

Lewis, obviously besotted by the Golden State, at times seems to be writing for the California Tourist Board as much as for his fellow occultists. "Of all the strange and mysterious parts of the world there is none that is so filled with the elements of fascinating and alluring mystery as that of the country of California." There is no state like California he rhapsodized, where schoolchildren and adults alike sing songs praising their state, affirming its unique and exemplary nature—proof, for Lewis, that the Golden State was magical. The first half of the twentieth century was a time when California boosterism was at its height, the state working feverishly to encourage a westward migration, offering a warm, dry climate, a paradise on Earth. No wonder that Lewis's mysticism also partook of this civic pride. Just one more praise singer of California, the new Garden of Eden.

Lewis, though, suggested that mixed in among California's great citizens there might be actual Lemurians. Lemuria was a place of nine-foot-tall telepathic humans, the same beings who inspired the statues of Easter Island. "Many years ago it was quite common to hear stories whispered in Northern California about the occasional strange-looking persons seen to emerge from the dense growth of trees in that region," he wrote of Shasta. "They would run back into hiding when discovered or seen by anyone. Occasionally one of these oddly dressed individuals would come to one of the smaller towns and trade nuggets and gold dust for some modern commodities. These hidden Lemurians," Lewis wrote, "were tall, graceful, and agile, having the appearance of being quite old and yet exceedingly virile. They gave every indication of what one would term *foreigners*, but with larger heads, much larger foreheads, head-dresses that had a special decoration which came down over the center of the forehead to the bridge of the nose, and thus hid or covered a part of the forehead that many have attempted to see and study." They speak with a type of British accent, and will not allow themselves to be photographed. The overall description is of a class of people just a little bit off, but not so much that you'd notice right away. By Lewis's description, anyone who struck you as a bit strange, whose actions didn't add up, may very well have been a Lemurian. Just ask the residents of Mount Shasta—they've certainly met a few people like that.

● ● ●

The word "utopia," as coined by Thomas More, literally means "no place," a nonexistent space. Both Atlantis and Lemuria are utopias: places that don't exist, that we can fill with meaning precisely because there are no facts against which to measure that meaning. They are whatever we put into them. They rose from the depths of the oceans in the second half of the nineteenth century as refuges against the rising tides of modernity, offering a pair of enchanted realms that could exist alongside the modern world while critiquing it. But this all would seem to depend on the continued belief that there are no extant traces of Atlantis or Lemuria, such that none of these assertions can ever be fact-checked. But decades after Blavatsky's death, this began to change. Harvey Spencer Lewis's Lemuria became the culmination of a different line of thought: what if Lemuria—or at least parts of it—survived, and could still be reached?

The fringe theories and conspiracies that stick best are those that strike that perfect mix of specificity and vagueness—enough specificity to seem grounded in fact, but not so much detail you can prove it one way or another. Ultimately, all it took to kindle the legend of Mount Shasta was the proposal that things were somehow different there, and that some of the people you met there might be a little unusual. The visitors and the pilgrims did the rest. People see what they want to see.

And so they came to the mountain. By the late 1930s, park rangers at Shasta reported that the mountain's hiking trails were stuffed with seekers looking for an entrance into the underground caverns of Lemuria, where they hoped to find Lewis's mythical race of telepathic superbeings. Among those who flocked to occult religions during the Depression, hoping for some measure of freedom from a life where capitalism had failed them and left them bankrupt, the rock beneath the mountain's surface had become as important as its surface. Mount Shasta now contains within it Plato's philosophy, Donnelly's comparative anthropology, Sclater's discarded geology, Blavatsky's mysticism, and Lewis's California boosterism. Alongside the igneous rock that makes up the mountain are these other, stranger layers that continue to contribute to Shasta's geology.

[4]

DISPATCHES FROM
THE DESERT OF BLOOD

B ath County, Kentucky, is what you might call the borderlands. Literally on the border of West Virginia, it's a borderland in a more abstract sense: it's neither here nor there, a place of in-betweenness. But once, for a brief moment, Olympia Springs had been a someplace, a place deserving of national attention and scrutiny. Because it was here, on a bright spring day more than a hundred years ago, that the skies rained meat.

FLESH DESCENDING IN A SHOWER, blared *The New York Times* on March 3, 1876. AN ASTOUNDING PHENOMENON IN KENTUCKY—FRESH MEAT LIKE MUTTON OR VENISON FALLING FROM A CLEAR SKY. Mrs. Allen Crouch, the *Times* reported, was outside her home, about two to three miles from the tiny town of Olympia Springs. She was in her yard making soap, "when meat which looked like beef began to fall around her. The sky was perfectly clear at the time, and she said it fell like large snow flakes, the pieces as a general thing not being much larger. One piece fell near her which was three or four inches square." The meat, she estimated, fell in an area roughly one hundred yards long and fifty yards wide.

The inexplicable meat shower quickly became a national news story, and before the month was out the *New York Herald* had sent a correspondent out to learn more about this "carnal rain." The people of Olympia Springs were in complete agreement that Mrs. Crouch was a reliable source, "too good a woman to be guilty" of any kind of hoax or deception. The skies had been clear that day, the sun shining brightly, she recalled, with only a light, westerly wind. She had been home alone with her grandson when the meat began to fall; she first asked her grandson what it was, to which he replied, "Why grandma, it's snowing!" Only when she heard a large piece of meat hit the ground behind her, making "a snapping like noise when it struck," did she grab her grandson and run inside in panic.

The fall lasted only for a few minutes, and, as Mrs. Crouch told the *Herald*, she had a vague idea that "my husband and son, who were away, had been torn to pieces and their remains were being brought home to me in this way." At the same time, though, she was also "impressed with the conviction that it was a miracle of God, which as yet we do not understand. It may have been a warning, as 'coming events' are said to 'cast their shadows before.'"

Mrs. Crouch estimated that there was "not less than half a bushel" worth of meat. The largest piece was as long as her hand and an inch wide, gristly, as if torn from the throat of some animal. After the fall, the hogs, the chicken, cat, and dog about the farm had started eating it "freely"; they seemed to "like it well," though the dog got sick some time afterward.

After the news reached the town, Harrison Gill, who owned the titular springs and whose veracity was "unquestionable," came out to the Crouch farm and saw pieces of meat still stuck to fences and scattered about the ground. Gill and Crouch's husband took up some samples and bottled them in alcohol.

It was one of these samples that the *Herald*'s correspondent tried to get a local Irish railworker named Jimmy Welsh to "sample." Welsh agreed to do it for a dollar, but after two or three "unsuccessful efforts to get it into his mouth," he asked for crackers to go along with the meat, then whiskey, before finally "remembering" that it was Lent and refusing to touch it altogether.

Others, however, were braver than Welsh; a butcher named Frisbe tasted the meat: "I did that at the springs in the presence of several persons," he testified, "some of whom told me it was a dangerous experiment, but I told them my constitution would stand as much of it as a rooster's or a cat's." Frisbe meant to swallow it, but after a few chews spat it out. "I have handled all kinds of meat," he said, "and I never tasted anything like it before. I am not prepared to say for certain that the taste resembled that of either fish, flesh, or fowl. . . . It looked more like mutton than anything else that I can compare it to."

Another local resident, Joe Jordan, bit off a piece of it, then quickly spat it out. "I did not keep it in my mouth long enough to perceive any taste," he told the *Herald.* "It was about a week after it had fallen before I saw it. I squeezed some of the pieces I had, and a brown mucous came from it. Some of the meat was very dry, like dried beef. It was elastic and thin. . . . The smell was offensive in the extreme, like that of a dead body."

While the residents of Olympia Springs struggled with their gustatory experiments, scientists and scholars were likewise struggling to figure out what had fallen on the Crouch farm on that fine March day. As reported in *Scientific American,* Leopold Brandeis of Brooklyn investigated a sample he'd been given and pronounced it nostoc, a colony bacteria that can swell up after a rain to appear as a jellylike mass. Because of its sudden appearance after rain, it's long thought to have fallen from the sky, nicknamed variously "star jelly" and "witch's butter." The Kentucky Shower of Flesh, Brandeis triumphantly declared, was "nothing more or less than the 'Nostoc' of the old alchemist." Noting that its flavor "approaches frog or spring-chicken legs, and it is greedily devoured by almost all domestic animals," Brandeis was sure the meat shower was "entirely in harmony with natural laws."

This would be fine, except that, as Mrs. Crouch and other reports had indicated, there had been no rain in the area, eliminating the nostoc possibility. In mid-March, a doctor named Lawrence Smith reported on his findings, arguing it was the dried spawn of some kind of reptile, "doubtless of the frog."

The debate over the mystery meat raged on. A letter to the editor soon arrived at the *Scientific American* from A. Mead Edwards of the Newark Scientific Association—Edwards, too, had thought it was probably nostoc, but he reported that Dr. Allan McLane Hamilton of New York had received a sample of the meat, and under microscopic investigation determined that it was lung tissue—either from a horse or a human infant (the structural similarities between the two being too close to differentiate). Edwards soon got his hands on the meat and was able to confirm Hamilton's findings. Edwards sent out for other samples (including Smith's in Kentucky), which he determined to be cartilage and muscular fibers and some connective tissue.

If it truly was horse meat (or, shudder, from an infant), where did it come from? The most commonly accepted explanation for the Kentucky Meat Shower is a pack of vomiting vultures: feasting on some decaying horse corpse in the area, they may have been startled suddenly, and, taking flight, sought to lighten their load by disgorging the contents of their stomachs.

But if it was a flock of vultures, why were no such creatures reported by any of the eyewitnesses? Neither Mrs. Crouch nor her grandson had seen anything but clear skies, and the sheer number of vultures required to vomit up that much meat would, one reasons, surely have been noticeable. What, then, could it possibly have been?

●   ●   ●

For Charles Fort, a rogue historian of the early twentieth century, the Kentucky Meat Shower meant something else altogether. He wasn't interested in proving, beyond a shadow of a doubt, what happened over Bath County that day. What mattered to him was sparring with those who claimed they *did know* what happened. Fort dismissed Brandeis's "proper explanation" of nostoc; what rain could have caused the substance to swell, particularly since multiple accounts described it as "dried"?

Fort was a journalist with a strong distrust of authority who collected seemingly unexplained and inexplicable historical accounts, which he gradually gathered together in four books published from 1919 to 1932. All manner of strange events: reports from Allahahad, India, when in April 19, 1836, fish fell from the sky—they could not be eaten, "in the pan, they turned to blood." A rancid butter or grease, nicknamed "stinking dew," fell in Munster and Leinster in the spring of 1695, and again in Limerick and Tipperary, Ireland, that November. A shower of frogs "which darkened the air and covered the ground for a long distance" fell near Kansas City, Missouri. And in Toulouse, France, in August 1804, a "tremendous number of little toads" seemed to fall from "a great thick cloud that appeared suddenly in a sky that had been cloudless."

More fishes from the sky above the valley of Abedare, Glamorganshire, February 11, 1859, likely young minnows. Fishes—including one ten inches long—rained on the streets of Boston in June 1841, and they fell in Derby a week after that. Strange fish appeared all over the ground after a massive earthquake in Ecuador in 1797, and again in the 1861 earthquake in Singapore.

Fort not only researched and reported on various anomalies, but he repeatedly pointed out that the accepted scientific explanation often failed to accurately explain anything. Rains of frogs and fishes, most skeptics will tell you, are the result of waterspouts, when a small tornado moves over a body of water, picking up a group of small aquatic animals that are then deposited elsewhere. But Fort scoffed at this proposal: what kind of tornado only picks up one species of animal? In such a hypothesis, he noted, "there is no regard for mud, debris from the bottom of a pond, floating vegetation, loose things from the shore"—only the "precise picking out of frogs or toads."

His writings could not have come at a more opportune time; if Charles Fort had not existed, it would have been necessary to invent him. More so than any crank who came before him or since, Fort changed the way we saw the strange, and would alter the trajectory of belief for so many things that came after him. The two most widespread fringe movements that would dominate the coming decades—cryptozoology and UFOlogy—would not have happened in the way they did without Fort, who laid the groundwork for how to comprehend the incomprehensible. The twentieth century was a Fortean time, when things didn't quite add up.

◦ ◦ ◦

Fort developed his anti-authority stance from an early age, fleeing an abusive home at seventeen to work as a cub journalist in Albany, New York, before moving to New York City in 1892, when he turned eighteen. There he lived in packed tenements, eking out a living writing for the *Brooklyn World* at eighteen dollars a week, toiling out fiction in his spare time. He never made a name for himself as a fiction writer, but his work was strong enough to attract the notice of Theodore Dreiser, who thought Fort's early stories "the best humorous short stories that I have ever seen produced in America," and would in time become his most powerful champion.

But by 1912 Fort had largely given up fiction. He had been married for years, but now he met the true love of his life: the main branch building of the New York Public Library, which had opened a year earlier and would become his mecca. The NYPL was the antithesis to nearby Columbia University, for its mission was to lower barriers to access, not institutionalize them. Fort walked to the library five days a week, stayed until lunch, walked home, and filed his scraps in pigeonholes lining his apartment, then wrote in the afternoon. He collected all manner of information, scraps, and ephemera, poring over scientific journals and antiquated news reports.

In 1916, an inheritance arrived that made him financially comfortable, but he still toiled on his writing, focusing on two books that would never see the light of day. Known as *X* and *Y*, Fort would later burn the manuscripts, so what we know of them now is mostly from letters from the time between Fort and Dreiser. Both were nonfiction, in the grand tradition of cranks and conspiracy theories: *X* posited that there was a race of aliens on Mars that controlled humanity through radio waves, imputing a hidden force behind our day-to-day travails and frustrations. Y, meanwhile, argued that there was a hidden continent at the South Pole.

Neither went far; despite Dreiser's dogged proselytizing, first X and then Y were rejected by Manhattan's publishers. Both books were not just failures of publishing; they were, as best we can understand them now, failures of imagination. Fort was interested in a critique of institutional science, but his alternatives were just as problematic: bizarre theories with little support or reason behind them. As Damon Knight explained, Fort believed that "there were, in science, only believers and cranks, and because he would not be a believer, he became a crank." He set out to follow in the footsteps of Donnelly, Blavatsky, Cervé, and dozens of others—positing radical nonsense as an alternative to mainstream science or religion.

Dreiser's failure to leverage his star power for X and Y was certainly, in hindsight, fortuitous. For, had either been published, Fort would likely have gone on to be largely forgotten, one more minor eccentric like Donnelly, a curious footnote in the landscape of American letters, no more. But instead Fort continued to toil at the library each day, researching constantly. In July 1918, he wrote to Dreiser that he had "discovered" his next book, Z, the product of some twelve years of research. But despite the similarity in title, Z would look nothing like X or Y.

In order to make his earlier book, X, make sense, he'd trimmed hundreds of pages from the original manuscript, cutting out all sorts of ephemera and digressions that didn't fit his thesis. But these scraps continued to gnaw at him; the "hypnosis" of these stubbornly strange facts held him fast. These tidbits and bits of information had a place neither in his crank philosophy nor in mainstream science; they were excluded from both orthodoxy and unorthodoxy. But yet, he realized, they remained, they compelled, they demanded some kind of response.

When he sent his new book to Dreiser in the spring of 1919, he heralded it as not just a book but a "religion." (Fort was never one for humility.) No longer calling it Z, its name befit a new theology: *The Book of the Damned.* "A procession of the Damned," he proclaims in the opening pages. "And by damned, I mean the excluded. We shall have a procession of data that Science has excluded." Fort's book would critique what he called the "exclusionists": those scientists who tended to exclude anomalous or unexplainable phenomena if it didn't fit with their preconceived notions or theories.

Dreiser took it to his publisher, Horace Liveright, demanding he publish it. When Liveright protested, arguing that he'd lose money on it, Dreiser responded, "If you don't publish it, you'll lose me." Appearing at the tail end of 1919, *The Book of the Damned* sold well enough to go into a second printing and led to some minor notice, enough to lead to three subsequent books—*New Lands* (1923), *Lo!* (1931), and *Wild Talents* (1932)—that would further catalog the unexplained, the poorly explained, the anomalous, and the purely bizarre. "There is no way of judging our data," he'd write in *Lo!* "There are no ways, except arbitrary ways, of judging anything."

All of these strange accounts he'd been collecting for years: of falling frogs, blood rains, floating cities, mysterious airships hovering over Chicago, thunderstones, ball lightning, angel hair—all of it could now be gathered in this repository for rejected evidence, this book of the damned. None of it need serve any thesis other than that such things *exist*, and must somehow or another be taken into account.

[5]

BELIEVE NOTHING

C harles Fort has become—well, if not a household name, then a name inextricably linked with a certain kind of news of the weird. For more than four decades, the British magazine *Fortean Times* has kept track of "the world of strange phenomena," gathering together all sorts of unknown and unexplained reports under its heading of Forteana. There's a reason we don't speak of things being "Blavatskyan" or "Donnellyan" like we do "Fortean." Fort's name became an adjective because he changed how we view the world around us, opening up an entirely new way of seeing.

The world of religion and magic, demons and angels, had been made to share the stage with the world of science, of laws and theorems. Both are totalizing systems: if you believe in an omnipotent and omniscient God, then anything—no matter how unusual—is the work of that God, and no matter how strange it seems you can trust in the fact that God works in mysterious ways. Likewise, science's laws are all-encompassing. Unlike these universal explanations, the word "Fortean" is itself a kind of placeholder: it doesn't designate anything beyond the inexplicable, the unclassifiable. On the questionnaire, it is the box marked "other."

Like the cranks before him, Fort had a dim view of scientists and their working methods. But his rejection of science wasn't entirely motivated by ignorance or superstition. In the half century before he began

The Book of the Damned, the field of science had changed dramatically. No university in America offered a PhD until Yale's Sheffield Scientific School in 1861, followed a decade later by the University of Pennsylvania and Harvard. Johns Hopkins (in 1876) and Clark University (in 1889) organized graduate education around the idea of "pure" research, science "for its own sake." During this same time, professional organizations sprung up across the disciplines; now to be a scientist meant to belong to an elite, like-minded group who had all trained at elite universities.

The last two decades of the nineteenth century saw scientific inquiry become an increasingly specialized field, one where well-connected Ivy League graduates held a near monopoly. Initially, universities drew the scientifically minded because they offered material support and the time to pursue projects without regard to their profitability. But soon these universities became the *only* place where pure science was seen as legitimate. And it's no accident, of course, that by organizing itself into tightly guarded professional disciplines centered in Ivy League institutions, scientific inquiry had become a matter of class. Science was for the rich.

So Fort was not lashing out against science per se; rather his celebration of the odd and unexplained was a by-product of how we organize knowledge and learning, and who is and isn't allowed to speak. "It seems to me that the exclusionists are still more emphatically conservators," he would later write. "It is not so much that they are inimical to all data of externally derived substances that fall upon the earth, as they are inimical to all data discordant with a system that does not include such phenomena." Just as the division of knowledge into science and religion led to a proliferation of conspiracy theories, so too did the organization of science into academics and professionals, unwittingly unleashing a new breed of amateurs, cranks, and conspiracists. It's also worth recalling that much of nineteenth-century science was obsessed with proving various social beliefs: that white Europeans were genetically superior to other races, or that teenage girls who sat in school desks all day long did irreparable damage to their reproductive organs. Fort was not wrong in seeing ideological biases behind supposedly objective science.

While cranks like Donnelly were using science to advance their pre-conceived ideas and fantasies, Fort rejected the scientific bureaucracy that had mushroomed into existence in the previous few decades.

More important, what made Fort fundamentally different was that he wasn't offering an alternative vision of the world. Conspiracy theories always involve *theories*—that is, they always offer a positive argument, an explanation to fit the facts (or lack thereof). What made Fort different was that, at his best, he rejected this in favor of a purely negative critique: he was content to point out errors with other theories without positing his own. You can see it in the name of the Fortean Society's magazine: *Doubt.* In an age of newspapers and radio, Forteanism was a return to radical Cartesianism: like Descartes, the goal was simply to doubt anything you could not know for sure.

"We hear much of the conflict between science and religion, but our conflict is with both of these," Fort would later explain. Like so many writers before him, he would inhabit that no-man's-land between the scorched-earth warring factions of science and religion. "Science and religion always have agreed in opposing and suppressing the various witchcrafts. Now that religion is inglorious, one of the most fantastic transferences of worships is that of glorifying science, as a beneficent being." But with his new direction, he would also reject the wild theories that had marred *X* and *Y*: "I believe nothing of my own that I have ever written," he proclaimed. To say that nothing could be taken on faith was, of course, the complete opposite philosophy of cranks like Lewis or Blavatsky—they argued that since science was incomplete, contradic-tory, or wrong, *all that was left was faith.* It was one or the other: science or faith. Fort rejected both. Fort embraced doubt.

Above all, Fort's work is sublime. When the eighteenth-century phi-losopher Edmund Burke defined the term "sublime," he used it to refer to something that was both awe-inspiring and terrifying, yet harmless from the viewer's perspective. A thunderstorm, for example, may be deadly if one is caught in the middle of it, but if one is viewing it from one's warm, cozy living room, its effect is purely aesthetic, and we can take a pure joy from it. Fort's accursed facts are likewise sublime. To find oneself in the middle of, say, a rain of meat or frogs, or an earthquake that turns the sky red and causes black hail—these things would be terrifying to experience. But to read about them through historical accounts engenders another emotion: not terror, but a strange wonder. As one biographer, Jim Steinmeyer, put it: "Fort had discovered that it wasn't merely houses that were haunted; our reality is haunted, our textbooks are haunted, our sciences and understandings are haunted."

● ● ●

Fort's impact, though immense, is hard to quantify. His book sales were decent but never remarkable; his fans were dedicated but never legion. He is not unlike Lou Reed's legendary rock band, the Velvet Underground. In 1982, the musician and producer Brian Eno was talking to Reed, who'd told him that the Velvet Underground's debut 1967 album, *Andy Warhol*, had only sold thirty thousand copies in its first five years—to which Eno responded, "I think everyone who bought one of those thirty thousand copies started a band!" The same could be said for Charles Fort—his first book sold well enough to go into a second printing, but was never a publishing success; his subsequent books had likewise lukewarm sales. And yet so many of Fort's readers went on to become writers in their own right, and his legacy and influence changed science fiction.

Among Fort's ideas was something he called the "London Triangle," an area contained between Worcester and Hereford in the north, Reading and Berkshire in the south, and Colchester, Essex, in the east. Fort chronicled a number of strange occurrences that took place inside this boundary line: an 1884 earthquake, accompanied by a reddish sky over

Colchester, followed by a large quartz stone falling from the sky the next day, rain as black as ink falling in the subsequent days, followed by black hail and snow. Vincent Gaddis took this concept and shifted the geography for a 1964 article on the "Bermuda Triangle," which went on to become a pop occult mainstay.

Fort influenced science fiction authors through the century, from John W. Campbell to William Gibson, providing an enduring wellspring of inspiration, along with films such as *Close Encounters of the Third Kind* and *Magnolia*, with its rain of frogs. And that's just the fiction. Fort's impact on supposed true accounts—of strange creatures, of flying objects, of unexplained phenomena of all kinds—would prove immeasurable.

Fort saw newspapers as our collective memory, a memory that could be faulty, spotty, jumbled, incomprehensible. Rather than treat history as some sort of homogenous memory, a univocal voice, Fort gathered up all that didn't belong, that didn't fit the dominant narrative. Reading Fort is vertiginous: he pelts you with one anomaly after another, a rain of weird facts descending on you without mercy.

The danger, of course, is in seeing science as static, as many cranks often do. In 1919, we had not yet discovered Pluto as the ninth planet, nor had we once again cast it out of the planetary pantheon. We did not understand DNA, had not yet split the atom, had not broached string theory or invented the internet. Fort wasn't necessarily wrong in using science as his target; his error was in assuming it wasn't a moving target.

He also tended to misunderstand the scientific process he was critiquing. Take the story of the Kentucky Meat Shower: scientists, rather than belonging to an obtuse, inaccessible monolith that refused to investigate the world, were actively debating the cause of the meat shower—trading hypotheses, testing evidence, adapting conclusions as need be. That there was never a single, definitive answer to the question does not mean that all of scientific inquiry is suspect, nor does it mean one need adopt the most far-fetched conclusion.

As long as he was simply cataloging anomalies and asking questions, Fort's work hummed with a secret, dangerous knowledge. But when he did propose theories for these anomalies, however provisional, they quickly sounded absurd. He repeatedly suggested that the cause of frog, fish, and blood rains was what he called a Super-Sargasso Sea: an undefined atmospheric condition that gathered up various substances, holding them in suspension, until, like normal clouds, it would become dense enough to rain something bizarre down on the Earth. There are "oceans of blood somewhere in the sky," he suggests at the conclusion of *The Book of the Damned*, a "substance that dries, and falls in a powder—wafts for ages in powdered form—that there is a vast area that will some day be known to aviators as the Desert of Blood. We attempt little of super-topography, at present, but Ocean of Blood, or Desert of Blood—or both—Italy is nearest to it—or them."

The other danger in Fort's approach, of course, was in failing to give science any credit, even when it was clearly in the right. During the Scopes Monkey Trial, Fort ridiculed both sides, and he often slipped dangerously into false equivalences between science and ignorance. He ridiculed Einstein and Bohr, and wrote of "dark cynicisms" about the origins of fossils. How much of this was serious, and how much provocation? It's difficult to know for sure, but passages like this open his work up to antiscience cranks, who were free to see in it unorthodox orthodoxies that Fort himself objected to. "The great trouble," he wrote to Edmond Hamilton at one point, "is that the majority of persons who are attracted are the ones that we do not want; Spiritualists, Fundamentalists, persons who are revolting against Science, not in the least because they are affronted by the myth-stuff of the sciences, but because scientists either oppose or do not encourage them."

Chief among these were his friend and acolyte Tiffany Thayer, a young novelist who had first written to Fort after falling in love with *New Lands*. Thayer would go on to found the Fortean Society, a small group dedicated to promoting Fort's work and that included Dreiser, screenwriter Ben Hecht, and a handful of other writers who would carry on Fort's legacy. After Fort's death, Thayer took control of most of Fort's notes and papers, and in turn left them to the New York Public Library, where they now reside.

The Fortean Society promoted skepticism and discouraged dogmatism, though Thayer himself would prove a poor example of this. Through the pages of *Doubt*, Thayer would argue for various conspiracy theories, including the baseless notion that Franklin Roosevelt had colluded with the Japanese over Pearl Harbor to gain entry into World War II, as well as the idea that fluoride and vaccination were both government plots to control society.

"The conspiracy theory has the same religiosity as the supernatural," Jim Steinmeyer notes, "the same way that atheism requires faith." Thayer was no doubt a conspiracy theorist, but Fort represented the opposite. After all, a hallmark of a conspiracy theory is that it is all-encompassing: everything is further proof of a grand, hidden design, and nothing is chance or random. The conspiracy theorist ultimately creates a system that accounts for everything. In this way, it is itself a kind of science or religion: a grand unified theory that seeks to explain all of creation (its only problem is its specious and unsubstantiated basis). Fort rejected such totalizing beliefs entirely out of hand; there was no system, no matter how grand or clever, that could account for everything. There was always a remainder, something left out, something damned.

What Charles Fort offered was a means of looking at these strange events that militated against ideology seeping in, which remains, a hundred years later, his most valuable gift. But it's easy to forget how that gift is supposed to work. I put the question to science fiction writer Jack Womack, who's spent a lifetime collecting Fortean books and ephemera (and, in 2016, donated a significant portion of his UFO library to Georgetown University): what does it mean to truly follow Charles Fort's methodology? Womack offered the following precepts for being a true Fortean—even if, he allowed, "we may have our continued doubts about gelatinous skies":

A.   *Know that anything can happen even if it hasn't happened yet.*

B.   *Be doubtful but open-minded. Take a large shaker of salt, nonetheless, to keep yourself reminded.*

C.   *Bear in mind the lessons of history and science. [This is probably the most difficult for many.]*

D.   *Remain optimistic, where possible. Be humorous, if circumstances warrant.*

E.   *Seeing is not believing, but start with believing your own eyes.*

F.   *Regard perceived patterns, whether in clouds or in politics, as coincidence or accident, to a point.*

G.   *Remember truth outdoes fiction every time.*

That level of open-mindedness, it seems, requires an almost religious level of devotion. Following any thread of anomalous material makes it clear how easy it is for anyone, even those with the best intentions, to cloud over their vision with preconceived notions. The difference, finally, between a Fortean and a crank, is that the latter looks to the strangeness of the world for confirmation of what they already believe. That even Charles Fort was sometimes guilty of this behavior suggests it may be impossible for any of us to be purely free of bias—to one degree or another, we're all cranks.

Donnelly and Blavatsky had sought a landscape that could be perpetually enchanted, forever resistant to the reach of modernity and rationality. While Fort may have spoken of New Lands in the sky, he was not seeking a place that could remain immune to disenchantment, but rather an outlook itself, something that could transmute a particular set of phenomena into the perpetually enchanted all around us.

PART II

THE END OF MONSTERS

---·---

Regardless of the degree of belief he gives to their existence in the more or less remote past, the modern traveler to far-away places no longer fears meeting a centaur, unicorn, sphinx, phoenix, roc, dodo, dragon, gargoyle, mermaid, behemoth, pegasus, seven-headed hydra, lamia, mantichore, satyr, or other fabulous creature—many of them partly human—which stud the accounts of earlier seagoing and land tourists. Nevertheless, belief in the existence of strange monsters, as yet unrepresented in contemporary zoological gardens, continues today almost as strong as in the days of Marco Polo, Benjamin of Tudela, Pliny, Sir John Mandeville and other trail blazers into the vast unknown when so-called civilization was restricted to Europe and near-by parts of Asia Minor and northern Africa.

—CURTIS MACDOUGALL, *HOAXES*

N ear the end of its run, the Altamaha River in Georgia explodes into a labyrinthine network of tributaries and marshland, fanning out into a maze of spillways and streams before reaching the Atlantic Ocean. Just to the north of this lacework of waterways is the town of Darien, with its high bluff overlooking the delta. I'd come in early March, the air crisp, a strong, steady wind covering everything. The winter sun, still low on the horizon, blotted out detail and contour—but there was a wild magic in the swampland nonetheless as I worked my way past trees draped with tinsel-like moss, piles of oyster shells, stagnant water carpeted over with green algae.

It had been almost twenty years to the month since the big sighting. A beautiful May day in 1998, the temperature had been different: warm and inviting—the kind of weather that draws children and young people out, almost by instinct, to rivers and ponds. The three boys—Rusty "Chewy" Davis, Bennett Bacon, and Owen Lynch—had been swimming in the Altamaha River when they saw a creature emerge from the water. "It was gray and brown and it had stuff all over like seaweed and grass," Davis, eleven years old at the time, later told the news. His friend Bacon, also eleven, had just jumped into the water when Davis and Lynch saw the creature, swimming less than ten feet away. As they shouted to him to get out of the water, Bacon turned and saw a large, scaly tail right in front of him; as he scrambled to get out of the water he scraped his stomach on the dock. He'd come about as close as anyone ever has to Altamaha-Ha, the mysterious water monster of Darien, Georgia.

Before coming to the Altamaha Delta, I'd stopped at the Darien visitor center, which sits in what was once a furniture outlet mall off the freeway. Acres of paved parking lot now sit empty, rows of low-slung storefronts all boarded up. The visitor center and an antique store are the only businesses left open.

SEE DARIEN'S SEA CREATURE, a faded sign exclaims. HAVE YOUR PICTURE TAKEN WITH HIM, BUT DON'T GET TOO CLOSE! Inside, the visitor center is dominated by "Altie," as the locals know it: a massive fiberglass model of the cryptid built by sculptor Rick Spears and donated to the town. Looking vaguely like a plesiosaur, the Altamaha-Ha river monster balances on her chest, her body arching up behind her, tapering into a long tail that spirals up toward the center's ceiling, with a flat, diamond-shaped appendage at the end. Her head is turned, as if to meet your eyes as you enter, looking straight at you with a gaze that is both benign and inquisitive. Whatever terror Bennett Bacon and his friends might have experienced when they faced the creature feels misplaced, looking at this model. Altie's job now, after all, is to welcome you to Darien.

Cryptids these days are all about tourism. Nearly every well-known cryptid has a hometown, and nearly every one of those towns has embraced their local celebrity. Whether or not they're given fearsome names like the Loch Ness Monster or the New Jersey Devil, most now have diminutive nicknames: Nessie, Altie, Caddy (a sea serpent said to be living off the Pacific Northwest coast) and her cousin Cassie (named after Casco Bay in Maine on the opposite coast). Whatever their origin stories, eventually such figures become part of the fabric of the local community. When Burlington, Vermont's minor league baseball team had a contest to decide on a new name, the town voted to name the team after Lake Champlain's most famous resident, the sea monster Champ. (The management ultimately decided "the Champs" might be a bit too cocky given the team's dismal record that year, so they chose the Vermont Lake Monsters instead.)

As I roamed the swamps around Darien, it occurred to me that I did not expect, in any real sense, to see Altie. I've been on numerous ghost hunts, and one thing that's clear is that any night in a spooky hotel or decaying house will produce all sorts of "evidence": strange noises, beeps, and squawks on your Ghost Box or K-II meter or whatever other technology you have on hand, "orbs" and other mysterious lights on your photographs. Whether you take this to be proof of the paranormal or not is often a question for the beholder, but there's always a lot of noise in which to search for signals.

Cryptid hunting, on the other hand, offers far fewer chances for false positives and confirmation biases. The odds of a massive, heretofore unseen creature bursting out of the wilderness are slight, and the odds of finding some traces—a footprint, some scat, a foul odor—aren't that much better. While ghost hunters often amass mountains of what they claim to be evidence—EVP recordings, photos, and videos—a cryptozoologist may go her or his life with only one or two sightings, and often those are undocumented. Robert H. Rines spent much of his life searching for the Loch Ness Monster based on a single sighting in 1972: "I had the misfortune of seeing one of these things with my own eyes." By the time he'd retired in 2008, he had precious little else to show for his work. Cryptid hunting is the art of disappointment.

All the same, there's something about it that changes your attitude to the natural world. Hunting—even for the most die-hard killers—is on some level a communion with nature, becoming one with the environment so as not to scare the deer or duck you're preying on. It means being aware of the snapped twig, the leaf rustle, the brown-on-brown blur at the far edge of the tree line.

Cryptid hunting is this, but something else again, since your quarry is not of this known world. It is training yourself not just to see nature as it is, but to try to place yourself in the middle of a complex ecosystem moving all around you with little concern for your presence. It is all that, and then trying to train yourself for what's different, what's out of place. In a world of camouflaged animals, silent stalking predators, and elusive prey, you're looking for something far more hidden.

I spent hours along the banks of the Altamaha. Once I got away from the road, the stillness overtook me, and I settled in a mostly dry patch not far from the bank, watching the shorebirds and listening to the rustle of the trees as the wind pulsed through them. I'd left behind the only other humans I'd seen—fishing off an overpass—and plunged deep into the delta's wilds. I never saw Altie, but it's hard to say that the experience was a disappointment.

On the way back through Darien I stopped at the local café for a surprisingly good cup of coffee, and fell to talking to Carl, the owner. Yes, he told me, there are seekers who come to Darien looking for the river monster, but even in the peak months there aren't many; situated between Savannah to the north and the resort community of Jekyll Island to the south, there's not much here to keep tourists in Darien. I mentioned how successful the area around Loch Ness had been at marketing their monster, and that perhaps in this regard Darien had "missed the boat," hoping the dumb pun would lighten the mood. But Carl took this fact surprisingly hard, and just responded, dismayed, "Yeah, that's the story of this county."

Finally, I asked him: Do you believe the stories? Have you ever seen the monster? What do you think it is? "I know folks who swear up and down they've seen it," he told me, wiping down already-clean tables out of what must have been habit (I was the only customer). "But most of the fishermen here, they'll tell you the same thing: it's just a manatee that got confused and swam upstream into fresh water."

Why, I find myself wondering, isn't the natural splendor of this place beautiful enough? Certainly, for many of us, simply being in nature is its own reward. But for at least some segment of the population, the natural world is only as good as the secret denizens it hides. Why the need to go poking in about the trees and underbrush looking for unseen creatures? What drives us to populate the forests and lakes and deserts of the world with thunderbirds and the chupacabra, Bigfoot and the Loch Ness Monster?

[6]

THE LINNAEAN SOCIETY OF NEW ENGLAND
VERSUS THE GLOUCESTER SEA SERPENT

During the dog days of August 1817, a strange creature appeared off the coast of Massachusetts. Over a series of weeks, Gloucester Bay, thirty miles northeast of Boston, became home to what appeared to be some kind of sea serpent, spotted not just once or twice, but by dozens, if not hundreds, of local residents.

Eyewitness accounts varied on specific details, but the overall form of the sea serpent was clear. Amos Story saw it midday on August 10, for about ninety minutes: it had the head of a sea turtle, he would later explain, and it was approximately fifty feet long, its diameter about that of a man's body, dark brown in color. James Mansfield also put it at forty to fifty feet long. Solomon Allen, who saw it on the twelfth, thirteenth, and fourteenth, thought its head was the shape of a rattlesnake but the size of a horse, about eighty to ninety feet long, and half a barrel in diameter. Epes Ellery also saw it on the fourteenth, just after sunset, with fifteen to twenty people, with joints the size of a "two-gallon keg," a flat head, and a mouth like a serpent. It appeared to have a series of humps or protuberances along its back, such that when it swam near the surface these humps could be seen trailing behind its head. William H. Foster described its dramatic ability to change course: it would "move in a straight line west," he recalled, "and would almost in an instant, change his course to east, bringing his head, as near as I could judge, to where his tail was." Foster described its speed as close to a mile a minute.

Matthew Gaffney was in the bay on the fourteenth when the serpent appeared not more than thirty feet from his boat. Its head, Gaffney recalled, was as large as a four-gallon keg, at least forty feet long, with a white belly and a dark head. Fearing for his safety, Gaffney fired at the monster, but if he hit it, the serpent was unfazed: it turned toward Gaffney's boat and swam directly under it, only to resurface a hundred yards away.

By the end of August, the sea serpent of Gloucester Bay had become a spectacle; crowds were thronging to the beaches to get a glimpse of the creature, and they were not disappointed. It was regularly sighted, both by those out on boats and those on land. It drew the curious all the way from Boston, including Daniel Webster, who joined a friend on a visit on August 17 to see the beast.

After a week of sightings, the Linnaean Society of New England found itself involved. The society had been formed in 1814 in Boston to advance the nascent professionalization of science. Its members were well-respected people in the community of course, but crucially they were made up of university professors and trained scientists, instead of simply aristocratic amateurs. It fell to three men—John Davis, Jacob Bigelow, and Francis Calley Gray—to investigate the matter and report back.

These men were hardly cranks. Under George Washington, Davis had served as the comptroller of the Treasury of the United States and later as the United States attorney for the district of Massachusetts; he was also president of the Massachusetts Historical Society and a fellow of the American Academy of Arts and Sciences. Jacob Bigelow taught botany at Harvard and was the driving force and architect behind Mount Auburn Cemetery. And Francis Gray was a member of the Massachusetts House of Representatives, John Quincy Adams's private secretary, and president of the Boston Athenaeum. These were among Boston's best and brightest, and they approached the matter not as credulous crackpots but as serious scientists.

The Linnaean Society set out to identify the beast, dispatching Lonson Nash, a justice of the peace, to depose the witnesses, gathering sworn affidavits from a dozen eyewitnesses as to what they'd seen. But having accomplished this work, their research hit a wall: other than evaluating similarities and differences among the accounts, there wasn't much more they could do. But then on September 27, a farmer named Gorham Norwood working in a field near Loblolly Cove killed a sea serpent.

● ● ●

This was by no means the first sighting of a mysterious sea serpent. Stories of such beasts are legendary, stretching back centuries. There was the sea swine (a fish with the head of a pig, four feet, and a forked tail, plus an extra set of eyes on its hind legs and a bonus eye on its belly), the sea horse (not the diminutive creature we know today but a full-sized aquatic equine), and the terrifying Ziphius (with its razor-sharp, swordlike back, it would supposedly swim under ships and then surface, splitting the boat in half so it could feed on the sailors). These figures hovered on the edge of maps, filled out the pages of medieval bestiaries, and populated stories and songs of mariners. But if sea serpents had existed for centuries, by the nineteenth century the world had changed around them, and a new scientific community of naturalists and zoologists had arrived—people who were not content to allow such monsters to simply exist in the realm of myth.

Sixty years before the Gloucester sightings began, Carl Linnaeus had published the tenth edition of his *Systema Naturæ per Regna Tria Naturæ, Secundum Classes, Ordines, Genera, Species, cum Characteribus, Differentiis, Synonymis, Locis* ("System of Nature Through the Three Kingdoms of Nature, According to Classes, Orders, Genera and Species, with Characters, Differences, Synonyms, Places"), and with it firmly established a taxonomy that could encompass all life on Earth.

Binomial nomenclature—the naming system in which a plant or animal is defined by a genus name and a species name—had first been developed by brothers Gaspard and Johann Bauhin in the sixteenth century, simplifying many Latin names of various plants down to a two-term system. Linnaeus took this idea and ran with it. He began to use it consistently in his descriptions of plant life, and then expanded it to the rest of the animal kingdom. Linnaeus's system initially had five levels (kingdom, class, order, genus, and species), though zoological nomenclature has since grown to encompass eight different levels. The genius of Linnaean classification is both its comprehensiveness and its flexibility. Anything could now be measured against known species, compared for similarities and differences, and then located in its proper place accordingly. Correspondingly, if a new animal is found that does not fit easily into the established classification system, the system itself can be amended.

In a single stroke, the Linnaean classification system wiped monsters off the face of the map. There might still be unknown beasts and fearsome creatures out there, but now they each would have a family, a genus, a species; no matter how strange an animal might be, it was now under the rubric of scientific study and discussion. Thus, the medieval world's monsters and wonders were, one by one, either incorporated into this taxonomy or excluded as myth. The kraken became the genus *Architeuthis*, the giant squid; the sea serpent became *Regalecus glesne*, the giant oarfish.

The Linnaean Society of New England, then, was not interested in a monster; they were interested in a new species, something they could categorize and taxonomize. They sought not the glory of the hunt, nor did they seek to drum up hysteria over some demonic new intruder. They simply wanted to understand what kind of an animal this sea serpent was: Where did it fit in relationship to other animals? Was it a fish or a snake? Did it require its own genus, its own family, its own order? Were there other creatures out there like it, waiting to be discovered?

So the discovery of an actual specimen from Loblolly Cove was of major importance, as it would allow Davis, Bigelow, and Gray to dissect and analyze its anatomy, and to better understand how it related to other species. What they found was a curious creature indeed. In many aspects, it resembled an eastern racer (*Coluber constrictor*), a snake common to New England. But this animal was different, for it had a series of strange ridges or "protuberances," forty in all, running down the length of the creature's back. Not only did these ridges seem to comport with eyewitness accounts of the serpent's humped nature, but they also seemed to distinguish it from a common eastern racer. After a thorough anatomical investigation, the Linnaean Society of New England concluded that they were indeed looking at a new species, which they named *Scoliophis atlanticus* ("scolio," crooked, "phis," snake).

But was the specimen they'd examined the same sea serpent that had been sighted in the bay? On the one hand, this one had been found on land, not at sea. On the other, it was significantly smaller: barely five feet, a far cry from the forty- to ninety-foot estimates.

Davis, Bigelow, and Gray considered this and decided that the most likely explanation was that this strange serpent was a juvenile of the larger creature sighted in the bay. Noting that sea creatures often deposited eggs on beaches, and that a juvenile boa constrictor is significantly smaller than an adult, they decided that their specimen was none other than a baby sea serpent.

For the next thirty years, *Scoliophis atlanticus* appeared in naturalist guides of the time, a new but generally accepted entry into the Linnaean taxonomical system. The stuffed specimen itself was put on display in a museum in New Haven, Connecticut (its lower jaw had been destroyed when Norwood killed it, so it had to be reconstructed using cork, bird quills, and other material). It was still there when the British geologist Charles Lyell saw it. Lyell, less credulous than others, suggested that what he was looking at was no juvenile sea serpent—rather, he judged, it was likely nothing more than a garden-variety *Coluber constrictor* with some kind of spinal deformity.

Lyell's appraisal was confirmed by none other than Jacob Bigelow's own son, Henry Jacob Bigelow, by then an eminent physician in his own right. Bigelow purchased the serpent from the museum and dissected what was left of it, confirming that the strange spinal ridges that had been so compelling to his father were likely a case of rickets.

What of the sea serpent's massive length, though? If it was just a five-foot snake with a vitamin deficiency, why had it seemed so massive to observers? David Humphreys had an answer, which he had proposed when he'd originally related the event in a series of letters to Joseph Banks of the Royal Society of London. "This difference of opinion, as to the length," he wrote to Banks, "perhaps may be partly accounted for on the principle of what sea-faring men call *looming*. Owing to the state of the atmosphere, or the point of view, the same floating spar appears sometimes 40, and at others, 100 feet long." This is a somewhat unsatisfying conclusion, and hard to test so long after the original sightings. But still, the scientific community may have justly assumed that this would be the end of any discussion of mysterious sea serpents and water beasts. But history is like a lake in Scotland: it's always a bit murkier than you expect.

[7]

SPECTACULAR TAXONOMY

Nessie hunters sometimes envision themselves as part of a grand, long tradition that stretches back centuries. They like to point to an early account of the life of Columba, the Irish saint who came to Scotland in the mid-sixth century and encountered a monster in the river Ness. But cryptids are a distinctly modern phenomenon, and they exist not in the world of saints and miracles but scientists and taxonomies. Nessie's story starts not in the sixth century, but, just like the Gloucester sea serpent, in August.

On a fine, clear night in 1930, three young men were fishing out on the waters of Loch Ness. According to the *Northern Chronicle*'s subsequent article on the encounter (titled simply "What Was It?"), at about 8:15 P.M. the three men claimed they'd seen a "great commotion" some six hundred yards away, when "the fish—or whatever it was—started coming toward us and when it was 300 yards away it turned to the right." Its abrupt turn sent a two-and-a-half-foot wave that rocked their boat violently. "We have no idea what it was," the eyewitnesses told the *Northern Chronicle*, "but we are quite positive it could not have been a salmon." There would not be a follow-up to the report for another three years, but something had stirred in Loch Ness.

In 1933, Nessie returned, and the sightings began to multiply. After a story in *The Inverness Courier* on May 2, 1933, dozens of witnesses claimed to have seen the monster, and by the end of the year national news outlets were also carrying stories of Nessie. If Daniel Webster could once have traveled to Gloucester Bay to see its legendary inhabitant himself, most of the world who read about Nessie could not; for everyone who flocked to Loch Ness to get a glimpse of the creature, thousands more could only read about it in newspaper reports. And some of those reports were more reliable than others.

During that initial frenzy of reports, the *Daily Mail* sent famous big-game hunter Marmaduke Wetherell out to Loch Ness to hunt for the monster. On December 20 he proudly announced he'd found evidence of a set of massive footprints leading to the water's shore. But researchers at the Natural History Museum in London quickly deduced that Wetherell's footprints were made by a dried hippo's foot—the kind that were popular at the time for use as exotic ashtrays and umbrella stands. From the start, scientists who'd hoped to take the phenomenon seriously had to be wary of hoaxers like Wetherell, and such hoaxes would plague the study of the Loch Ness Monster from then on.

The single best piece of evidence for the existence of the creature had appeared in April 1934, when the *Daily Mail* published the famous "Surgeon's Photograph" (named for gynecologist Robert Kenneth Wilson, who didn't want his name used): a single shot of the creature's neck and head rising up from the water, a solitary traveler across a gray-dark sea. The arc of the neck, the head straight forward—both give the creature a strange sense of melancholic beauty.

The Surgeon's Photograph became the hallmark of Nessiedom: a grainy trace that was evocative but not conclusive, hinting at the shape of a thing that remained almost entirely concealed beneath the waters. Writers like to cite Ernest Hemingway's "iceberg" theory of minimalist prose: "If a writer of prose knows enough about what he is writing about he may omit things that he knows and the reader, if the writer is writing truly enough, will have a feeling of those things as strongly as though the writer had stated them," Hemingway writes in *Death in the Afternoon*.

"The dignity of movement of an ice-berg is due to only one-eighth of it being above water." As with icebergs, so, too, with water monsters; what was beneath the surface mattered as much, if not more, than what was on film. Other photos would follow, along with sonar records and film footage, but none have had the iconic allure of Wilson's simple image.

Nessie, in some sense, benefited from the media technology of her day: in lieu of ubiquitous cell-phone cameras and HD technology, she is a creature of the grainy, out-of-focus shots, the blur in the water. These images were printed in newspapers and cheap, pulpy periodicals, which often had no compunction about cropping the images for dramatic purposes, and regularly distressed their resolution for economy's sake—all of which only heightened their mystery. The poorer the quality, the more authentic the image appears.

In November 1934, seven months after the Surgeon's Photograph appeared, a scientific conference was held on the matter at the Linnean Society in Piccadilly, London, during which they reviewed some footage taken by a Nessie observer that September. The footage, taken through the mist from three quarters of a mile away from its subject, was difficult to make sense of, and opinions differed at the Linnean Society as to what, exactly, it depicted. Some proposed it to be a seal; others thought it might be a killer whale. Others argued that if it was a seal, it would have been seen on the banks of Loch Ness, as seals are wont to do. At least one attendee saw an otter. Sir A. Smith Woodward reminded the group that if Nessie *was* a surviving Mesozoic animal, there would be evidence of her peers in the fossil records. Martin Hinton, then deputy keeper of zoology at the Natural History Museum, argued that the "monster" was a composite beast, made up of a living seal who'd been caught on film; various erroneous observations of various animate and inanimate things; and tradition and superstition.

Once again, eminent scientists weighed in on what to make of these reports, but unlike in 1817, these biologists did not endorse the notion that Nessie was a new species. Stanley Kemp, director of the Marine Biological Laboratory at Plymouth, perhaps summed it up best by simply saying he had no idea what it was. For the time being, the scientific establishment let the matter rest.

Soon enough, it seemed like the monster's fifteen minutes of fame were up. During the Depression, Loch Ness had provided an interesting escape: a strange, dreamy possibility of some unknown frontier. Once war broke out, though, British attention shifted elsewhere (though Mussolini's in-house newspaper, *Il Popolo d'Italia*, did proclaim that Nessie had been killed by a German bombing raid). The legendary inhabitant of Loch Ness seemed to fade back into the mists of obscurity.

● ● ●

It would fall to a nonpracticing family doctor, someone with no formal training in zoology and who had never published a book before, to draw Nessie back out. Constance Whyte had lived along Loch Ness for twenty years, and spent ten years writing her 1957 book, *More Than a Legend: The Story of the Loch Ness Monster*. She not only rejected the findings (or lack thereof) of the Linnean Society twenty-three years earlier, she made that rejection a basic part of her pitch.

"The Loch Ness story challenges beliefs which are integral to the makeup of most established zoologists," she wrote in a direct assault on the scientific establishment. Whyte's book was written for a general audience and with a common folk wisdom, and it argued that the problem with trained biologists was their willful ignorance, their acceptance of dogma, and their refusal to accept observational evidence directly in front of them.

This close-minded approach made it difficult for those who *were* willing to search for Nessie; since a serious, scientific search of the lake's waters would be prohibitively expensive for amateur researchers, the refusal of the scientific academy to put up the funds made it impossible to know one way or another for sure. "Official research is so controlled," Whyte seethed, "that it is extremely difficult for a young scientist with a hunch to go out and follow it up."

Whyte's book reawakened the slumbering beast that was Nessiedom. Nessie had quickly become a polarizing issue around the very institution of science itself—its universities, natural history museums, zoologists, and laboratories. To believe in Nessie, Whyte argued, meant rejecting science.

But did the opposite hold? Did being a scientist mean, more or less, that one had to believe Nessie a hoax? Denys Tucker wasn't so sure. Tucker had been a rising star in ichthyology when he was hired at the age of twenty-six by the Natural History Museum in 1949 as its curator of fishes. He'd visited Loch Ness in March 22, 1959, two years after Whyte's book had rekindled interest to see for himself what the fuss was about. While there, he saw a dark hump moving across the water that didn't match anything he knew about aquatic life. He recognized it a year later in a short film of the creature that Tim Dinsdale had made, and came to the conclusion it was a *Cryptoclidus*, a long-necked plesio-saur that went extinct 65 million years ago.

When the Natural History Museum's board learned that one of their star curators was entertaining the existence of Nessie, they were not amused. The museum had fallen for a supposed piece of Yeti scalp a few years earlier (the scrap of flesh was actually from a pig), and it had been forced to admit that their "objective identification" of the hoax had been "written off by the faithful as mere incompetence on our part." They were not about to be taken in again. A memo that went out to all staff read: "The Trustees wish it to be known that they do not approve of the spending of official time or official leave on the so-called Loch Ness Phenomenon. . . . They take this opportunity of warning all concerned that if as a result of the activities of members of the staff the Museum is involved in undesirable publicity, they will be gravely displeased."

Tucker, however, would not back down, so the museum fired him. It was as though they hoped to make a lesson out of him by ostracizing him from his workplace, his professional standing, connections, and the privileges that they brought. Entertaining the idea of mythical beasts wasn't just bad science; it would leave you outside the very community of scientists, alone and bereft. The monster had claimed its first victim.

But the sightings, spurred on by Whyte's book and those that followed in her wake, continued. From 1962 to 1971, the Loch Ness Phenomena Investigation Bureau held something of a monopoly on searches and sighting operations, organizing amateur photographic and filmic expeditions in an attempt to catch a glimpse of the creature. As Tucker's experience had shown, though, the creature had become something of a litmus test: Were you open to the possibility of the marvelous? Or were you stuck in the close-minded rut of the scientific establishment? In 1974, naturalist Gerald Durrell accused the scientists of labeling otherwise "observant, intelligent witnesses" as nothing more than "drunk, insane, hoaxers or partially blind and all definitely mentally retarded," simply for reporting their observations. The searchers had stopped looking for just a single animal; they were looking to overturn the entire edifice of the academy, the entire disciplines of zoology and biology.

o   o   o

Unlike the Gloucester sea serpent, the Loch Ness Monster divided the world into believers and scientists. The Linnaean Society of New England may have been wrong identifying a sick snake as a new creature, but (while they were ridiculed for their error) they weren't cast out of the scientific establishment like Tucker was. By the twentieth century, the natural sciences had professionalized to a degree that entry into that world—with the prestige and resources that came with it—meant accepting a certain level of seriousness. Hunting for mythical beasts was not becoming of a modern scientist. But the flip side was hardly better: in favor of Nessie were hoaxers like Wetherell and various other cranks putting forth distinctly antiscientific ideas, relying on dubious eyewitness accounts, and given to confirmation bias and wishful thinking.

And then in January 1982, a number of scientists and researchers—many of whom had become pariahs in their own fields for their interests in water beasts and other cryptids—came together to find a third way, forming the International Society of Cryptozoology. As the name implied, this new group and their magazine, *Cryptozoology*, would professionalize the science of hidden beasts. Using rigorous scientific methods, researchers would conduct serious studies, guided by an open-minded skepticism.

Cryptozoology also remains one of the best examples of something like an organized Forteanism: a field devoted to Fort's principles of extreme doubt, avoidance of dogma and established authority, and a tangential, somewhat skeptical relationship to institutionalized science. This was a field, they believed, that could be separated from the hoaxes and hucksters, and elevated to a level of seriousness that rivaled other disciplines. Paleontology, for example, worked on extinct animals, of which there was no direct evidence but traces in the fossil record. Why couldn't cryptozoology, which also relied on traces, be taken just as seriously?

Cryptid hunting had long been a rebuke to science, to the arrogance of those who assumed they knew better than ordinary observers; now instead it would reconfigure itself as cryptozoology, no longer a critique of science but instead its imitation. The search for the Loch Ness Monster need not be a repudiation of science, if it was handled right.

But there was pushback, primarily from the amateurs, the working-class hunters who spent their weekends and free time with nothing but a camera, who did not come from academic backgrounds, and who feared—not without reason—that they'd soon be marginalized in this new field of cryptozoology. Pushback from the people who'd turned to cryptid hunting as a rejection of science, who now bristled at having to once again share the limelight with stuffy academics. One Bigfoot hunter, René Dahinden, said that if he ever did capture a specimen, he would only sell it to the scientific community for the right price; otherwise, he threatened, "the evidence is going to lay out there and rot away and I wouldn't move a finger. I don't give a damn about science. I couldn't care less about science." This remains the fundamental contradiction embedded in the search for hidden animals: is the field an explicit rejection of the scientific establishment, or does it mirror it, a parascientific pursuit working in tandem with the more established fields of biology and zoology?

Perhaps both. The words "cryptid" and "cryptozoology" were first coined by Bernard Heuvelmans, who held a doctorate in zoology but had far more success as a cryptid hunter than a zoologist. In his definition he purposely built in a very specific idea of wonder. A bizarre beetle, a new kind of tree frog, an interesting deep-sea fish—none of these, for Heuvelmans, qualified as cryptids. To count, a candidate must have at least one trait that was "truly singular, unexpected, paradoxical, striking, emotionally upsetting, and thus capable of mythification." To count as a cryptid, the creature must be itself a critique of science, a rejection of the everyday. They don't just go beyond the reach of science; their mere presence is an affront to it.

Cryptids are fundamentally the product of a post-Linnaean world. They are what cannot be captured by science, what does not fit into this totalizing system of classification. Cryptids resist all attempts at categorization; to believe in cryptids is to refuse the proposition that science can find a taxonomical place for every living thing. Cryptids are the remainders.

Cryptids don't just live at the geographical margins, they exist perpetually at that margin between the scientific and the fantastic. Insist too heavily that they are mythical, and believers will respond with physiology, breeding habits, child-rearing techniques. But push on these scientific aspects too much and the creatures disappear once again back into the fog. Cryptozoology lives on this bright and unsettled line between amateur hunters and serious scientists, as a rejection of science and an earnest parody of it.

The aim of cryptozoology, as George Simpson once put it, is to "demythify" these once mythical beasts: "to search hopefully to find the objective, living animal from which the myth developed." The search for cryptids is not just a search for a reenchanted wilderness; cryptids are not fairies, unicorns, or leprechauns. They are mythical but not mystical. Rather than a reenchanted wilderness, the cryptozoologist seeks a reenchanted science: a science of adventure and discovery, a romantic science of discovery that the cryptozoologist feels has been lost in an overly technocratic age.

The Nessie cottage industry, meanwhile, had become such a juggernaut that few could afford to pay much attention when, in 1975, Marmaduke Wetherell's son Ian admitted that he, his father, his stepbrother, and others had conspired to fake the famous Surgeon's Photograph: Wetherell, humiliated when his footprint hoax was revealed, set out to get revenge on the *Daily Mail*, building a small model of Nessie, staging a photograph, and then passing it through to a doctor friend whose reputation, they rightly assumed, would confer legitimacy.

In 1986 came another revelation: Nessie enthusiast Henry H. Bauer revealed that the monster itself was born of a tourist campaign—at least according to the writer David Gerahty, who confessed to conjuring up the monster first in a roman à clef, *Marise*. "In the early 1930s I, with two young partners, ran a publicity service in London," Gerahty wrote to Bauer. They had been offered a small contract by a group of hotels near the Loch to help drum up more business. At the same time, another client of theirs, a real estate agent in British Columbia, had mentioned that he had helped invent the legend of Ogopogo, a sea serpent supposedly living in Lake Okanagan. "This was corn in Egypt," Gerahty wrote. "The Lossiemouth member of the firm then told us that for centuries a legendary creature was supposed to dwell in Loch Ness. We had never heard of it." Nonetheless, over "several pints of beer," Gerahty and his group became "midwives of the reborn Loch Ness Monster. All we had to do was to arrange for the Monster to be sighted. This we did and the story snowballed. Thousands went north to see it and see it they did. It was, of course, pure hokum." Even with this proof in hand, Bauer continued to believe in the monster. Some things matter more than proof.

Ian Wetherell's confession again resurfaced in the early 1990s, when David Martin and Alastair Boyd dredged it up and tracked down the last surviving member of the conspiracy, Wetherell's stepson, Christopher Spurling, who confirmed to them in 1991: "It's not a genuine photograph. It's a load of codswallop and always has been." It's not a genuine photograph of Nessie, then, but it's still a photograph—and it still invokes all of the wonder and mystery that photographs offer.

Ultimately, the story of Loch Ness is a story of a lake, a lake deep and dark and mysterious, yet one right in front of us, well known and well inhabited. How much of our life is spent next to such places, places that seem well known but whose depths we've never fully plumbed? The cryptozoologist believes, on some level, that humanity is not yet in complete possession of the natural world, does not yet hold dominion over it. It is a rejection not just of a Linnaean view of the world, but of a religious one as well, a rejection of God's command to Adam to take dominion over the natural world. For how can we take dominion over the world if its corners remain murky?

[8]

THE EDGE OF THE MAP

n the collections of Seton Hall University in South Orange, New Jersey, there's a round ceramic disk, about the size and shape of a cobblestone, with the barest image of a face on it. Two eyes in a mushroom-shaped head, a mouth opened in a howl or scream of some kind. Radiocarbon dating puts its age at about seven hundred years old, which would make it one of the earliest known images of the Jersey Devil.

The Lenape knew it as Mësingw, a spirit being vital to preserving the balance of the forest. Mësingw ("Living Solid Face," "Masked Being," or "Keeper of the Game"), according to Herbert C. Kraft, who devoted his life to researching and documenting Lenape culture, was of prime importance to the Lenape. Of all the manetuwàk (spirit beings whose job it was to care for and maintain the world that Kishelëmukòng had created), Mësingw had one of the most important jobs: looking after the animals of the forest and ensuring their health and safety. Mësingw could sometimes be seen riding through the forest on a large buck, covered in long black hair from head to toe like a bear. The right side of his large, round face was colored bright red, the left side colored black.

Alternately revered and feared, he ensured the prosperity and prevalence of vital game for the people but could also, if displeased, ruin a hunter's luck, or "break his speech," causing him to stammer uncontrollably, or scare him to death. Mësingw, for the Lenape, kept the forest in balance, mediating between humanity and animal life. When white settlers came to the land where the Lenape lived, they saw images and masks of a strange creature who, they were told, lived in the forbidding wilds of the Pine Barrens, the edge of the settled world. As they heard tales of Mësingw and saw the masks and effigies of the god, they saw him not as a figure of order but of terror.

Whatever prowled the foreboding Pine Barrens, early settlers thought, it was not Christian. And in the early Puritan imagination, fevered with thoughts of Satan and divine punishment, Mësingw merged with another local legend: the Leeds Devil. Stories tell of a "Mother Leeds," who was in labor with her thirteenth child when she uttered, out of exasperation or pain, "Let this one be a devil!" resulting in a monstrous birth, the hideous creature fleeing the house as soon as it was birthed.

"Mother Leeds makes no attempt to love or nurture her offspring, and, rather than mourn his loss, is relieved to be rid of him," Frank Esposito and Brian J. Regal write in their study of the Jersey Devil. "It is the female—a self-centered, uncaring, unloving mother—who bears the brunt of the blame." This story, Regal and Esposito note, has some basis in fact: Anne Hutchinson, the Puritan leader who was expelled from the Massachusetts Bay Colony in 1637, later gave birth to a "disturbing mass that bore little resemblance to a child" (what was likely a molar pregnancy, in which a nonviable fertilized egg implants in the womb, resulting in a malformed mass of cells). Another apostate, Mary Dyer (who was later executed for converting to Quakerism), likewise gave birth to a deformed child who was taken as proof of her heresy. Mother Leeds "becomes a scapegoat for various fears about witches, non-Christians, and women in general," Esposito and Regal explain. "She is an outsider, rural, uneducated, and prone to supernatural and superstitious beliefs and who has sex with the devil."

The Devil itself, meanwhile, likely took its name from Daniel Leeds, a well-respected and influential early New Jersey writer, but one who increasingly flirted with unorthodox ideas. He brought English astrology with him to America, publishing astrological charts in his popular almanacs. So the Leeds Devil's emergence as early American folklore came at a time when there was a fair amount of anxiety over colonials living outside of the carefully controlled Puritan power structure.

The early years for European settlers in America were filled with strife, everything from unexpected crop failures, conflict with the indigenous populations, and a general inability to adapt to new conditions and climate so far from England and Europe. As with many communities under siege from external forces, the early colonists responded by enforcing a strict religious and governmental hierarchy; dissent could simply not be tolerated, lest the whole colony fail.

The Leeds Devil prowled at the edges of a tight-knit community, a warning to all who might step out of line. Cryptids have since come to occupy these places, almost exclusively: marginal locations on the edge of the known world. The dense redwood forests of Northern California; the deep, forbidding lochs of Scotland; the impassable Himalayan peaks; or the deserts along the border of the United States and Mexico, where the goat-sucking cryptid the chupacabra is often seen. It was here that one caught in 2007 by a local rancher: "I'm not going to tell you that's not a chupacabra," veterinarian Travis Schaar, who examined the creature, told the Associated Press. "I just think in my opinion a chupacabra is a dog."

Anthropologists use the word *liminal*, from the Latin *limins*, or threshold, to describe those moments and places of transition, places where the rules are fuzzy, the laws suspended. These are the frontiers between here and there, between the "savage" and the "civilized." The sunken continents of Atlantis and Lemuria dreamed up by Ignatius Donnelly and Helena Blavatsky were liminal places, border regions halfway between the known world and a mystical realm beyond our ken. The mysterious denizens of such places have gradually been replaced by Yeti and Nessie, whose purpose remains the same: to patrol the edges of the map.

· · ·

Monsters have always patrolled the margins of the map. In distant lands lived barbarians, cannibals, and wild, unimaginable creatures. Travelers' narratives, such as Sir John Mandeville's mid-fourteenth-century chronicle, brought back stories of the horrific and marvelous from far-off lands. Mandeville's fictional travelogue reported of distant islands where one could find "ugly folk without heads, who have eyes in each shoulder; their mouths are round, like a horseshoe, in the middle of their chest. In yet another part there are headless men whose eyes and mouths are on their backs. . . . In another isle there are people whose ears are so big that they hang down to their knees." Such wonders populated maps of the period; Roman cartographers had sometimes used the phrase *HIC SVNT LEONES*—"Here be lions"—to denote unexplored incognita; medieval cartographers updated this with fanciful images of sea serpents, kraken, and dragons.

These distant races inspired wonder—a sense of the magic and the mysterious in the far and distant world, precisely because they lived on the edges of the known world. Medievalist Karl Steel notes that medieval natural historians understood wonders primarily in terms of where they stood in relationship to civilization: "In the bestiaries and medieval natural history tradition in general, unicorns, dragons, and other wonders are not associated with a particular place or habitat," he says. "Medieval wonders live at the edge of the conceptual map: the further you get from home, the weirder things get." In the travels of Sir John Mandeville, wonders don't begin to appear until after he's passed through Jerusalem; the routes between England and the Holy Land were well documented. But after that, the landscape turns wondrous. By their very strangeness, monsters determined the boundaries of the regular world.

Such tales were less about accuracy and more about creating an organized world of the civilized and uncivilized—marked, first and foremost, by strange monsters. Credibility didn't matter to an audience who themselves were likely never to see such places, and besides, people who'd never ventured this far were in no position to fact-check a traveler's assertions. A sense of wonder, divorced from the obligations of veracity, was precisely the point.

Some of these distant species were gradually assimilated into a Linnaean taxonomy as they were definitively collected, observed, and cataloged (the giant squid, for example, or the panda bear). Others, though, simply vanished, receding into the mists of myth. Such creatures could only exist so long as there were unknown corners of the map; as the explorers fanned out over the seas and mountains and it became a small world after all, there were fewer regions that could plausibly be inhabited by monsters.

The birth of cryptids—of strange creatures that exist beyond the reach of civilized humanity—is in part a response to this end of wonders. For the most part, cryptozoologists are re-creating those species that are not only beyond the grasp of understanding, but whose realm is specifically in the margins, where they are free to transcend scientific classification.

Cryptids require physical spaces that can't be fully reached, fully documented, fully inhabited by civilized people. They require the borders between places, the edge lands. Cryptids are nothing without their habitat, and their habitat was, at least for a time, destroyed by colonialism and capitalism throughout the nineteenth century, as the "blank spaces" on the map were filled in, and as cultural differences were more and more assimilated through trade and tourism.

*   *   *

European settlers to North America romanticized the idea of a frontier, a dividing line between civilization and savagery, and such a concept would be integral to the country they founded as it spread west toward the Pacific Ocean. The frontier was amorphous in its location and definition, and mythical in its pull on white settlers—it was less a place than a state of mind. But creatures like the Leeds Devil were important for this border, too, since they reminded settlers what happened if they moved too far, too fast, into the savage and virgin lands.

The Leeds Devil was an important myth so long as there were settlers in New Jersey living along that liminal borderland, but by the nineteenth century the creature was rarely mentioned in the press or in the local folklore. Once the frontier moved, leaving only civilization, there was no need for the same kind of monstrous figure to patrol that line and keep the civilized on their side.

New Jersey's devil isn't the only cryptid who can trace its genealogy back to this collision of indigenous and settler cultures. In the Illinois town of Alton, just across the Mississippi River from St. Louis, along a parkway that navigates between the river and sheer rock walls, is a small parking lot and a picnic area. There, on a bluff overlooking the river, is an image of a ferocious animal: its body is scaly and appears in profile, covered by wings that run the length of the creature, painted blue and red, above four sharp talons. Its face is vaguely human, but with deer antlers and fangs, a reptilian tail coiling about its body. The painting is huge, towering several stories above the ground, halfway up a massive rock face.

This is the Piasa, another figure with a stable history within a Native population that found itself changed by the appearance of Anglo settlers. On the far edge of the parking lot, chiseled into a massive piece of granite shaped like an arrowhead, is the legend of the Piasa. According to the Illini, a winged monster had made its home on the bluff and would carry off adult deer for food, occasionally devouring the Illini themselves. Deciding that they needed to be rid of this menace, the people turned to Ouatoga, the tribe's chief, who fasted and prayed to the Great Spirit for a means to defeat the Piasa. After a month of fasting, he was given the answer: the Piasa was vulnerable beneath its wings. Ouatoga went to a large clearing, offering himself as bait for the Piasa; his twenty greatest warriors, meanwhile, waited in the woods at the edge of the clearing, their bows drawn. As the bird swept down to attack Ouatoga, the chief held fast to the ground, wrapping his hands in thick roots to keep from being carried off. Struggling to lift him, the Piasa raised up its wings, and Ouatoga's warriors fired, hitting the bird where it was most vulnerable, and killing it.

We don't know when the painting of the terrifying bird first appeared above the waters of the Mississippi, since what we know of the Piasa painting comes not from surviving Illini tales, but from the explorers who were the first Anglos to see it. It was first recorded by white explorers in 1673, when Jesuit Jacques Marquette and Louis Jolliet traveled from Michigan down the Mississippi. "While Skirting some rocks, which by Their height and Length inspired awe," Marquette later recalled, "We saw upon one of them two painted monsters which at first made Us afraid, and upon Which the boldest savages dare not Long rest their eyes." The Piasa he saw were depicted as being "as large As a calf; they have Horns on their heads Like those of deer, a horrible look, red eyes, a beard Like a tiger's, a face somewhat like a man's, a body Covered with scales, and so Long A tail that it winds all around the Body, passing above the head and going back between the legs, ending in a Fish's tail. Green, red, and black are the three Colors composing the Picture." Marquette was not just impressed with the startling and terrifying images; right away he and Jolliet recognized the artistry and skill that went into them: these two monsters, he continued, "are so well painted that we cannot believe that any savage is their author; for good painters in France would find it difficult to paint so well,—and, besides, they are so high up on the rock that it is difficult to reach that place Conveniently to paint them." Twenty-five years later, another explorer, Louis Hennepin, would similarly remark of Alton's paintings, "which the boldest Men durst not look upon, there being some Enchantment in their Faces."

In 1883, S. H. Russell gave a fuller recounting of the image: "a picture cut into the surface of the rock to the depth of half an inch or more," it had originally been painted "red, black and blue, as portions of these colors were still adhering to the rock." The Piasa, Russell recalled, "had the head of a bear, directly facing the river below; the mouth was open, plainly showing large disproportioned teeth. On its head were the unmistakable horns of an elk. The upper portions of the horns were red, while the lower portions, together with the head, were black. The body was that of a fish confusedly colored with all three colors; it also showed distinctly the marks of scales, resembling in their order those of a fish. The wings were expanded to the right and left of the face, as if in the act of taking flight, extending probably from sixteen to eighteen feet from point to point. The legs were those of a bear, armed with the talons of an eagle. The tail was wrapped three times around the body, twice back of the wings, once forward, terminating in the shape of a spear head. The most prominent features were the wings and head, the latter being covered with a long beard or mane."

At the time, the Mississippi was itself another borderline for the United States; the Piasa, like Mësingw, stuck out to the white explorers as one more ferocious monster patrolling the edges. But as settlers pushed the border—and North America's inhabitants—farther west, the Piasa lost its power to terrify. With no one to revere or fear it, the cliffside painting faded, and then was destroyed altogether in the 1860s, when workers blasting rock in nearby quarries caused a rockfall that obliterated the cliffside and the Piasa with it.

●   ●   ●

By then, the Jersey Devil was lying dormant, mostly forgotten. But then in early 1909, a flurry of sightings reestablished its preeminence as the southern New Jersey creature of note. This new reappearance was occasioned by curious, unexplained hoofprints that began to appear in the snow on streets and in people's backyards. They were caused, the *Trenton Evening Times* surmised, by "some strange animal not yet classified by scientist or nature-faker." It was during this time the creature took its most iconic form: as an emaciated horse standing erect, with bat wings—an image that first appeared in the *Philadelphia Bulletin* in 1909. Anomalies, of course, would always be rife along the frontier between civilization and savagery—after all, who knew for sure what was out there, and who could say for sure what devilish magic the barbarian might be capable of? But there was no place for such unknowns in the city. Instead, they were quickly corralled into a money-making hoax, and in a world tamed and civilized, the stage was set for the return of the Devil, in its third guise: as bunk and kitsch.

Whatever the source of the original footprints, soon hoofprints were being manufactured, and reports planted in the press by a man named Norman Jeffries, a press agent for Charles A. Bradenburgh's Ninth and Arch Street Dime Museum in Philadelphia. After they'd sufficiently stoked the public's curiosity, they announced that they'd captured a live Jersey Devil. In reality, they'd taken the most exotic animal they could find, a kangaroo from an animal trainer in Buffalo, New York, and then attached wings to the poor animal and painted stripes on it. Displayed in captivity, a stagehand offstage would poke the kangaroo with a long stick with a nail on its end, sending the tortured creature jumping and shrieking toward the audience.

It drew crowds and convinced at least some people who should have known better. Curtis MacDougall writes that at least one expert from the Smithsonian felt that this Jersey Devil "bore out his long cherished theory that there still existed in hidden caverns and caves, deep in the interior of the earth, survivors of those prehistoric animals and fossilized remains," assuming that this maligned and abused creature on stage was some kind of ridiculous pterodactyl.

It wasn't long before the hoax was revealed, and although the attraction was initially successful for Bradenburgh, after a few weeks they closed it down and sent the tormented kangaroo back to Buffalo. But despite its short time in the limelight, the Dime Museum monster came to define the Jersey Devil in the twentieth century. As a hoax, the Jersey

Devil had offered a means to manage anxiety over those Fortean anomalies. Believers were gullible rubes. The Jersey Devil had become a means of patrolling civilization itself.

But after Bradenburgh's ruse was exposed, sightings of the creature only increased, though whatever supernatural terror it may have once inspired seems to have largely disappeared. The Jersey Devil's current manifestation is more of a mascot, a source of pride, a reflection of a certain kind of attitude in the state (Asbury Park now holds an annual festival for the Devil). In a 2017 article by Molly Fitzpatrick, the creature is depicted as a neon-aqua demon with sunglasses, drinking a Slurpee and wearing an "I Love NJ" T-shirt. The Jersey Devil, Fitzpatrick argues, is the story of a "disturbing urban legend that has been feared and loved, co-opted, and commodified. Like any long-surviving organism, he's eminently adaptable." New Jerseyans may not believe in the Jersey Devil, but they claim it for their own nonetheless.

*   *   *

The Piasa, too, would see its fortunes reverse, after a strange incident two hours from Alton, in Lawndale, Illinois. On July 25, 1977, at about 8:30 P.M., ten-year-old Marlon Lowe was playing with two friends in the backyard of his home near Kickapoo Creek. His mother, Ruth, was nearby watching them when she noticed two giant birds overhead. Before she had time to determine what kinds of birds they were, one swooped down and grabbed Marlon, picking him up by his shirt and attempting to carry him off. Horrified, Ruth ran after the bird, screaming at it to let her son go. After a short distance—accounts vary as to how far and how high Marlon was carried—the bird let go, and the two creatures flew off.

After she determined her son was okay, Ruth Lowe called the county sheriff's department. What if this animal attacked other children? What if someone was successfully carried off? It was, after all, a matter of public safety. But her report was met with scorn—who could believe such a story? One animal conservation officer came to the Lowes' house and went through a series of bird photos with Marlon's mother, but none matched; his verdict: "I don't think the child was picked up." There is no bird in North America strong enough to pick up a fifty-pound child like that.

But unlike so many other sightings, the Lawndale incident had multiple witnesses, and they were all consistent in their descriptions of what they saw: two huge, black birds, white rings on their long necks, with long, curled beaks, and wingspans of more than ten feet. It's as hard to dismiss the account as it is to accept it.

As reports of cryptozoological giant birds spread throughout Illinois, the legend of Alton's Piasa was reborn. What existed previously as a story from a culture that had long been forced out of Illinois became an increasingly convenient means of explaining this strange bit of Forteana. A destroyed rock painting documented only in settlers' diaries took on a strange new life, elevating a local "news of the weird" story into something mythical, even transcendental. Local interest grew, and in 1999 the terrifying bird was once again returned to the side of a bluff overlooking the river, painted by the local artist Dave Stevens. (Stevens had no choice but to base the image on those early settlers' descriptions, since there's no extant trace of the original.) The story of Marlon Lowe's abduction and the Piasa gradually became conflated, even though their connection is tangential at best. Now, accounts of the Lowe abduction regularly feature the tale of the Piasa as a backstory on websites sponsored by Enjoy Illinois, the state's office of tourism.

The Piasa and the Jersey Devil are monsters that change with the times, and in the process, earlier cultural traditions are lost and overwritten. A cryptid like this is a sort of palimpsest, in which each successive generation takes the same source material and reinscribes on it their own fears, prejudices, and inside jokes. The Jersey Devil is a perfect emblem for American culture, in which an indigenous folk belief is transformed into a morality tale, which is in turn remade first as a swindle and then as a harmless entertainment and source of regional pride.

To say, then, that monsters, or cryptids, live on the margins, is always to be asking *whose* margins, *whose* civilization. As soon as you label the cryptid as the thing on the outer edge of civilization, then you are, de facto, announcing where civilization ends.

And yet, cryptid hunters are still looking for the Jersey Devil; north, in the Hudson Valley of New York, one cryptid hunter suggested to me that the Bigfoot she was in search of may have been none other than Mësingw. Laura Leuter, cofounder of the Devil Hunters, a modern cryptid-hunting group dedicated to finding the Jersey Devil, says she doesn't think it's the Leeds Devil, but something more inexplicable. "I do believe that there is something out there," she explains. "While I love the legend, I don't actually believe that a woman cursed her baby. If that were true, many more of us would be devils out there."

[9]

THE HOME INVASION

Three thousand miles from Darien, on a different coast facing a different ocean, sits Fort Bragg, California. Fort Bragg and its sister town, Mendocino (to call them cities would be a stretch; combined their population is under ten thousand), hug a desolate, beautiful portion of California coast. The nearest major city is Santa Rosa, two hours away. To get to Fort Bragg from Highway 101 means a winding, treacherous drive through Jackson State Forest, fifty thousand acres of coastal redwoods that locals call "the Moat."

Out here on the edge of the Moat was where Bud Jenkins and his wife used to live. On February 7, 1962, Jenkins's wife's brother, Robert Hatfield, a Crescent City logger, had been staying with them, and had stepped outside around 5:30 in the evening, when he heard the Jenkinses' dogs barking. Looking to see what was causing the commotion, Hatfield turned and saw a creature standing "chest and shoulders above a six-foot-high fence" at the back of the property. "It was much, much bigger than a bear," he later recalled. "It was covered with fur, with a flat, hairless face and perfectly round eyes."

Hatfield went inside to tell his hosts, and the three of them set out searching for this strange creature; coming around the side of the house, Hatfield ran straight into the thing, which knocked him to the ground and then chased the three of them back into the house. As they tried to shut the door, the creature threw its weight against the door, blocking them from closing it. Finally, Bud Jenkins went to get his gun. "I'm going to shoot the damn thing," he yelled—at which point the monster relented and fled.

Afterward, Jenkins found a sixteen-inch footprint and an eleven-inch dirty handprint on the side of the house. The Fort Bragg Bigfoot incident was one of a cluster—all of which seemed to be pointing to the same thing, that we were on the verge of a major new discovery, of something hidden and new in the Northern California wilderness. More and more such sightings had been happening in the past few years, as though the logging camps and suburban towns pushing farther into the coastal wilds were disturbing the habitat of something undiscovered that had been living alongside us for years.

Suspend, for a moment, your disbelief of a wild and ferocious creature who nonetheless knew enough English to understand Jenkins's threat and knew to flee before it got itself shot. The story of Bigfoot—and the many other names he travels under—is, after all, the story of such confusions between human and animal. It is the story of the creature uncannily close to us, encroaching from the wilderness into our homes, battering on the door, threatening to come inside.

* * *

Creatures like Bigfoot aren't new; they've been around for centuries. What changed in the 1940s and '50s was their *realness*—they'd stepped out of the mists of legend with their big feet and began stomping all over the news. Bigfoot and its siblings—Sasquatch, the Yeti—have long been recognized by folklorists as variations on an archetype known as the Wild Man. The Wild Man legend is old and spans many cultures: in Tibet, they're known as *mi rgod* ("wild man"), *gangs mi* ("glacier man"), or *Mi shom po* ("strongman"). In Lepcha, they are known as *Hlo mung* or *Chu mung* ("mountain goblin" or "snow goblin"). You can find them in medieval Europe, too: a sixteenth-century French manuscript of

Names, Weapons, and Coats of Arms of the Knights of the Round Table opens with an illumination of two men holding a coat of arms: each of them is covered entirely with blue hair (except for their hands, feet, faces, and knees), with long hair and full, ZZ-Top-esque beards. Usually the story involves some large, hairy figure, like a man but different, harassing a town, stealing food or livestock, and drinking from the town's water supply. Usually in these stories, the villagers eventually swap the water for fermented milk or other alcoholic soporific and the Wild Man falls asleep, allowing the villagers to kill or capture him.

These legends are of a different sort than stories of sea serpents and water beasts. "Creatures like the Loch Ness Monster and Bigfoot" remain an easy shorthand for people who don't know the term "cryptid," but these two enduring examples are very different animals, and they live on opposite ends of a hidden spectrum. And the existence (or lack) of either of these two creatures would have very different ramifications.

In 1978, two psychologists surveyed mainstream scientists on their beliefs that either the Sasquatch or Nessie existed; while most didn't respond, and 10 percent of respondents provided "abusive comments of one kind or another," the results from those who did engage in the question were nonetheless illuminating. More scientists surveyed were willing to entertain the possibility of Nessie existing than Bigfoot or its relatives (23 percent of respondents versus 13 percent). But given the two of them, more than half (57 percent) of the respondents would view the theoretical discovery of something like Bigfoot as having a severe impact on science, whereas only 3 percent of respondents felt similarly about Nessie.

Water beasts, no matter how fanciful and elusive, are really not much different than the colossal squid or the oarfish—bizarre underwater creatures we rarely get glimpses of and don't understand very well. Were we to find definitive proof of a water beast like Nessie, it would be exciting, and should the animal prove to be a dinosaur, a major revelation. But ultimately, such a discovery would find itself slotted into Linnaeus's taxonomy, rendered from myth to science. Some Nessie hunters may see themselves as opposed to scientific institutions, but should definitive proof of a Loch Ness Monster ever be found, there's no doubting that it would be seamlessly merged with the existing field of natural science and zoology.

Wild Men like Bigfoot are different—they are, in a word, abominable.

In 1921, British explorers received permission from the government of Tibet to summit Everest, in exchange for weapons they could use against China. The first reconnaissance expedition by British explorers, led by Lieutenant Colonel C. K. Howard-Bury, ended in failure. But Howard-Bury did report that on Lhakpa La, more than twenty thousand feet in altitude, the expedition "came across tracks in the snow" that seemed humanlike. Howard-Bury's Sherpa porters concluded that these were the tracks of "the Wild Man of the Snows." While Howard-Bury himself was dubious, the discovery caused a sensation among Tibetans. It wasn't long before the news reached an Anglo journalist in Calcutta, Henry Newman, who wrote a short article on this startling "discovery." Newman's article, the first on the Yeti written for Western audiences, fatally garbled the original Tibetan term *metoh kangmi* (which means "manlike wild creature"). Newman misrecognized *metoh* as *metch*, mistranslating "wild" as "filthy" or "dirty." Despite this error, the name Newman gave the creature stuck: "the Abominable Snowman."

Despite (or, more likely, because of) its faulty translation, Newman's name worked; it was "like an explosion of an atom bomb," according to cryptozoologist Ivan Sanderson. "Abomination," a word that captures both metaphysical horror and physical disgust, is the word that the books of Leviticus and Deuteronomy use to describe a host of immoral and sinful behaviors, along with various other activities considered "unclean." But it also gets used to refer to various animals, according to whether or not it is permissible to eat them: the ox, goat, sheep, and antelope are "clean," while the camel, hare, and the rock-badger are "abominations"; the pig is an abomination, too.

Mary Douglas, in her 1966 anthropological classic, *Purity and Danger*, rejected the idea that these dietary laws had something to do with sanitation and health: the prohibition against pork couldn't have had anything to do with early fears of trichinosis, or the pig's open-minded attitude toward eating trash, mud, and other gross things, because none of this would apply to the hare or the camel. Rather, Douglas reveals, what's at issue is how we humans categorize the world: wild game like the sheep and antelope share a similar category with domestic food sources like cows (cloven-hoofed ruminants), while "unclean" animals violated these theoretical categories. Camels are ruminants but don't have cloven feet, while pigs have cloven feet but are not ruminants. The abominations of Leviticus, Douglas writes, "are the obscure unclassifiable elements which do not fit the pattern of the cosmos. They are incompatible with holiness and blessing." Abominations violate the boundaries of categories we've erected; they are on the border between here and there, and are unclean as a result.

An abomination doesn't just mark the limit of civilization, it troubles the boundaries themselves, it interrupts the categories we use to make sense of the world.

Unlike the Loch Ness Monster, the chupacabra, or some giant thunderbird, a Wild Man necessarily straddles the worlds of the human and the animal, with one big, hairy foot in each realm. Would such a creature prove to be a missing link of some kind? Could it use tools? Would it have a language? Would it have rights? Wild Men raise these questions because they trouble the line between human and nonhuman. If most cryptids offer a reflection of how we see the animal kingdom, what sets Wild Men apart is that they reflect how we see ourselves.

[10]

LOST IN TRANSLATIONS

The fascination with Wild Men began in Everest, with the *metoh kangmi*, the Abominable Snowman, or as the Nepalese Sherpas called it, the Yeti. While legends of such creatures had existed in Nepal for untold time, for westerners, the Yeti was merely stepping in to fill a role that once belonged to dragons. For centuries, Europeans didn't climb mountains for fear of the dragons who lived at their summits. In 1708, naturalist Jakob Scheuchzer collected a taxonomy of the various dragons that supposedly lurked in the Alps, gathered from various local legends and municipal reports. These strange guardians of the mountain peaks not only stood guard against all who would summit them, but also reminded any would-be climber that mountains, too, lay at the edges of the map, and that here, too, be dragons. (Even today, mountain climbing is sometimes referred as "killing dragons.")

Once man replaced God as the measure of all things, however, the mountain's summit became increasingly attractive; what better vantage point from which to survey all that man now had dominion over? By the nineteenth century, avid mountaineer and biographer Leslie Stephen (better remembered now as the father of Virginia Woolf) called to his fellow Europeans to seek out new and higher summits, to climb and explore nature, in a book he called *The Playground of Nature*. To summit a great mountain was not only to test the limits of human prowess, it was also to assert the limits of human mastery over the natural world: here there be playgrounds.

But Europeans who came to summit Everest could never quite shake that ingrained belief that some monstrous creature might be guarding the peaks, and as soon as they arrived in the Himalayas they heard (and seized on) strange stories of mythical monsters. The tracks discovered by C. K. Howard-Bury's 1921 expedition, the *metoh kangmi* mistranslated by Henry Newman as the Abominable Snowman, would be—like the Jenkinses' bestial houseguest in Fort Bragg who knew enough English to run at the mention of a gun—an amalgamation of different things, some human, some not.

As more and more white adventurers came to Nepal seeking the world's tallest mountain, stories seeped out about this weird and wild creature. One explorer from 1937 described seeing tracks that "were certainly not those of bear. They were roughly circular, about 8 inches across and 9 inches deep, and the remarkable thing was that they were all on the same axis and not 'staggered' to right and left as in the case of other four-footed animals." After being told by the Sherpas he'd hired that such a creature fed only on humans, he responded that if that was true the creature must be hungry, since no humans had been in that part of the Himalayas for years. The Sherpas, he reported, "were not so amused as I expected."

The closest thing to "proof" came in 1951, during an expedition led by Eric Shipton. On November 7, Shipton, Michael Ward, and Sen Tensing came across a set of tracks that, they felt, could only have belonged to the Yeti. They'd been somewhat distorted due to the bright sun, but were still recognizable as large oval impressions, longer and broader than those made by boots, with three large toes and a broad thumblike toe on one side.

What that big toe suggested was something that walked upright, something humanoid. Yet no human could walk barefoot in the snow in such inhospitable places. It was like a riddle: what walked like a man in a place where no men walked? Whatever this creature was, it seemed hard not to believe that it would be related to *Homo sapiens* in a shocking, uncanny way. "Hitherto I had been open-minded, perhaps a little sceptical, on the subject of the Yeti," Shipton would later write in his autobiography, "but now I became convinced, particularly by the unmistakable evidence of the toes, of the existence of a large, ape-like creature, either quite unknown to science or at least not included in the known fauna of Central Asia. For, whatever creatures had made those tracks, they were neither bears nor human beings. Sen Tensing and I were both well acquainted with the tracks of both species of Himalayan bear; and people do not wander for miles over snow-covered glaciers with naked feet."

Photographs of the Shipton prints renewed the world's fervor in the possibility of the Yeti. In 1959, six years after Edmund Hillary and Tenzing Norgay summited Everest ("almost together," as Hillary described it), Hillary was attempting to raise money for an expedition back to Everest to study the effects of low oxygen in high-altitude climates, and he dangled the prospect of the Yeti as a potential side benefit of his trip. "In the early stages of the expedition, when the men must acclimatize themselves to the intermediate heights between 14,000 and 19,000 feet—then we are going looking for the Yeti," he explained in a *New York Times* article. "We are approaching the problem with unbiased minds, seeking only to find some tracks and then to try to discover what is making them, be it bear or Yeti, monkey or man!"

Raising money to hunt the Yeti was always the biggest obstacle, even more so than scientific skepticism. One of Constance Whyte's complaints about mainstream science was that official research was too tightly controlled, so much so that young scientists and amateurs lacked the resources to hunt for cryptids. If this was true of a lake in northern Scotland, it was doubly true of the Himalayas—simply getting there was a logistical challenge, to say nothing of the resources required to mount a serious expedition in search of a Yeti. Tom Slick offered an antidote to this. A wealthy scion from an oil family, Slick developed a fascination with science from an early age, and throughout his life supported a number of scientific research initiatives. The Texas Biomedical Research Institute of San Antonio, Texas, was founded by Slick as the Foundation of Applied Research in 1941; Texas Biomed has done important work on heart disease and Ebola, and has helped develop vaccines for hepatitis B and other diseases. In addition, Slick had an almost naive belief in world peace, organizing a series of conferences designed to bring international partners together to further this goal.

But Slick also spent much of his life fascinated by the possibility of cryptids, and with his curiosity and his largesse, he was able to fund various expeditions in search of the Yeti in the Himalayas and Bigfoot in North America. His ability to reconcile serious science with pseudo-science is best captured in an undated fragment of writing in which he lays out the difference between two kinds of technical progress: "evolutionary" and "revolutionary." In the evolutionary method, "one little piece of new knowledge, a small step forward from previous knowledge is laboriously added, brick by brick, until a worthwhile accomplishment results. This is the method of university research and of the great research laboratories that have grown up, particularly in America." Slick saw this as not only the dominant mode of scientific inquiry, but also the "most certain and safest way" to scientific advancement and new technological innovations.

The revolutionary way, by contrast, is "the way of the gifted inventor, or the adventurous explorer. It is the skipping of the small steps and arriving at a radical advance, perhaps more by intuition or by daring trial and error than by entirely logical reasoning." With the rise of universities and professional schools, the bureaucratization of the scientific field, the evolutionary method, he said, "is taking care of itself, it is the method today of safe careful conservative work of teams helping each other." But such institutions were, almost by definition, inimical to revolutionary thinkers—isolated geniuses, adventurous speculators, and explorers, whose talent and creativity, Slick warned, society was in danger of losing. "The trend of our society is the other way, toward security instead of risk, towards the cautious instead of the bold, towards protecting what we have rather than advancing. Today the revolutionaries need encouragement." Slick was very much in the mold of today's Silicon Valley; he was, in techspeak, a disrupter, convinced that he could upend the staid and hidebound scientific discipline through a single revolutionary stroke that would challenge everyone's perceptions, change the game entirely, allow for a new level of chaos that would let new players into the game. The Yeti was his killer app.

Slick made an initial reconnaissance trip in the mid-1950s to see if he could learn more. Around the same time, an Irish-born tea merchant named Peter Byrne announced that he was going to mount an expedition to find the Yeti, though he lacked financial backing. As Byrne later remembered, he'd encountered a group of men in Nepal in the spring of 1956, including Tenzing Norgay, who mentioned that an American named Tom Slick was looking to fund an expedition to find the creatures. Byrne wrote to him immediately.

The expedition, financed by Slick and headed by Byrne, began in March 1957. During the two months they searched the mountains, Byrne and Slick found tracks they believed to be Yeti, but no solid proof. A second expedition in 1958, however, turned up word that a monastery in Pangboche had a preserved Yeti hand. "The temple had a number of Sherpa custodians," Byrne later recalled. "I heard one of them speaking Nepalese, which I speak. He told me that they had in the temple the hand of a yeti which had been there for many years. It looked like a large human hand. It was covered with crusted black, broken skin. It was very oily from the candles and the oil lamps in the temple. The fingers were hooked and curled." The monks had put the hand on display, and it had become a local tourist oddity, drawing visitors who'd donate to the monastery in order to see it.

The monks were in no mood to part with their hand, which was a valuable source of donations, even for scientific purposes, though they did let the expedition photograph it. Byrne returned home, as it were, empty-handed.

Back in London, Byrne was asked by Slick and primatologist William

Charles Osman Hill to try again to retrieve the hand, though Byrne relayed how the monks had been; Osman Hill had inspected the photographs and concluded that the hand could not have come from a gorilla, chimpanzee, or orangutan. Slick suggested a plan: if the monks would not part with the hand, could Byrne steal a finger and replace it with a human finger? Hill produced a brown paper bag, dumping its contents on the table: a human hand. "It was several months old and dried," Hill told the BBC in 2011. "I never asked him where he got it from."

So Byrne went back to Nepal in 1959, and back to the monastery. In order to make the switch, he was obliged to find the monk standing watch and get him drunk enough that he passed out; once alone, he cut off one of the Yeti's fingers and replaced it with the ersatz digit.

But how does one smuggle the finger of a cryptid out of the country? Getting it from Nepal into India was easy, but Indian customs agents could be difficult. Here, too, Slick had a plan: he arranged for Byrne to go to Calcutta's Grand Hotel to meet none other than the actor James Stewart and his wife, Gloria. Thinking that celebrities would be less likely to be questioned by customs, Byrne had Stewart's wife hide the finger in her lingerie case in order to get it back to England unnoticed.

The theft of the Yeti finger from Pangboche is a textbook example of Western hubris, of course, and a cavalier attitude that Western scientific curiosity trumps all other needs. But Christian Europe has a rather long history of the theft of body parts from various monasteries and churches: during the medieval period in particular, the theft of human relics was a widespread problem. In Catholic churches, relics of the saints—a sliver of shinbone, a vial of blood, a finger—were sources of great power; they were also, as with the case of Pangboche's Yeti hand, a source of tourist income, as they would draw religious pilgrims. As such, enterprising monks would often plunder Roman catacombs in search of bones to pass off as belonging to saints, and rival monasteries and churches would occasionally steal valuable body parts from one another.

In the Middle Ages, this kind of relic theft had a specific name: it wasn't known as stealing, it was known as translation. Oftentimes, the would-be translator would first "pray" to the saint, who would appear in a vision and tell the translator that he or she wanted their relics stolen, thus giving a sort of supernatural license for the theft.

Back in England, the finger had no power—its DNA has been tested repeatedly over the years, and it was abundantly clear that it was human. In a distant, candlelit monastery, it had an allure, a mystery, but taken from its context, its magic quickly dissipated.

                                 o   o   o

Tom Slick, undaunted, continued to search for cryptids, bankrolling expeditions and going out on his own. And while he focused on the rugged quest of adventure and firsthand observation, he didn't reject the scientific establishment. Unlike other hunters in the field, he was more than happy to work with primatologists and zoologists and compare notes. His initial 1957 expedition with Byrne had enjoyed the scientific backing of the San Antonio Zoo, and would rely on two consultants, one of whom was Harvard anthropologist Carleton S. Coon.

Though he tried to downplay it in his public life, Coon took the prospect of the Yeti's existence seriously. His major work of anthropology, *The Atlas of Men* (1954), had argued that modern ethnic groups had formed separately, each evolving from *Homo erectus* independently, and only later reconverging into the species *Homo sapiens.* Coon's theory has long since been debunked; even at the time, he was in an active war with Columbia University anthropologist Franz Boas, who argued instead that there was no genetic difference between ethnicities. Coon believed that the Yeti, if it existed, would bolster his claims significantly. Serious study of a Yeti, he argued, "would be of incalculable help to those of us who are trying to find the origins of human behavior." Coon saw the Yeti as a potential game changer, an animal that could illuminate something fundamental about humanity. He wasn't a primatologist, and didn't care about it as a new species; as an anthropologist, he wanted to know what the Yeti might say about *us.* The existence of other cryptids may change how we see the world around us, but the existence of Wild Men has always been about who we are in the world around us.

Coon's involvement in the Slick expedition came about via *Life* magazine: when word was first announced of the project, *Life* offered Slick twenty-five thousand dollars for the rights to any photos of the Yeti, and the magazine's editor, Henry Luce, separately approached Coon about launching a rival expedition. Coon spent a good deal of time working out the logistics of such an expedition, and there was some talk of him joining Slick and Byrne, though at the last minute Slick decided on a much smaller group, and Coon never got his chance to hunt the Yeti.

During World War II, Coon had worked for the OSS, the intelligence agency that would subsequently be reorganized into the CIA, and he remained a fervent anticommunist. Nor, strangely, was Coon the only one to have intelligence ties. Tom Slick did as well, at least according to Loren Coleman. Slick owned an air freight company, Slick Airways, which, Coleman has argued, may have been used by the CIA for clandestine operations, with or without Slick's knowledge. (Slick's niece, Catherine Nixon Cooke, on the other hand, denies any connection in her 2005 biography, *Tom Slick, Mystery Hunter*, citing the lack of any evidence in Slick's papers.)

What is clear is that by 1961, the FBI had opened a file on Slick due to his international peace efforts, worried that his overtures to China may have been some sort of national security threat. And what is also clear is that many of the men involved in the Cold War hunt for the Yeti had some connection to American, British, Russian, or Chinese intelligence, and that it was no secret that the hunt for the Yeti had some geopolitical impact.

In 1959, the US Embassy in Nepal sent the State Department a document regarding the proper protocol for hunting Yeti: any such hunts involved paying five thousand rupees to the Nepalese government for a permit, and the animal may not be killed except in cases of an "emergency arising out of self-defense." All photographs are property of the government of Nepal, and any news or reports of the creature must be submitted to the government before being disseminated to the press. As the National Archives suggested when it declassified the document, "Of course, the existence of this document doesn't mean that the U.S. Government believed in Yetis. The memo was instead a strategic move to demonstrate the U.S. support of Nepal sovereignty." On every level, it seemed, the Yeti was being employed by various governments for political purposes.

And whether or not the Yeti hunters were actually working for Western intelligence, the Soviet Union felt comfortable proclaiming they were. "Soviet Sees Espionage in U.S. Snowman Hunt," *The New York Times* reported in April 1957. The Kremlin wasn't entirely wrong in assuming that the mountain climbers in the Himalayas had other motives. In 1965, American military intelligence with the help of India tried to put a plutonium-powered sensor device on top of the Himalayan peak Nanda Devi (25,645 feet high). Mountaineers attempted to summit the mountain and assemble the device, with the goal of aiming it at China to observe any nuclear activity and missile launches, but were stymied by the weather and stashed the device midway up the mountain, hoping to retrieve it the following year. When they returned, they were unable to find it; perhaps the Indian government had secretly returned and absconded with it, but more likely it had simply been buried by an avalanche and is still there somewhere on the mountain.

Nepal, a tiny country surrounded on all sides by global superpowers jockeying for supremacy during the early years of the Cold War, had developed an immense strategic importance, and whatever its interest to mountain climbers and cryptozoologists, there was no escaping this fact. The hunt for the Yeti was inescapably tied to Cold War politics.

The legend of the Yeti was born of a Western misunderstanding of local Himalayan culture, but it quickly became a means of Western entanglement in Himalayan geography, a means of using myth and folklore as a smokescreen for intrigue. And cryptids never arise out of a vacuum. The Yeti became a topic of interest because of a renewed fascination with mountains and mountain climbing, which in turn triggered a collision of cultures. But it's not clear that this alone would have been enough to sustain Yeti fever; instead, this collision of cultures happened on the slopes of a contested borderland between Cold Warring super-powers. Whether the Yeti was cover for covert operations or merely a strange set of coincidences on the high Himalayan slopes may be a mystery forever buried in the CIA's archives or the mountains' glaciers. But the Yeti's history is a stark reminder that blank spaces on the map are never truly blank.

[11]

MEN, AND WILD MEN

I t was the time of the Wild Men. In late summer 1958, around the
same time that Peter Byrne was puzzling over the mystery of the
Pangboche hand, a group of Northern California loggers began to
talk about a strange creature that appeared to be repeatedly ransacking
their campsites: food was stolen, tents were overturned, and equipment
was strewn everywhere. The only trace of any animal that they found
were large tracks, too big to be bears. They nicknamed this mysterious
creature "Big Foot," and after the local paper, *The Humboldt Times*,
reported on the story, the legend began to grow.

Whether loggers in the California redwoods or mountain climbers in
the Nepalese Himalayas, Wild Men sightings came from groups of men
cut off from regular society, bonding together in difficult situations.
Daily life depended on what the military calls "unit cohesion"; Bigfoot
and other myths could have been an important part of that. Stories of
strange creatures could often take the form of practical jokes or other
hazing rituals; such jokes, Joshua Blu Buhs suggests, "served to initiate
novices and cement relations on the job." Buhs suggests that "tales about
legendary creatures also helped those who worked far from civilization
to manage their anxieties. Inchoate fears about an unknowable nature
were congealed into slightly ridiculous forms—the will-am-alone, for

instance, was a kind of squirrel that dropped pellets of rolled lichen onto sleeping lumberjacks, causing nightmares—and thus the fear was made to seem absurd, too." Perhaps it mattered less if the creature was real than how a group of men came together in isolation.

These stories weren't new, after all. Legends of the Chetco Monster of Myrtle Point, Oregon, a Wild Man–type creature that threatened logging camps, date back to 1890. "The Chetco Indians believed there were man-animals in the woods," one account explained. "They claimed that for generations they had shared their hunting grounds with fierce-looking hairy creatures that walked upright like men. The strange beings were not human, or animal, neither friendly nor hostile. They were simply there, like every other man or wild creature, so the Indians left them alone." In the white loggers' accounts, however, the Chetco Monster had turned deadly, killing a search party in an account that bears more than a strong whiff of resemblance to *Beowulf.* Of course, there are no recorded unexplained deaths of loggers from the time period, but that hardly mattered to the tellers of such stories.

So Bigfoot itself wasn't particularly new. But something had changed in the late 1950s that let this old campfire story jump from an isolated logging team to pop culture, from a camp to campy. Buhs also connects the culture of 1958 to Bigfoot's mainstream crossover success. In the decade after World War II, masculinity itself was undergoing a crisis. Men who'd fought in a great war were now readjusting to a life of domestic placidity and workplace drudgery. The 1950s were a time of economic prosperity in the United States, to be sure, but such economic gains came with a radically reenvisioned sense of a man's role: no longer someone who worked with his hands, he now worked a desk job, he was tethered to a suburban house and familial obligations, and his world was one of consumerism. This masculine malaise helps explain the massive popularity of men's adventure magazines, with their tales of flesh-eating weasels, quicksand, and cobras. Magazines with names like *True Adventures* and *Real Life Action* played to the nine-to-five stiff, giving him an alternative fantasyland in which to reimagine himself as liberated from the womanly bonds of the material world, living off the land with only his skills and his hands. Free once more.

Into this pulp fantasy world stepped a giant pair of feet. When Ivan Sanderson began publishing his articles about Bigfoot, he did so not only in niche magazines that appealed to the weird and esoteric, but also in *True,* which meant a much larger, mainstream audience, one primed to respond to stories of an ancient Wild Man mythos returned to liberate the 1950s working-class Joe.

◦ ◦ ◦

If there was a poster boy for the intersection of masculinity and cryptozoology, it was, of course, Tom Slick. He was the archetype of the heroic cryptid hunter: dashing, attractive, and wealthy, embodying a great deal of what the future of cryptozoology might hold. And then, on October 6, 1962, the dream came crashing back to Earth. Tom Slick and his pilot, Shelly Sudderth, were en route from Canada to Phoenix, Arizona, to visit family when something went wrong with their Beechcraft Bonanza and the plane went down somewhere over northwest Montana, killing both on board.

Something else had died with Tom Slick. For decades, writers like Charles Fort and Constance Whyte had railed against the scientific establishment, arguing that their near monopoly on the research power necessary for new discoveries was being bottled up by close-minded thinkers of the academy. Someone free of prejudice, doing honest work with an open mind, could be successful in finding hidden beasts. But such expeditions could be costly, and they required the backing of major museums or universities.

Tom Slick should have been the turning point. Able to fund expeditions free of the myopia of the academy, he could bring open-minded researchers into the field and find what no scientist was willing to look for. And he did bring them into the field, but, as before, those he funded found nothing. The connection between cryptid hunting and science was, even under the best of circumstances, tenuous, and often required charismatic individuals like Slick to bridge the gap; the loss of these in-dividuals often meant severe, sometimes permanent setbacks for those trying to mainstream cryptozoology.

● ● ●

By that point, stories of Bigfoot had merged with another local leg-end. Years before the Willow Creek incidents, a teacher on Chehalis Indian Reservation named John Burns had collected Wild Man stories in 1929 from his students of a creature they called *sæsq'ec*, and which Burns anglicized as Sasquatch. Burns's article was a serious attempt to document folklore, but when it appeared in the magazine *Maclean's* on April 1, 1929, some viewed it as a hoax, and it was mostly forgotten until Bigfoot hunters in the 1950s resurrected it, giving the monster known only for its feet a proper name.

A familiar pattern began to emerge. As with the Yeti, in Sasquatch white men had begun to seize on preexisting mythologies that they quickly adapted to their own needs. Colonization, in its normal pattern, depends on dismissing indigenous beliefs as superstitious, and enforcing Western rationalism and Christianity as part of a "civilizing" process. But as colonial empires like Britain and the United States came close to a complete homogenization of their territories, some at the fringes of these cultures became seized with a sudden nostalgia. Not unlike sports mascots with their racist caricatures, or hippie boutiques selling dream catchers and peace pipes, the Wild Man lore of the Chehalis and the Nepalese had become a way for white people to romanticize what they were destroying, and a way for disaffected members of the colonizers to find a kind of melancholic reflection in these endangered cultures.

Now, indigenous histories are ripe for plunder by cryptozoologists seeking confirmation of their beliefs. In the histories of the Nuxalk Na-tion, located on the central coast of British Columbia, Canada, there are stories of supernatural beings like the *sk'amtsk*, a water monster, and the *sniniq*, a Sasquatch-like creature. They are the kinds of stories that cryptid hunters have taken as proof of the existence of undiscovered species. When I spoke to Snxakila (Clyde Tallio), a Nuxalk orator and historian, he suggested that much of this misses the point entirely.

When I asked Snxakila if he could explain these monsters and what their role was in Nuxalk culture, he instead told me the history of the world—from the time of Creation through to the Time of the Ancestors and into the time of today. Supernatural figures like the *sk'amtsk* are not anomalous beings that can be pulled out of the fabric of the world and talked about in isolation. They are woven into all of time, and any history that recounts their existence or purpose is interconnected with every other aspect of creation.

These spiritual histories are integral to the Nuxalk, and they not only explain the world as it is and as it came to be, they also provide guidance and perspective on contemporary matters. A history involving a *sk'amtsk*, for example, might be a meditation on what happens when a problem goes unaddressed. Or they might be stories told to the young to help teach them how to behave. Snxakila remembered hearing stories of the *sniniq* when he was a kid; "as children," he told me, "we hear these stories, and they help us focus on what our values are, and what our worldview is." Cryptid hunters who come here, he told me, "never get the true meaning" of these histories; "they're interested in their own agenda, in furthering their schemes, to make a name for themselves. It really does get annoying."

These histories became endangered when the Canadian government banned the Pacific Northwest potlatch ceremony (where they were recounted) in 1885, a deliberate attempt to cripple the ability of Canada's First Nations to maintain their culture and language. The ban, which lasted until 1951, did serious and lasting damage to the original nations of North America, who still, decades later, are working to preserve their way of life. At the same time, these histories were appropriated—and still continue to be appropriated—by white anthropologists and writers, who take the stories for their own benefit (including, perhaps most notably, the famous anthropologist Franz Boas, who wrote about the Nuxalk nation in 1898). "Academics have come to take our stories," Snxakila told me, "to get their PhDs and write their books."

The cryptid hunters are part of this problem—one more group of white interlopers, who don't understand the histories or what they mean and who seek to use them for their own fame. "When people come in hunting for these beings, they're misinterpreting our histories," Snxakila continued. "They're not looking for how those stories work. It's not about whether or not that being really exists in the land."

o   o   o

Sometimes, though, these stories can flow in the opposite direction. In 1975, the anthropologist Henry S. Sharp spent a summer with a group of Chipewyan on the shores of South Lake (east of the Great Slave Lake), living with them as they hunted for the coming winter. Immediately, he noticed, there was a significant tension between two brothers, George and Wellington, that developed through the summer into an open rivalry (those were not their real names; Sharp changed the names for privacy, making it difficult to confirm his story). They were sons of an established patriarch, and now each was working to set up his own family and broaden his influence. George was in his late twenties, small and agile, with a sense of humor and a perpetual sense of wonder. Wellington, five years older than his brother, was more practical and focused on establishing an income both through trading and as a tour guide for wealthy white people interested in hunting and fishing in the northern Canadian wilds.

During the early summer months, Wellington was far more successful at hunting caribou than his brother, creating a low-key tension that began to build as the heat rose and various unexpected setbacks stymied George's fortunes. And then in June, a wealthy American arrived: identified by Sharp only as Corky, he'd hired Wellington to take him fishing for a week. He was, Sharp observed, already suffering the debilitating effects of his ambition: founding and franchising an extermination company had brought him wealth, but at the cost of his own health, as he seemed in perpetual pain and racked by tension. Nonetheless, he'd managed to pick up a bachelor's degree from the University of Cincinnati by taking night classes; it was there, Sharp noted, that Corky "had acquired an interest in Atlantis, Mu, and other comparable ideas. One of these ideas was Bigfoot or Sasquatch."

And so Corky and Wellington spent the week together, Wellington leading the expedition and Corky regaling him with stories of Sasquatch. At night, when Wellington would return to camp, he'd tell the others the various stories he'd heard from Corky. The most popular ones were about Bigfoot, which Wellington translated as *bekaycho* (*be*, third person singular; *kay*, foot; *cho*, large), which the children in particular were eager to hear more of. He mixed in what he'd heard from the American with Chipewyan legends of *udzena dene*, an unpredictable or dangerous person, a bogeyman. Such monsters could often take the form of white interlopers who directly threatened the Chipewyan or the land, or otherwise acted in inexplicable or confusing ways.

As for Wellington, he didn't believe in Bigfoot; he would always be careful to relate his stories as something he'd "heard from Corky," adding a layer of plausible deniability. Wellington knew such stories, of course, but he knew them as myth and folklore, the kind of things told to children to scare them into behaving. If pressed, he would reply noncommittally, "I've never seen one."

But the stories spread among the children at South Lake, including Sharp's own American four-year-old daughter, who told the other children that she'd seen Bigfoot on television in a car commercial, which added another layer of veracity to the cryptid's existence. Corky left after a week, but his impact on the camp would last the summer.

Meanwhile, the brothers' tempers rose steadily, eventually to the point where the two stopped speaking. Then, weeks later, George disappeared on a hunt; when the others found him, he wouldn't stop talking about his encounters with a *bekaycho*. Though Sharp and others realized he had likely seen a group of archaeologists during field work in the area, George would not be dissuaded. Wellington ridiculed him at first, but soon thereafter Wellington found tracks near his stockpile of meat, and soon he, too, was warning of a *bekaycho* in the area. Realizing that their winter food might be at risk from this mysterious creature, George and Wellington made the decision to hunt the *bekaycho* together and headed out in search of the beast.

They never found the monster, but the hunt had another effect: it healed the rift between the two of them. Sharp remains convinced that the tracks they had seen were the work of the archaeologists, but he also recognized that at some point that was less important than the fact that these two brothers had found a way to reconcile their relationship while allowing each to preserve his own masculinity. All summer long the two had been in a pitched rivalry over who was the bigger man; the arrival of Bigfoot allowed them to unite forces against an even larger foe. Its mere presence, it seemed, allowed each brother to feel as though he were a man.

[12]

BELIEVING IS SEEING

I was so terrified I couldn't even blink my eyes," is how Harold Nelson described his run-in with the Montana Snowman on September 11, 1968. He'd been traveling through the west in a camper, and had pulled off the highway for the night near Billings when he heard a racket outside; when he opened the door, he later told the men's adventure magazine *Saga*, he was face-to-face with a Wild Man.

"I was frozen with terror," he said. "It had an apelike face but it was definitely not a gorilla. The head was slightly pointed, sloping down like the sketches of cavemen. The whole body was covered with a reddish-brown hair. There were a few spots of white hair along the edge of the enormous shoulders. It stood erect, like a man, and must have weighed 600 or 800 pounds. He was big—real big."

Nelson fired a shot; he missed, but it was enough to scare off the creature. He soon thought the beast might be going back to gather some friends, so Nelson drove off in a fright, not stopping until he'd reached a gas station, where an attendant calmly listened to his story. "He said other motorists going through had seen these beasts along the highways. I decided not to report the incident. The police would say it was a bear, the attendant told me."

What if he had hit the creature—and what if he had killed it? "I think about the legal aspects a lot," Nelson told *Saga*. "What would have happened if I had shot that Montana Snowman? The thing is definitely part human. Would it have been murder?" (Contemplating such "human" rights violation, the government of Skamania County, Washington, made it a felony to kill a Bigfoot a year later, punishable by up to a ten-thousand-dollar fine and five years in prison—though its "emergency" adoption on April 1 suggests it may not have entirely been an earnest gesture.)

Nelson's story came about in a year of renewed urgency, since Bigfoot had, the previous fall, become extremely real. On Friday, October 20, 1967, two men, Roger Patterson and Bob Gimlin, had announced to the world shocking news: they claimed to have cast a female Bigfoot's prints during an expedition near Bluff Creek in Northern California. Even more sensationally, they had caught her on film.

The Patterson-Gimlin film, the most famous footage of Bigfoot (Big-footage?), had come about as the result of an odd pairing of two unlikely men. Roger Patterson was, by nearly all accounts, something of a con man, always in search of another get-rich-quick scheme. Gimlin was a quiet veteran of the Korean War who spent his days taming horses and doing odd jobs around his home in Yakima, Washington. When Patterson had first approached his friend about hunting Bigfoot on Mount St. Helens, Gimlin turned him down, but the two began taking camping trips through the Pacific Northwest backwoods, riding horses while Patterson plied Gimlin with stories of Sasquatch. When word came out that a logging camp in the Six Rivers National Forest had found its equipment inexplicably disassembled (perhaps Bigfoot was a member of Edward Abbey's Monkey Wrench Gang), Patterson was finally able to convince Gimlin to go with him to check it out.

The original Patterson-Gimlin film is just under a minute, but on

YouTube you can find a more complete reel with additional materials, which contribute to the context and the mystery of the experience. The opening shot is of a silhouetted Gimlin astride a horse, wearing a cowboy hat—as if to announce to the world that this film is just one more John Wayne movie. It pans leisurely to the top of the tree line, revealing nothing but the splendor of the California wilderness. This is, so far, just introductory material. Background, both literally and figuratively.

In found footage films like this, there's always a wondrous sense of expectation, like a horror film. Everything before you is so banal, so ordinary. It's beyond boring. And yet you know something is coming. You know that unlike every other uninteresting home movie you've ever been forced to watch, something *awaits* at the end of this one.

Weaving among the trees, it jumps to another shot, this time again of Gimlin on his horse, leading a pony with supplies away from the camera. As with the silhouette, this single shot of a cowboy walking away, his back to us, into the wilderness, seems to convey a story much larger, a melancholic farewell to a way of life. We follow him for about thirty seconds, as though he's going to disappear into the woods for good, one last glimpse of the last cowboy. And then the camera jars to the left, a blur, to an outcropping—and a seated figure you wouldn't even have noticed if it didn't move slightly. For barely a second it's there, and then another cut.

A long, slow pan up a hillside, revealing nothing. Then another cut, Gimlin on his horse once more. The tree line behind him a shockingly bright swath of red, a mix of both autumn foliage and the deterioration of the chemicals on the film stock. Whatever it was is gone.

We're now two and a half minutes into a three-and-a-half-minute film, and so far the only thing we've seen is a second-long blur. Crypto-zoologists, of course, focus on the end of the film, but the first two thirds are vitally important. Like the carnival barker outside the freak-show tent, their job is to get the viewer primed and ready for something, to build suspense, to hype the main event. Every second you spend scanning the tree line or watching Gimlin on his horse builds more tension, more anticipation. Your senses are keen, focused, on high alert. And what you're focusing on, while you search for the Wild Man of Northern California, is a plaintive image of a cowboy on horseback, lost and searching.

Then the action starts: the image shaky and chaotic—Patterson is running, carrying the camera, so the shot is nothing but a blur. Then he stops, and for a few brief moments the back of the creature is visible against the trees, before Patterson is up and running again, trying to get closer. At about 2:51, he stops again, this time for the longest uninterrupted view of Bigfoot. A quick but unhurried stroll toward the trees, arms swinging at her sides. At some point she notices the men, and in an iconic gesture turns her head over her right shoulder to look back at them, not breaking her stride. A few seconds later, she's gone.

The film is a hoax. While Gimlin and Patterson described their quarry as a female, she walks with a male's gait, and her physiology is contradictory: her head, with its sagittal crest (the ridge of bone that runs lengthwise along the top of the skull in some animals), implies a large, powerful jaw used for chewing low-calorie plant material. But herbivores need a lot of internal digestive systems to handle all that plant material, and the figure Patterson filmed lacked the kind of large, protuberant belly that is common in ruminants. "The wildman on the screen was impressive unless you understood biology," Buhs concludes, "in which case it started to look like an impossibility."

Still, the footage is impressive. Like the Surgeon's Photograph, it's an iconic image, something boring deep into a shared human consciousness that resonates even after you admit it's fake. The film has all the hallmarks of another film that had captivated the 1960s with its amateur feel: the film that caught the Kennedy assassination. The Patterson-Gimlin film would seem to imitate the aura and mystery of Abraham Zapruder's home movie, in which the banal was transformed into the momentous over a few frames of film. The Zapruder film, as one of Don DeLillo's characters puts it, is "powerfully open . . . glary and artless and completely steeped in being what it was, in being film. It carried a kind of inner life, something unconnected to the things we call phenomena. The footage seemed to advance some argument about the nature of film itself."

Don Abbott, a cultural anthropologist who was also involved in hunting Bigfoot, captured its paradoxical nature best: "It is about as hard to believe the film is faked as it is to admit such a creature really lives." (For years, the film and its reputation dogged Gimlin. Long after Patterson died of cancer in 1972, Gimlin found himself caught between the skeptics who were convinced he was a con man, and the believers who staked everything on his experience. The film, he told *Outside* magazine in 2016, "ruined me.")

The Patterson-Gimlin film, just like the Surgeon's Photograph, bears out Kevin Young's maxim: "Hoaxes prove that believing is seeing." Whatever is in those documents is what you choose to put into them, whatever you *need* them to be. "The hoax is rather a kind of coded confession," Young writes, "revealing not only a deep-seated cultural wish but also a common set of themes—or feints or strategies—that add up to a ritual."

What is that cultural wish? The *Saga* article recounting Harold Nelson's experience had not only raised the specter of Bigfoots all along the Montana highways, it also raised the problem of what rights they might be entitled to. "Your imagination wouldn't have to stretch too far to see some fascinating political problems if Snowmen are real," an unnamed attorney in the *Saga* article stated. "As a human, they would have the same rights as any other citizen. This would include the right to vote, own property, enter into legal contracts and, of course, be responsible for their acts. . . . The government would undoubtedly decide they were wards of the state. The politicians would create another government bureau to manage their affairs. Some politician would start thinking about the Snowman vote and we would have another poverty program!"

Bigfoot stories are always, eventually, about race: the Wild Man is the dark, uncivilized other of the white imagination, who is both beneath the white man and yet free in ways he can only dream of. (Unsurprisingly, one early account of Sasquatch described it as "negro black.")

No one understood this better than Carleton S. Coon. While he was advising on Yeti expeditions, he was also advising white supremacists such as his cousin, Carleton Putnam. Putnam was a member of an organization called the International Association for the Advancement of Ethnology and Eugenics, which attempted to make the scientific case for white supremacy. Putnam believed that "social status had to be earned," and that black Americans had failed to earn a coequal place among white society. Putnam was taken by Coon's argument that different ethnicities had different biological origins, and in July 1959 reached out to him for guidance; Coon invited him over to his house to talk further. Throughout 1960 the two men kept up a correspondence. As Putnam worked on his racist manifesto, Coon offered advice on how to avoid controversial sources and reach the widest audience, while managing to keep his fingerprints off the final product and free of any negative association with Putnam.

It's possible that Coon's racism and his cryptozoology were two distinct passions, but it makes more sense to see them as two sides of the same coin. For an anthropologist like Coon, invested in finding some sort of scientific basis to justify his racism, Wild Men lore offered a compelling narrative, a chance to prove a scientific basis for his white supremacy.

◦   ◦   ◦

B ut still, there was the footprint! The Shipton footprint—the best preserved and best documented evidence of something trekking through the Himalayas that wasn't quite human. Unlike the Patterson-Gimlin footage, there was far less evidence to suggest it was a hoax, and even less evidence to explain what it was.

The most serious consideration of the Shipton footprint would come in 1972, via John Napier, the Smithsonian primatologist and one of the few well-regarded biologists to really tackle the Wild Man problem with his book *Bigfoot: The Yeti and Sasquatch in Myth and Reality*. Napier's engagement with the question of the Wild Man should have been heartening for cryptozoologists: here was a noted and respected scientist taking the possibility of the Yeti seriously. But if they'd hoped that meant Napier would finally vindicate their beliefs, though, they were in for disappointment.

Napier dove deep into bipedal physiology, laying out how the weight of a primate or a human makes a footprint first through the heel (the heel strike), then the outer border of the sole, then the inner border (when the body is immediately above the supporting foot), and finally the ball of the foot as the figure pushes off (the toe off). He discussed how variants of extant Sasquatch footprints suggested two different kinds of stride, a near impossibility in a single species, given how fundamental locomotion is to an animal's development. He discussed the possibility of fakes (requiring, he surmised, a "conspiracy of Mafia-like ramifications").

A close examination of the Shipton photograph suggested to Napier that the heel area was the result of sublimation, not the heel strike common to bipedal animals. But even still, he was unable to convincingly prove that the Shipton footprint was simply an animal's print that had melted and refrozen into an uncanny shape. "I only wish I could solve the puzzle," he lamented, "it would help me sleep better at night. Of course, it would settle a lot of problems if one could simply assume that the Yeti is alive and walking about the Himalayas on gigantic feet with two big toes on each foot, and leave it at that." But believing in that hypothesis presented other problems: "Such an assumption conflicts totally with the principles of biology as we know them. Rightly or wrongly, in the absence of any other forms of natural evidence, I would rather put my money on biological principles than on imaginative speculation."

Unable to prove the thing existed, Napier did his best to redirect the question from biology to sociology. "Bigfoot, the living animal, if it exists, must be part of nature. Bigfoot, the legend, which undeniably exists,

is part of human culture." Take Bigfoot seriously, he urged, but not literally. He did not think it made sense to simply dismiss the phenomenon;
rather, he wanted those interested in the question to redirect their line of
inquiry: even if it has no basis in fact, it's still a part of our collective
yearnings and fears, and as such it's something with which we have to
grapple. "Man needs his gods—and his monsters," he concluded, "and
the more remote and unapproachable they are, the better."

One of the hallmarks of the cryptid is that it eschews civilization: as
Everest has become crowded with rich tourists, there have been fewer,
not more, Yeti sightings; of course, the reasoning goes, the Yeti is fearful
of humans, and thus must have retreated off the mountain to more forbidding ranges. To claim to see a cryptid, then, is not just a novel victory;
it is also a boast that you too have left civilization, that you are welcomed
by nature in a way weekenders and casual explorers are not. What people are seeking in cryptids is their own escape from the world of humans
from which they come. Further, to persist in the belief of a forest preserve where unknown creatures still exist is, of course, to persist in the
belief that there may be some wilderness forever unspoiled or untouched
by us.

Like Everest, the forests where Bigfoot roams may not have this same
allure for much longer. Traveling through Northern California, the
widespread devastation resulting from the state's forest fires is increasingly common: once dense, lush, and impenetrable forests are now bare
hillsides, blackened stumps, and denuded branches, where nothing can
hide. As we lose our last wildernesses to climate change, what will become of the strange creatures who once lurked there?

Meanwhile, a new creature has been lately spotted on the slopes of
Everest: the wealthy adventurer, who appears in droves each year to
summit the crowded mountain. You can find traces of its scat all over
the mountain, since frozen human shit can't be buried and doesn't de-
compose in such cold weather, meaning that the leavings of hundreds of
mountaineers is creating a slow-rolling ecological problem. And unlike
the Yeti or Sasquatch, there are plenty of corpses to study, since not a

year goes by that people don't die up on Everest and leave behind corpses, which are often too difficult to remove.

The thing about Everest is that above eight thousand meters, you have barely enough resources to save yourself: if a companion in your party begins to succumb to the elements, you have no choice but to leave them to die while you continue your climb to glory. Such trade-offs are inevitable in war and natural disasters, of course, but only on Everest do people pay tens of thousands of dollars for the opportunity to turn their backs on their dying peers. The commercialization of the world's highest peak, one of the last untouched places on the map, the farthest reach from civilization, has created a place where hundreds of tourists each year pay to choose between common human decency and a bit of narcissistic glory, revealing far more about themselves than any mythical Yeti might have. On a clear day in May you can stand at base camp, gaze up at the sacred summit, and see the brightly colored pelts of these mysterious beasts. Who are these strange creatures, who look like men?

PART III

IN THESE PERILOUS TIMES

———————◆———————

If we knew exactly what the flying saucers were . . .
we would have solved the mystery, returned to boredom,
and stopped thinking again. I hope we never
really solve the mystery of the saucers.

—RAY PALMER

We must loosen our thinking, let our imaginations fly
with the winds, and, above all, we must *want* to think!

—MORRIS K. JESSUP, *THE CASE FOR THE UFO*

Garrett has seen things in the sky he can't explain. He's lived in Lancaster, New Hampshire, most of his life. Lancaster is a tiny town, just a few thousand people, a stopover between the capital, Concord, and Canada. Everything you might want from a picturesque small New England town, and very little else. An affable, levelheaded guy in his late fifties, Garrett is as rational and sober an eyewitness as you could ask for.

Sunday afternoon, the only place open is a brew pub, and the people here are talking about conspiracies. Our server also raises and sells steer; she's trying to get one couple interested in buying two thousand dollars of fresh beef her family just butchered ("Enough to get you through the entire year!"). Trying to close the sale, she gets going about Monsanto, how toxic they make the land, how bad beef raised on Monsanto corn is. "They do crazy things. It's insane. It sounds like a conspiracy theory," she says, "but . . ." and then trails off. There's discussion of the number of people with hormone imbalances, things seen on YouTube videos that speak to the poison in the water and in our food.

I'm just about to leave when Garrett and Lisa arrive. They look like they've been together long enough that they don't have much to say over drinks, so they relish a new conversation. Lisa says she's Catholic, and while she doesn't know anything about UFOs, she definitely has seen "demonic experiences." As for aliens: they wouldn't conflict with her religion—"God is vast," she says—but she just hasn't seen anything that would fit the bill. "I choose not to believe," she says finally.

Garrett, though, is different. He's good, he says, at judging distances—"If I'm on a mountaintop and I see smoke, I can tell you how far away it is." That's why the light he saw on Route 3 fifteen years earlier was strange. In 2005 or so, he was driving with a coworker toward Twin Mountain at night, from Route 115 to Route 3 South, when they saw it. For about five miles, they followed it, talking about what it could be. "It was midway in the sky—not a jet, not a star, not a satellite. Maybe a helicopter, but it wasn't moving." One by one they proposed hypotheses, dismissing each one, unable to satisfactorily identify the light, until it finally passed out of sight behind them. He still doesn't know what it was.

I'm far from Area 51 or the usual places associated with UFO sightings, but that doesn't mean there aren't stories out here in rural New Hampshire. When Lisa was a child in the 1970s, she heard her uncle talk about UFOs. And she remembers how they used to talk about a couple from New Hampshire that had been abducted. Back then, everyone knew about the Hills.

The night of September 19, 1961, Betty and Barney Hill were driving down Route 3 through the White Mountains of New Hampshire on their way back to Portsmouth. A biracial couple, Betty and Barney had been returning from a trip to Canada and had anticipated getting home sometime between two and three in the morning. They reached Lancaster at some point after midnight, which is when they first noticed a single bright light that seemed to be following their car. They continued down Route 3 through the mountains, the light keeping pace. At one point Barney stopped the car so they could get a better look at it; through binoculars, it appeared to have a row of windows, and Barney, thinking it was just a plane or helicopter, walked out into a field to get a better look at it. Something happened out there to change his mind, though, and, overcome with fear, he rushed back to the car, driving off with

Betty and their dog in a panic. Later, a strange "beeping" noise started coming from the back of the car; both of them felt drowsy, but they managed to make it home. It was 5:00 A.M.

Route 3 is now intertwined with Interstate 93, and the path through the White Mountains feels much less remote. I didn't wait until midnight to begin my drive, but it was late enough when I retraced the Hills' journey. I thought of the words that Barney had used to describe this area—"the barren hostility of the wooden area"—and his desperate wish to see another motorist, anyone he could flag down and ask about the light in the sky. But that night they were completely alone, not another car on the road.

It's almost impossible to imagine that now: during the entire drive, I don't go more than a minute or two without seeing another car. Sixty years ago, this might still have been the wilderness, a borderland between the outposts of civilization, but no longer. Trucks barrel past me constantly. Looking out my window in hopes of seeing mysterious lights quickly becomes a hazard, as there's too much traffic to take my eyes off the road for long. My GPS is reassuringly counting down the miles to Concord. Cruising a two-lane freeway at 70 miles per hour, it's impossible to feel as Barney must have felt, alone in the terror of the unknown dark.

After their strange drive, Betty went to the library to try to make sense of what had happened, and there a copy of Donald Keyhoe's *The Flying Saucer Conspiracy* helped cement her fears that something had happened to them. Betty's sister had also claimed to have had an encounter with UFOs, which may have primed Betty to think along these lines. Barney, however, remained agnostic about the night's events. Betty began having increasingly strange nightmares, and a month after the event, sat down with two flying saucer investigators—one of whom, Robert E. Hohman, noted the short distance between remaining on their drive and the two hours it took them to finish their journey, and asked them, "What took you so long to get home?"

The question terrified them—they'd somehow lost two hours and couldn't account at all for the missing time. Betty began to believe her nightmares were, in fact, memories that had been suppressed. The two began a series of hypnosis sessions with Dr. Benjamin Simon in an effort to determine what had taken place.

Each under separate hypnosis sessions, Betty and Barney began to recall a mysterious event, where an alien saucer had landed and taken them on board. Barney described the vehicle as looking "like a—big—pancake. With windows—and rows of windows, and lights. Not lights, just one huge light." The occupants were, as Betty described them, short (five foot to five foot four), with large chests and long noses. They had a gray complexion, blue lips, and black hair, and wore matching blue uniforms. Once on board, the couple was split up and, Betty recalled, subjected to a series of physical tests in which she was disrobed, and a long needle was thrust into her navel as part of a "pregnancy test." At one point the leader left Betty's examination room to attend to Barney's, and when he returned he began touching her teeth, apparently confused that they could not be removed—and then, with a quizzical look, showed her Barney's dentures.

Why had these aliens—if they were real—chosen Betty and Barney Hill? What did they hope to learn from these physical examinations? Where had they come from? Under hypnosis, recalling the terror of first seeing the spacecraft before them, Barney had asked a question that would come to define half a century of sightings, contacts, and abductions: "*What do they want? What do they want?*"

FRAGMENTS

S hortly after he became a household name at the end of June 1947, Kenneth Arnold began receiving letters from a man named Ray Palmer. Arnold was newly famous for having reported seeing a series of unidentified aircraft: on June 24, 1947, he had been flying from Chehalis, Washington, to Yakima, taking a short detour to scout for the remains of a recently downed C-46 transport plane, when he saw nine metallic flying crafts near Mount Rainier, flying in an echelon formation at an extremely high rate of speed, faster than any known human technology. Arnold wasn't the first person to see something strange in the sky, but due to a collision of factors and accidents, his would become the most important.

Arnold's sighting was taken seriously across the country; whatever Arnold had seen, he was a credible and rational observer. Palmer, on the other hand, had been the editor of *Amazing Stories*, a science fiction magazine that lately had specialized in the increasingly fantastical and bizarre. But Palmer was beginning to transition from bizarre fiction to bizarre fact; he had left *Amazing Stories* and now was focusing on "real" stories of the paranormal with his new magazine (cofounded with Curtis Fuller).

Like *Doubt* and *Amazing Stories*, the title of Palmer's magazine was revealing: he called it *Fate*. He may have had a great deal of Fortean radical skepticism in him, but his new UFO venture would not be about doubt—it would be about accepting the coming inevitability. UFOs were here, the world had changed, and there was no going back. It was fate.

Palmer had tried to buy an original story from Kenneth Arnold about his Mount Rainier sighting, but Arnold demurred, sending the account he'd already offered the Air Force instead. Published as "The Truth About the Flying Saucers," it put the new venture on the map. Then Palmer came back to Arnold with an even wilder proposition: he wanted to send the aviator out to investigate another supposed sighting of a flying disk, this one also in the Pacific Northwest, near a place called Maury Island.

Set off from the mainland metropolises of Tacoma and Seattle, Puget Sound's Maury Island has long maintained its unique, isolated character. It's home to a marine preserve, the result of a decades-long battle between environmentalists and a Japanese-based mining company— and it now boasts some of the best views of Mount Rainier from the Sound, and a serene beach of Pacific madrones above eelgrass beds that wave in the water below.

If Maury Island seems like one of those bucolic places trapped in time and forgotten by modernity, at the time of the incident it was anything but. During World War II, the Army had established various observation posts throughout the island, and after the war, it began to convert those for long-term use (eventually, the Army would establish a missile base on the island's Sunrise Ridge). A longtime agricultural hub for the Puget Sound area, it had seen its Japanese population, many of whom were established and wealthy farmers, forcibly removed; only a quarter would return to Maury Island after the internment orders were lifted.

On June 21, 1947, three days before Arnold's Mount Rainier sighting, Harold Dahl had been in a patrol boat with his son Charles, their dog, and two other men, looking for scrap lumber, when they'd claimed to see six metallic objects shaped like donuts hovering at about two thousand feet in the air with no obvious signs of propulsion. As the four men watched, one of the ships appeared to experience some kind of trouble; it dipped and wobbled, causing another craft to come to its aid. After a few minutes, a cascade of what looked like thin metal sheets and scrap fell from the troubled craft's center, followed by another substance that looked like black lava rock. This black substance was hot; it steamed as it hit the water, and one of the chunks landed on Dahl's son's arm, scalding it. Another piece hit their dog, killing it. Two days later, one of Dahl's coworkers, Fred Crisman, went out to investigate and claimed to see a single aircraft, similar to Dahl's descriptions, disappearing into a thundercloud.

For two hundred dollars, Arnold agreed to go check it out and report back what he'd found out. The June 21 incident would turn out to be just the beginning. Of all the sightings, hoaxes, delusions, alleged cover-ups, and other associated weirdness, none were as bizarre as the Maury Island Incident—which, better than any other chapter in the UFO saga, would capture the coming age.

From the start, though, nothing seemed to add up. At first, Dahl refused to talk to Arnold, and none of the supposed evidence he'd promised was forthcoming. The photos Dahl had taken could not be found. There was no trace of the dog who'd been killed by errant spaceship magma; Dahl told Arnold that they'd unceremoniously tossed the corpse into the bay. Nor was there any trace of Dahl's son, who'd supposedly been wounded on the arm by the same ejecta, but now was mysteriously missing. Dahl eventually agreed to meet with Arnold, taking him to his secretary's house to show him the fragments of space metal that he'd recovered. But if the material was potentially a revolutionary scientific find, no one seemed to be treating it that way: Arnold noticed that Dahl's secretary was using one of the fragments as an ashtray.

Eventually, Dahl offered an explanation of sorts for his cagey behavior. The day after the incident, he told Arnold, he'd been visited by a man dressed in a black suit, driving a black 1947 Buick sedan, who took him out to breakfast before sternly warning him to say nothing about what he'd seen. "I did think it was rather fantastic how this gentleman happened to know what I had seen," Dahl told Arnold, "and I was quite sure that he hadn't talked to any of my crew and I know he hadn't talked to me before. In fact, I had never seen him before."

Meanwhile, Dahl's son would turn up later, busing tables in another state—either Lust, Montana, or Lusk, Wyoming, the stories varied—with no memory of how he'd got there, or any memory of the Maury Island Incident. (No hospital record of the injury to his arm ever emerged.)

By this time Arnold was no longer the only interested party in the Maury Island Incident. The Army sent two investigators, Captain William Lee Davidson and First Lieutenant Frank Mercer Brown, to evaluate the story. They met with Arnold, Dahl's coworker Fred Crisman (whose subsequent witness account of the spacecraft was even thinner than Dahl's), and another man, E. J. Smith, at the Hotel Winthrop on July 31. Much of the meeting was spent trying to get Crisman and Dahl to turn over the supposed fragments they had; Arnold and the Army investigators were dubious about the specimens, which looked exactly like aluminum, but Davidson and Brown took a portion of the samples with them, intending to fly back to Hamilton Field in Marin County, California, the next day to analyze the fragments. They didn't make it; their plane crashed en route, killing Davidson and Brown. The fragments were destroyed in the crash.

Only a matter of days separated Arnold's first sighting, an unexplained but credible sighting, vague on explanation but clear on details, and Maury Island: a story of inconsistent explanations and bizarre revelations that contained, in embryo, so many aspects of what would come to define UFO lore. Secret investigations by the Air Force; evidence lost in mysterious circumstances; an amnesiac witness; a "Man in Black" appearing from nowhere, warning civilians to stay away: it had all the ingredients of a great conspiracy theory. Tantalizing but fragmented eyewitness accounts, a careful mixture of specificity and vagueness, a lack of evidence and a corresponding explanation for that lack in the form of shadowy, malevolent figures. In conspiracy theories, less is often better: there's enough detail to pique interest, but everything else is left undefined—the conspiracy theorist then fills out the picture.

What's more, the Maury Island Incident would bring together the three main strands of what would come to define UFO sightings for the next half a century and beyond: credible witnesses of genuinely anomalous things (such as Arnold), a yearning for a mélange of sci-fi and mysticism (via Palmer), and the government. By the time Arnold wrapped up his investigation in August, he was no closer to understanding what had happened, but, as he admitted later, he and his friend Smith "both felt safer with a gun in our possession."

[14]

AN UNIMPEACHABLE WITNESS

To understand Kenneth Arnold's UFO sighting, the event that launched the postwar obsession with flying saucers, you first have to understand balloons. More than nine thousand of them, carried across the Pacific Ocean, made of nothing but wood, glue, and rubberized silk, bringing with them mayhem, chaos, and death. Designed by Toshiro Otsuki, the Japanese balloon bombs of World War II were no more than weather balloons outfitted with incendiary bombs and designed to follow the Pacific jet stream to the Pacific Northwest, the first-ever transcontinental weapon. The hope was to cause fires and panic; they were, depending on your perspective, largely ineffective (success rate was dismal), or surprisingly effective (given that such a wild idea worked at all). Weather patterns kept them from doing extensive damage, but they did have their effects: the only wartime civilian deaths on continental American soil happened one May day when a group of Sunday-school children and one of their chaperones accidentally triggered the balloon's explosives. Another balloon managed to cut the power lines at the plutonium processing plants at Hanford, Washington—which, had the untried backup power not worked, might very well have caused a nuclear meltdown. The balloons made it as far east as Detroit, but the US government was largely successful in convincing journalists not to report on them, to prevent the Japanese government from learning their long-shot weapons were actually effective. They became a bit of local folklore: well known to residents of the Pacific Northwest, who passed around word of them, but unknown to the majority of the American public.

By the end of World War II, the residents of the Pacific Northwest had been trained to watch the skies, to be always alert for unexplained or unexpected menaces above. Kenneth Arnold, who had a small business as a traveling salesman for fire control suppression systems, was no different in this regard. After years of driving all over Oregon, Washington, and Idaho, he'd earned his pilot's license in 1943 and bought a CallAir two-seater prop plane, and even though World War II was over, the Cold War had begun, and the people of the Pacific Northwest were still watching.

Arnold was part of a new generation that was taking to the skies. Prior to World War II, the only people flying were an elite class of aviators and hobbyists, but in 1939, the Civilian Pilot Training Act was passed to change that. One of many similar laws passed by various governments in the 1930s to encourage more citizens to take up civilian aircraft training, it helped ramp up civilian preparation for the impending war. From 1939 until 1944 the Civil Aviation Authority alone trained eleven thousand new pilots each year, propelling more and more people higher and higher into the air.

There they found wonders: a common sighting throughout the war were "Foo Fighters," strange balls of light that followed Allied servicemen as they flew bombing runs over Japan and Germany. Classed sometimes as static electricity, many pilots thought them secret Axis weapons designed to foul the ignition systems of bombers. (German and Japanese pilots, meanwhile, who experienced the same phenomenon, thought them Allied weapons.) The more people looked to the skies, it would seem, the more they found there.

That day in late June 1947, Arnold didn't know exactly what he'd seen. They were about fifty feet long, he judged, in a convoy that stretched about five miles. They were "bat-shaped," Arnold would later claim, "like a pie plate that was cut in half with a sort of convex triangle in the rear." And they moved, he said, "like saucers skipped over water." Whatever they were, he knew enough to worry they might be foreign, either a Soviet reconnaissance or perhaps a first strike. When Arnold landed in Pendleton, Oregon, he went immediately to the local FBI office, worried that he had seen some kind of remote-controlled Soviet weapon. But the FBI office was closed, so he went instead to the only newspaper in town, the *East Oregonian*, just minutes before the paper's deadline. Two reporters, Nolan Skiff and Bill Bequette, took down his story, churning out a brief report that made the front page of the June 25 edition. "Kenneth Arnold, with the fire control at Boise and who was flying in southern Washington yesterday afternoon in search of a missing marine plane, stopped here en route to Boise today with an unusual story—which he doesn't expect people to believe but which he declared is true," the story read. "He said he sighted nine saucer-like air craft flying in formation at 3 P.M. yesterday, extremely bright—as if they were nickel plated—and flying at an immense rate of speed. He estimated they were at an altitude between 9,500 and 10,000 feet and clocked them from Mt. Rainier to Mt. Adams, arriving at the amazing speed of about 1200 miles an hour. 'It seemed impossible,' he said, 'but there it is—I must believe my eyes.'"

Skiff and Bequette changed Arnold's description, turning his metaphor ("like saucers skipped over water") into literal description ("saucerlike"), a subtle but important shift. A batwing aircraft, after all, seems within the realm of what human technology could produce in the 1940s, but a flying disk was not. They had forged a literal thing—a flying disk—out of linguistic imagination, and this in turn would fuel thousands of imaginations to come. They had, in effect, created a second category of aircraft—one whose mechanism and purpose was unknown, something differentiated from fixed-wing aircraft. In the process, they gave a shape to every unknown object out there. The story was less than twenty-four hours old, and it was already distorted, on its way to becoming something else entirely.

The lore of flying saucers depended—as with cryptids—on a particular mode of transmission in their early days: the newswire. Bequette was obligated to also file the story on the AP's C wire, sending it out to other regional AP partners, for use in local news stories. One of the legacies of Samuel Morse, the newswire laid the groundwork for the very idea that news could be "objective." Before the telegraph, the notion that local news would be partisan was taken as a given, but wire services, in order to maximize their profit potential, had to strip out local tone and outlook (it didn't hurt that the telegraph put a premium on minimizing characters). Once news was designed to be shared and repurposed for hundreds of local papers and local markets, it had to lose whatever color the original reporter might have brought to the story. Merely the facts, objectively reported, condensed down to their bare minimum.

In the mid-twentieth century, wire reports would be a crucial vector for stories of Bigfoot, flying disks, and other news of the weird, which could be slotted alongside national and local news to fill space as needed. Arnold's story hadn't been verified or vetted, and yet overnight it was a sensation: a single eyewitness account propelled through the machinery of publishing, functioning mostly on autopilot, into the national consciousness. "Why are such whoppers believed?" Curtis MacDougall wrote in his 1940 history of hoaxes. "Man is ignorant, suggestible, influenced by the prestige of a newspaper printing them."

The AP report was much shorter, and changed key elements. It downplayed Arnold's admission that the whole thing seemed implausible, asserting confidently in its lede: "Nine bright saucer-like objects flying at 'incredible speed' at 10,000 feet altitude were reported here today by Kenneth Arnold, Boise, Idaho, [a] pilot who said he could not hazard a guess as to what they were."

By sending it out on the C wire, Bequette expected it only to reach regional audiences, but the AP's Portland editors picked up the story and sent it out on the main "trunk wire" to all AP affiliates. By the next morning the story was appearing as a page-one story across the country.

The credibility of Arnold's account, disseminated through the nominally objective form of the AP wire, helped catapult it directly into the world's consciousness. Even among those who were skeptical of what Arnold saw, few doubted that he believed what he'd seen, and few were ready to dismiss his account as hallucination or hoax.

Taken at their extreme, unidentified flying objects are not really any different than cryptids or any other Fortean phenomena. By definition "unidentified," once you postulate that they are aliens, or angels, or even Russian spy craft, you've taken a stab at identifying them and the jig is up. Arnold never offered a definition of what he saw: all he did was report the sighting. He'd gone to the FBI because he believed them to be some kind of threat, but in his account to the *East Oregonian* he had made no attempt to offer a hypothesis.

It was this, plus his reputation as an unimpeachable witness, someone sober and serious, trusted by his community, someone whose eyewitness account wasn't too exotic or far-fetched, that stayed consistent with each telling, with calculations and measurements as best as Arnold could make them, that gave his account such legitimacy. But like all neutral, credible observers, he soon found his tale co-opted by everyone who *did* have a hypothesis or an agenda.

[15]

WELDING

To really understand Maury Island, you first have to understand Ray Palmer. Palmer was in every way imaginable the opposite of Arnold: a provocateur and pitchman, someone unafraid to embellish for the sake of readership. Even more so than Arnold—or any of the numerous eyewitnesses of unexplained objects in the skies that would appear in the coming decades—Palmer would shape the story of flying saucers. Whatever people were *actually* seeing, Palmer already had a language and cosmology for those sightings, and as he slotted sightings like Arnold's into his grand mythology, it was harder and harder for many not to be influenced by Palmer, harder and harder to try to see with unbiased eyes.

Palmer had been editing *Amazing Stories* since 1937; he'd dreamed of writing for the magazine since he was a kid, a lonely child from Milwaukee who'd been crippled when he was seven after being run over by a milk truck. Science fiction became his escape, a fantasy world where anything was possible. But *Amazing Stories'* founder, Hugo Gernsback, was far less interested in fantasy than in science fact: he'd envisioned the genre as another avenue for testing the validity of scientific ideas, and wanted work heavily rooted in plausibility. (The magazine's original motto was "Extravagant Fiction Today—Cold Fact Tomorrow.") *Amazing Stories* profited under Gernsback's direction until the 1920s, when it began to face stiff competition from a proliferation of rival pulp magazines, and Gernsback, unwilling to sensationalize his scientific content, sold the publication. At its height, *Amazing Stories'* circulation was 150,000; now it was down to a tenth of that, and publishing only bimonthly. After a few ownership changes, it landed in the hands of Ziff-Davis, a publishing company far more interested in story than science. They hired Palmer as editor, and he began incorporating more and more fantasy, increasing circulation at the expense of plausibility.

Slowly, Palmer had turned Gernsback's science magazine into a rejection of science. "Science says nothing exists that can't be proved," he wrote in a 1946 letter. "With five meager senses, if you please. What about the invisible? You can't SEE that?" Scientists confronted with the unusual, Palmer complained, too often simply shrugged and said they didn't know. "They DON'T KNOW! . . . what poor, blind, dumb bastards. . . . Science—a cult. Scientists—priests. Fen—kneeling, trembling, adoring, befuddled, unthinking, stupid worshippers. Go ahead, take somebody's word for it. And HOPE they're right—if you're *lucky*. Don't question a thing. Never use your brain for DOUBTING. Doubt only what you're TOLD to doubt. Be a follower."

Palmer was one more soldier to pick up the banner against the institutions of science. His language and rhetorical flourishes often mimicked Charles Fort, but unlike Fort, Palmer had no qualms about championing mystical and mythical ideas over hard science. And yet, unlike Blavatsky, his motivations seemed distinctly commercial—he was more P. T. Barnum than crank, someone who understood that pushing back against professional scientists created the kind of taboo attitude that sold magazines.

His tour de force, though, would be something else altogether— though it's not fair to say it was his own invention. In 1943, Palmer handed one of his fellow editors, Howard Browne, a letter from a reader named Richard Shaver, asking him what he thought. "I read a third of it, tossed it in the waste basket," Browne later recalled. "Ray, who loved to show his editors a trick or two about the business, fished it out of the basket, ran it in *Amazing*, and a flood of mail poured in from readers who insisted every word of it was true."

When he mailed his first letter to *Amazing Stories*, Richard Shaver had been a free man for only a short time—he'd spent much of the previous years in and out of various psychiatric hospitals. The Great Depression had been hard for him: jobs were hard to come by and only with difficulty did he land a physically demanding, high-stress assembly-line job. His wife was an artist whose local reputation was solidifying, but her family didn't approve of Shaver. And then, in 1934, his brother Taylor died, which may have been the last straw in pushing Shaver into a mental breakdown.

He began hearing voices coming from the welding machine at his work. The voices, he would later explain, were sometimes soft, sometimes loud, and sometimes hidden within other noises, like "a fly buzzing by your ear." He came to understand these voices were being telepathically projected into his mind by mysterious rays whose source he could not locate. The voices, he quickly learned, would not communicate with anyone else but him.

While impossible to know for sure in hindsight, Shaver's description of these voices, most now agree, bear all the hallmarks of paranoid schizophrenia, a condition that often manifests itself in disembodied voices that are "projected" or broadcast from some hidden, often nefarious source.

Shaver's confession that he was hearing voices would lead to his first institutionalization; to compound his troubles, while he was institutionalized his wife died in a freak accident. The next twelve years were spent in and out of mental institutions, as his schizophrenia deepened. Biographers have had difficulty tracing his exact movements during this time because his recollections are half memory, half fantasy—he would gradually come to believe there were two different races, the good ones (theros) and the evil ones (deros), at war for his soul. Max, a dero, tormented him throughout the 1930s and early 1940s, while two theros, a woman named Sue and a blind girl named Nydia, would help him.

Ultimately, he was hospitalized at the Ionia State Hospital for the Criminally Insane, though the exact reasons for this are still unknown; also unknown are the conditions of his eventual release. But by the time he got out, he understood that talking about deros and theros was a quick way back to confinement, so he learned instead to channel his demons into writing, an outlet that allowed for him to manage his condition.

"This language seems to be definite proof of the Atlantean legend," Shaver wrote in his letter to *Amazing Stories*, which Palmer retrieved from the wastebasket. The language he referred to was his "Mantong" (Man tongue) language; in it, he assigned a concept to each letter of the alphabet—words could then be analyzed for how they bore out the combinations of those concepts: the word "bad," for example, would be composed of "B" ("be, to exist—often a command"), "A" ("animal"), and "D" ("disintegrant energy; detrimental"—the most important symbol in language), and hence to be "bad" would mean to be a detrimental, animalistic, and destructive force of some kind.

Shaver's alphabet ran in the January 1944 issue of *Amazing Stories*, a mix of numerology and apophenia that made little sense then and even less now. Palmer didn't care. He encouraged readers to try it out for themselves, playing to his recognition of the burgeoning fan culture that drove early science fiction. Palmer reprinted letters, interacted with fans, and tried various other techniques to get readers to feel as though they were a part of *Amazing Stories*. If the internet would come to be seen as the medium of best dissemination for conspiracy and stigmatized knowledge, it's impossible to understate the role of the pulp magazine as its predecessor. *Amazing Stories*, *Fate*, and other publications served as a clearinghouse for sharing ideas, connecting believers, refining facts. (*Fate* letter from a reader, Winter 1949: "It fills the need for circulation of little known fact . . . most people are reluctant to discuss the strange phenomena for fear of public ridicule.") The difference between this model and the internet, though, was that all of this was channeled through the central figure of the editor—Palmer and his cohorts—who could shape and drive the narrative, as well as be shaped by submissions from readers.

The Shaver Alphabet generated some reader discussion, a mix of earnest application and gentle ridicule, but by then Palmer had already written to Shaver asking if he had anything else; Shaver responded with a rambling, ten-thousand-word manifesto, "Warning to Future Man." Palmer promised to publish it immediately, though only after he'd extensively rewritten it. He also retitled it: "I Remember Lemuria!"

Under Palmer's editing, Shaver's manifesto became a sci-fi romance about an underground civilization. Palmer swapped out Shaver's Atlantis for the more Theosophical-friendly Lemuria, and stuffed it full of standard space-opera tropes: in a subterranean world, a "sub-Atlan" art student named Mutan Mion finds his art rejected by his teacher and descends deeper into Mu (populated by Titans and elder Atlans) to better understand the world and develop his art better. There he meets a love interest, fawn-girl Arl, who instructs him in the mysteries of Mu. They learn that radioactivity has poisoned the Earth's surface above, and that the civilization is planning to escape to a new star—but that the evil Deros are trying to stop them. Mutan and Arl escape to the planet Nortan, inhabited by a "pure" race of beautiful blond giants, led by Princess Vanue, who reveals a plan to rescue the sub-Atlans. The Nortans lead a battle against the evil Deros, liberating their captives. The story ends with the elder Atlans evacuating Earth, and Mutan's warning for future inhabitants of the sun's evil rays.

By reworking Shaver's hallucinations, Palmer did more than just turn a record of schizophrenia into pulp adventure. He yoked it to an occult history that had already reconceptualized Earth as a place filled with enchanted borderlands on the margins of civilization. The edge of the map could just as well be the planet's interior as some distant continent. He turned the focus of *Amazing Stories* from the future to the distant past. Shaver himself had made no mention of Lemuria, but Palmer's genius was in yoking Shaver's nightmare hallucinations to a free-standing Theosophical cosmology, which gave the former legitimacy and added novelty to the latter.

And, most importantly, he presented it as true. Palmer's gambit was in presenting Shaver's work as nonfiction: Palmer and Shaver's term for this would be "racial memory," the idea that Shaver was channeling an ancient race. It was an attempt to make memory itself uncanny, so that the unexplained and contradictory could be connected to these strange occult ideas of the past. Palmer was a canny showman, no doubt, a purveyor of Barnumesque bunkum, but his interest was always in wonder over truth. In 1977, he explained his use of the term "mystery" as something that should perpetually remain unsolved, something that will stimulate curiosity over definitive answers. Fiction was great, but it didn't trouble the same fundamental assumptions about our world, didn't gear the mind into wondering about those central truths, and couldn't elevate imagination into that level of the terrifying but captivating sublime. What Shaver's hallucinations offered Palmer's readers was neither science fiction nor science fact, but an enchanted world that reached all the way down into the Earth's bedrock.

Sales of *Amazing Stories* skyrocketed (Palmer had an extra fifty thousand copies of the "I Remember Lemuria!" issue printed, all of which sold out), all borne on the back of a tortured man's paranoid schizophrenia. It is an odd facet of our interest in conspiracy theories in general: the strange pleasure we take from another's paranoia. To be close to the mystery of mental illness, but to escape unscathed, seems to bring a strange rush.

The Shaver Mysteries would dominate *Amazing Stories* until 1948, when Palmer's publishers made it known they were done with them. But by then, Palmer was on to his next big thing. For two years he'd been seeding his audience with word of flying saucers: "If you don't think space ships visit the earth regularly," a 1946 letter from the editor read, "then the files of Charles Fort and your own editor's files are something you should see. Your editor has hundreds of reports (especially from returned soldiers) of objects that were clearly seen and tracked which could have been nothing but space ships. And if you think responsible parties in world governments are ignorant of the fact of space ships visiting Earth, you just don't think the way we do." It was time to shift gears; no longer would Palmer direct his readers' attention down into the Earth—it was time to look up.

For Ray Palmer, Kenneth Arnold's story was the key, and it launched his new magazine, *Fate*, heralding a fundamentally new age in sci-fi pulps. But when Palmer sent Arnold to investigate the Maury Island Incident, he kept one crucial piece of information from him: Crisman, the second eyewitness, had been a longtime writer for *Amazing Stories*, and someone who claimed to know about the Shaver Mysteries. One of his letters had even seemed to offer firsthand corroboration of the Shaver Mysteries. "For heaven's sake, drop the whole thing!" he'd written, explaining how he and a friend had fought their way out of a Deros cave with submachine guns. It was Crisman—hardly a reliable source at this point—who'd first tipped Palmer off to the story.

The Maury Island Incident was almost certainly—nearly everyone agrees—a hoax perpetrated by Crisman. But what a hoax it was. Arnold, the impeccable witness—clear-sighted, rational and objective, trustworthy and well-regarded—had found himself immediately enmeshed with Ray Palmer, a science-fiction provocateur who had been passing off Richard Shaver's schizophrenic letters as fact. And the net result of his involvement was entanglement in an obvious hoax that inadvertently cost the life of two men and the reputations of a good many others.

Despite their entanglement, Arnold and Palmer stand at opposite ends of a spectrum that would come to define the UFO phenomenon from the end of World War II to the present day. At one end, a serious scientific investigation of anomalous evidence, approached with a rational and open mind. At the other, fantasies imbued with occult mysticism, where pop culture and science fiction mingle freely with the objective world.

Would our view of UFOs have turned out differently if Palmer hadn't intervened so early on, putting a distinctly mystical stamp on the anomalous things that Arnold and others were seeing in the sky? Perhaps. But one group was bound to take these sightings seriously, with or without Palmer's salesmanship.

[16]

A JITTERY AGE

A month after Arnold's Mount Rainier sighting, something crashed in the desert. On July 8, 1947, the *Roswell Daily Record* reported that the Army claimed to have had "come into possession of a flying saucer," though details were sketchy on what exactly it was. A day later the Army had already backed off this story, informing news outlets that it was not a downed flying craft, that it was instead wreckage of a weather balloon.

The Roswell crash would be mostly forgotten for the time being, but sightings began to multiply. The same day that AP's Arnold story broke, the crew of United Airlines Flight 105 had seen a formation of five disk-shaped objects. And then on July 8, airmen at Muroc Field (now Edwards Air Force Base) saw three silver disks in the sky heading west. The proximity of these disks to a military installation helped convince the government to act. In late summer 1947, Lieutenant General Nathan F. Twining, commander of Air Materiel Command, issued an internal Air Force memo concluding, among other things, that there are "objects probably approximating the shape of a disc, of such appreciable size as to appear to be as large as man-made aircraft."

The emphasis on disk-shaped craft, of course, demonstrates how quickly the shorthand mistranslation of Arnold's original description had been accepted as gospel. Nevertheless, at the end of the year the Air

Force approved Project Sign, an investigation group whose mission was "to collect, collate, evaluate and distribute to all interested government agencies and contractors all information concerning sightings and phenomena in the atmosphere which can be construed to be of concern to the national security." Its security designation was "restricted," the lowest rating, which gave an early indication as to the likelihood that the Air Force was involved in a deep cover-up of alien technology. Nonetheless, they began interviewing eyewitnesses across the country; as Curtis Peebles notes, "Whenever a reporter went to interview a person who had seen a saucer, he found the Air Force had already been there." And then, barely more than a week after the formation of Project Sign, the project was given a renewed sense of urgency.

On January 7, 1948, Thomas Mantell, a pilot for the Kentucky Air National Guard, was flying a low-altitude navigational training mission with three other pilots. About 2:40 p.m. local time, they received reports of "an unusual aircraft or object . . . circular in appearance approximately 250–300 feet in diameter" over Mansville, Kentucky. Once the object was in his sights, Mantell began his approach. "The object is directly ahead of and above me now," he reported, "moving at about half my speed." He was at 15,000 feet by now, climbing steadily. "It appears to be a metallic object or possibly reflection of Sun from a metallic object," he continued, "and it is of tremendous size." Mantell and the two other pilots were now at 22,000 feet.

None of the pilots had supplemental oxygen onboard, necessary for flying at higher altitudes. Mantell's two comrades broke off pursuit at this point, lacking oxygen, but Mantell continued. "I'm still climbing, the object is above and ahead of me moving at about my speed or faster," he radioed. "I'm trying to close in for a better look."

Somewhere above twenty-five thousand feet, Mantell passed out due to lack of oxygen; his plane stalled out at thirty thousand feet, then entered a spiral dive, breaking up between twenty thousand and ten thousand feet. With Mantell's death, it was time to take the flying saucer craze far more seriously.

Still, in those early days there was no mention of aliens. In August 1947, a Gallup poll reported that while 90 percent of Americans were aware of flying saucers, no one thought they had anything to do with extraterrestrials. (Sixteen percent believed they were either US or Soviet secret weapons.) Most believed they were illusions, hoaxes, or other readily explainable phenomena. (No one talked too much about a shell-shocked nation still reeling from a cataclysmic war, one that left many of its pilots dealing with untreated PTSD, pilots who now found themselves in civilian settings, chasing phantoms across the night sky.)

Mantell's death spurred the Air Force to keep a keen eye on unidentified flying objects—even if they weren't Soviets or aliens and just hysteria or hallucinations, that didn't mean they couldn't get good pilots killed. The Air Force began gathering up eyewitness accounts, which they then would evaluate, looking for explanations that accounted for what people were seeing. They recruited a local professional astronomer, J. Allen Hynek, to explain sightings that might have celestial origins. (Project Sign concluded that Mantell may very well have been chasing the planet Venus, whose position in the sky would have corresponded with where multiple witnesses claimed to have seen the flying craft.) Most could be debunked or explained—planets or satellites, weather balloons, hallucinations. There were some, though, that continued to leave Air Force investigators stymied.

One immediate side effect of Project Sign was that the Air Force determined the shape of the standard narrative of flying saucer sightings. In their original mandate, they agreed not to investigate any sightings that happened prior to Arnold's famous Mount Rainier sighting. The Foo Fighters of World War II and other earlier sightings were excluded from their sphere of inquiry, and thus were eventually excluded from the mainstream history of flying saucers.

Eventually, two camps within the project emerged: those who believed that all sightings were, in some form or another, explained by terrestrial means, and those who believed that some kind of extraterrestrial intelligence was involved. In September 1948, analysts in the latter camp put together a legendary document: the "estimate of the situation." Edward J. Ruppelt, later head of the Air Force's UFO investigations, reported on the document's existence, but it's never been seen firsthand by civilians. (Ruppelt also claimed to have coined the term "UFO," as a more general catchall term for things that weren't necessarily shaped like disks.) But Ruppelt claimed that the document pushed the timeline back to before the Arnold sighting, and claimed that the document argued that the UFOs were real and of extraterrestrial origin. It was submitted to Hoyt S. Vandenberg, chief of staff of the Air Force, who sent it back claiming it lacked proof; the report was subsequently buried.

As a result, the culture in the Air Force changed; by the time Project Sign had been reorganized a year later as Project Grudge (later renamed, once again, Project Blue Book), the party line was now entirely that UFO sightings were all terrestrial in origin—either classified military projects, delusions, or hoaxes. (Hynek would later scoff that the change of names "signaled the adoption of the strict brush-off attitude to the UFO problem.") With Project Blue Book, investigators turned from the skies to the witnesses, seeking to discredit them or otherwise explain away what they'd seen. Like any institution, as it matured the Air Force defined what did and didn't count. The more it looked at random lights flitting about the sky, the less it saw.

This also meant a public relations campaign to downplay the supposed hysteria. Scientists were trotted out to explain that most of what people were seeing were hallucinations—or, at most, balloons (always balloons). A *Life* magazine article rounded up some of the more bizarre sightings and cataloged the most specious explanations ("In Chicago Mr. L. M. Wendorf said the disks were merely hallucinations which would disappear if U.S. citizens followed a correct diet. He recommended a menu including 50 dandelion blooms a day"), while drawing comparisons to the Loch Ness Monster and the *New York Sun*'s infamous 1835 moon hoax.

In a 1949 piece sympathetic to the government, Sidney Shalett wrote in *The Saturday Evening Post*, "The officers and technical experts

assigned to Project Saucer—a nickname for the top-secret Air Force investigative effort—sometimes get to feeling they're living in a dream
world, so utterly unfettered and mysterious are some of the reports they
are assigned to evaluate." It was as if the Air Force had become the nation's psychotherapist, tasked with vetting and dispelling an entire country's anxious psychoses. It was, as Shalett noted, a "jittery age."

This tactic almost immediately backfired: reports and sightings spiked.
People began to doubt the Air Force's methodology and motives, and
investigators and sleuths set out to figure out just what, exactly, the government knew. Donald E. Keyhoe not only had a long history publishing
fiction in pulp magazines like *Weird Tales*, he also was a retired major in
the US Navy, with connections in the Pentagon. When the men's adventure magazine *True* asked him to write an independently researched article on flying saucers, he leaned on these contacts in the military, hoping
to get the true story once and for all. Instead, Keyhoe was stonewalled.
Rather than making him go away, this tactic led him to believe there was
a cover-up; his article, "The Flying Saucers Are Real," alleged not only a
conspiracy but that the government had knowledge of extraterrestrials.
The Air Force reports, he claimed, "contradictory as they appear, are part
of an intricate program to prepare America—and the world—for the
secret of the disks." The issue of *True* in which Keyhoe's article appeared
sold out so quickly the magazine had to reprint it.

As sightings increased, the public relations effort became more truc-
ulent. A 1951 article in *Cosmopolitan* by Bob Considine (also written
with government cooperation) went after the "disgraceful UFO hoax"
with indignant fury. Considine played up the waste of government tax
money that had been spent on UFO investigations. (If you were forced
to pay for every fraud and swindle, Considine opined, "You'd raise hell,
and demand that Something Be Done!" And yet, he continued, "You're
paying for something even less enchanting: the daily cost of running to
ground every phony clue concerning the purely idiotic and wholly nonexistent 'flying saucers.'")

Considine did more than just attempt to debunk UFO sightings, he set out to highlight the true costs—both material, in the form of tax dollars wasted by the Air Force, and lives lost (well, life, singular, lost; his only example was once again Thomas Mantell). The phrase, "And nothing can be done about such frauds," is a constant refrain throughout the article, playing to people's fear of impotence in the presence of government waste and fraud. The *Cosmopolitan* article actively set out to humiliate and embarrass those who believed in UFOs, and to convince people it was not simply a "harmless" belief. Those who believed in flying saucers were not just wrong; they were stupid and dangerous.

But such tactics are not without consequences. Conspiracy theory researchers use the term "stigmatized knowledge" to describe those beliefs that are not just outside of mainstream, but actively ridiculed by mainstream culture. The defining line is often blurry and shifting (reading your daily horoscope may be considered more or less normal, whereas spending hundreds of dollars on psychics may not be). But the net effect is to separate the wheat from the chaff—half-hearted believers in UFOs drifted away as it became more fringe, but those who remained would become that much more hardened in their convictions, as it became clear that they were being dismissed by mainstream culture.

Nor did the government itself have a consensus about what these sightings were. By 1952, the CIA was beginning to openly question whether or not the flying saucer epidemic was a national security threat. Worried the Soviet Union might have the technology to manufacture flying saucers, the CIA turned to a panel of scientists led by H. P. Robertson, a physicist at the California Institute of Technology, to investigate. The Robertson Panel, as it was subsequently known, convened for four days in January 1953 to review the Air Force's "best" evidence for UFOs. The panel included a nuclear scientist, a geophysicist, a radar/electronics expert, and an astronomer, plus Frederick C. Durant, president of the American Rocket Society, and J. Allen Hynek. They reviewed evidence gathered by the Air Technical Intelligence Center (ATIC): eyewitness reports, blurry photographs, and two films—one of twelve bright objects moving across the sky taken at Tremonton, Utah, on July 2, 1952, and another from August 15, 1950, showing two points of light flying on an even course above Great Falls, Montana.

After four days they issued a report, in which they stated that "the evidence presented on Unidentified Flying Objects shows no indication that these phenomena constitute a direct physical threat to national security." Further, nothing they saw indicated "a need for the revision of current scientific concepts."

The Robertson Panel operated under the same assumptions that drove zoologists and biologists approaching cryptids. They were not completely closed off to the possibility, but what was being presented as evidence was far from conclusive. It was anomalous, to be sure, but it lacked anything material. They contrasted the ATIC work with the intelligence operation during World War II that led to the discovery of Germany's V-1 and V-2 rockets (Operation Crossbow): there, recovered hardware from a crashed plane had given investigators evidence of a new weapon and a direction for their intelligence gathering. The overwhelming conclusion of the Robertson Panel was that visual data in the form of blurry films of strange light blobs was not enough. Just like you needed a Bigfoot corpse, you needed a crashed spaceship.

The problem they did see, though, was in the public's fascination with such things. The continued emphasis on the reporting of the UFO phenomena, they went on, "does, in these perilous times, result in a threat to the orderly functioning of the protective organs of the body politic." They recognized the problem of false reports and of increased hysteria, and they realized that the Air Force was better served by de-emphasizing these anomalous sightings and debunking them wherever possible. There was a real strategic value, they understood, in educating the public about things that might cause strange lights in the sky—balloons, Venus, etc.—so as to keep the channels of communication open for legitimate security threats.

Of course, if you already believe in UFOs, as people like Donald Keyhoe did, then the government's reassurance that there's nothing to worry about will have the opposite effect. In 1956, Keyhoe got word that a group of flying saucer researchers might be interested in getting serious. Clara T. John and T. Townsend Brown ran a "flying saucer club" in Washington, DC, one of many informal groups throughout the country that gathered to discuss sightings and hypothesize how such craft might fly and what the coming implications might be. Brown, who had relocated to Washington in search of government funding for his Winterhaven antigravity space propulsion device, began to talk to John about an umbrella organization—a central place that could gather up all the available amateur research and pool efforts. Encouraged by UFO researcher Morris K. Jessup, in August 1956 they formally incorporated the National Investigations Committee on Aerial Phenomena (NICAP), the first civilian attempt to understand UFOs in a systematic, scientific, and open-minded manner.

If NICAP was originally intended to be objective, within a year Keyhoe had wrested control of the board and had turned its focus to coverups. He believed that the government already had evidence of UFOs, and he envisioned NICAP as a lobbying organization to force their hand. Under his direction, NICAP began a media blitz designed to pressure Congress into holding hearings. A tension that runs through civilian UFOlogy was right there at the founding of NICAP. Some civilian researchers wanted to use empirical science to get to the bottom of the phenomena; neutral and unbiased, they represented a good-faith attempt to simply understand. But these researchers could never fully disentangle themselves from those, like Keyhoe, who operated under the assumption that the government already *knew*, and that the work of civilian scientists was to unearth the truth. To this latter group, mainstream scientists who evaluated the data and saw no conclusive evidence of extraterrestrial craft were simply part of the same conspiracy.

Despite NICAP's lobbying, the military did not open up the inquiries and investigations to the public. Even after they had decided internally that there were no extraterrestrial forces at work and no security risks associated with UFOs, they still kept all material classified, preventing the public and disinterested scholars from evaluating the data the military had received and drawing their own conclusions. Writers like Keyhoe were successful because they were struggling with the question on many people's minds: why was a field of inquiry, legitimate or not, being kept from the public? It was one thing when professional scientists enshrined in universities and museums had closed off the natural world—at least they weren't working in secrecy. The postwar era, driven by the secrecy surrounding nuclear physics, had once again changed how we saw our physical surroundings. When writers like Keyhoe and others suggested that the rise of UFO sightings had to do with the atomic bomb, they were right in one sense: no longer could the pursuit of natural science be entrusted to public citizens.

By gathering all of the sightings and evidence under a classified program, the Air Force had basically made the study of the natural world a secret military endeavor. Falling meat, hairy humanoids, lost continents—none of these would seem to have national security implications, but bright objects moving fast across the sky might, and this distinguishing criterion elevated the UFO saga out of the longer, more diffused history of Fortean weirdness into a specific cultural relic of the early postwar years. If there is a dividing line between UFOs and other kinds of fringe phenomena—cryptids, lost worlds, or even ghosts—it's that from the start, UFOs were claimed by the government.

The Earth and the air above all now belonged to the state. And by the time the government began to come forward with fairly plausible explanations (many of which revolved around high-altitude balloons known as Project Skyhook), few were in any mood to believe them. As *The New York Times* noted in 1951, "Even if space ships manned by pygmies from another world are now dismissed the belief will probably persist that the whole truth has not yet been told and that information about some new weapon or some new type of aircraft is being withheld. But this is the price that must be paid for secrecy. Where there is secrecy, rumor, gossip and imagination take the place of news." Unlike other Fortean phenomena, flying objects would always be about something else—Communism, government secrecy, paranoia.

THE CALL FROM CLARION

Truman Bethurum had been out of work due to a strike when he agreed to take a job in Mormon Mesa, Nevada, as a swing shift maintenance mechanic, leaving his wife behind in Redondo Beach, California. Remembering stories of how the desert had once been the ocean floor, he set out one evening in July 1952 to hunt for seashells for his wife; taking a nap in his truck after midnight, he was woken by a group of small men in uniform.

At least, that's his story, in his highly implausible 1954 narrative of his alien encounter, *Aboard a Flying Saucer.* Bethurum tells of how he was welcomed by this group of aliens who live on the planet Clarion, a planet on the other side of the moon, inexplicably hidden from our sight. Much of the book involves his conversations with the ship's captain, a female alien named Aura Rhanes: "She wore no jewelry, not even a buckle on her belt. Her black hair was short and brushed into an upward curl at the ends, and she wore jauntily tilted on one side of her proudly held head a black and red beret. She was standing before a great wide flat topped desk, with her graceful hands resting upon it. Her bodice was of some fitted material which looked like black velvet, with short sleeves decorated with a small red ribbon bow. The top of her skirt, which I could see above the edge of the desk, was of the most radiant red material I had ever seen. It looked like wool and was set all round in small flat pleats."

Strip away the paltry attempts at physics and astronomy, and *Aboard a Flying Saucer* quickly reveals itself to be a rather conventional—and sappy—romance. While Aura Rhanes is indeed beautiful, the love story here is truly between Truman and his wife, Mary, back in the suburbs of Los Angeles. Having made contact, he sends her letters describing his ordeal, attesting to the veracity of it all, and inviting her up to see for herself.

Captain Rhanes, meanwhile, writes two letters to help Truman plead his case, one in Chinese, one in French. The French letter explains at length how the problems plaguing modern Earth society are feminism and its rejection of Jesus Christ. "We are Christians here and on this point we have not retrogressed as I see from here the dreadful gnawing at modern countries," she writes, warning Truman's wife, Mary, of spiritual decadence. "Try," she continues, "to convince him by your unlimited fidelity and your complete devotion, refusing to permit your hearth to revolt or to reproach past weaknesses. But, above all, learn to place your faith in God, and, by Christian effort which will be an example to him, try to lead him back to a sincere faith or to increase in him the practice of religion." God, it seems, has saved the Venusians, who do not have divorce or adultery "to the dangerous degree that it exists on the Planet Earth." The Chinese letter, a bit more succinctly, translates as: "Chinese women hold their husbands with love, if not they put them in chains."

Truman Bethurum was another blue-collar worker in a difficult climate, away from family and comfort, discovering wonder and a small amount of danger in the wilderness. The lesson of his book, once again, is the validation of the working-class man in a world that's changing around him, a reaffirmation not only of conservative values but of his place as head of household, with a faithful and demurring wife. (Even when delivered by transcendental space beings, though, the message doesn't always take: Bethurum's wife, Mary, eventually divorced him.)

The most extreme, ineffable, revelatory experience is almost immedi-ately banalized—aliens crossing vast distances with unimaginable tech-nology to repeat the most basic of Sunday School moralities.

The difference, of course, is these are not mute beasts half glimpsed in the forest or mountain peaks, but an advanced civilization (whose power sources include "antimagnetic," "plutonic," and "nutronic"), artic-ulate and multilingual, that represents the zenith of technology and cul-ture. Both Bigfoot and Captain Aura Rhanes are here to tell us how to be human. But the Wild Man legend exists to help us understand how we differentiated ourselves from the natural world, a way of explaining to ourselves what is beneath us. The alien narrative is aspirational: to show us what we must become.

○ ○ ○

The desert is contactee country, where mystics and occultists (along with ordinary people like Bethurum) claimed to have made com-munions with visitors from other planets throughout the early 1950s. "The whole thing about deserts," Ken Layne tells me, "is that deserts are where religions come from. It's with people on the edges of a city, or on a trade route or something, that you get Christianity and Islam." Layne runs *Desert Oracle*, a magazine and accompanying radio show out of his home in Joshua Tree, California, chronicling the natural and cultural landscape on the edge of civilization. It's not just religion that is born in the desert, he suggests, "but also that mysticism that comes with being out in the desert in a place that is inhospitable." The Christian mystics who holed up in caves in the Syrian deserts or lived on abandoned col-umns in Roman ruins—these people found in the desert an existence just on the edge of being, on the far reaches of the human.

It was out here in the Southern California desert that George Adam-ski began the contactee era. In April 1952, *Life* magazine ran a feature with the bold headline: HAVE WE VISITORS FROM OUTER SPACE? It took only a few short months for Adamski to offer a definitive answer to the question. Adamski was born in Poland in 1891, and came to the United States during the First World War. He spent his first few years in America working various odd blue-collar jobs, but soon switched to preaching a brand of mystical philosophy, which he called the Royal Order of Tibet. The main tenet of his religion seemed to be the imbibing of wine, which is to say the entire thing seems to have been a scam to allow Adamski to skirt Prohibition laws. During World War II and afterward, he and his wife operated a hamburger joint near the Hale Telescope on Palomar Mountain, which may have fueled his interest in astronomy and watching the skies. On November 20, he claimed, he was traveling in the deserts east of Mount Palomar with a few friends, when they saw a "gigantic, cigar-shaped silvery ship." Adamski went off to investigate alone, and there encountered a spaceman from Venus. A tanned man with long, sandy hair wearing a brown ski suit, in Adamski's description he seems straight out of a fashion shoot for some Nordic skiwear. Communicating telepathically, the Venusian explained to Adamski that he and his fellow extraterrestrials were worried about mankind's sudden development of atomic weapons.

Adamski's account of his encounter first appeared in a book coauthored with UFO investigator Desmond Leslie, *Flying Saucers Have Landed*. The first half of the book is a long, sober-enough treatise by Leslie, recounting evidence and the likelihood of extraterrestrials, before giving way to Adamski's short account. Taken as a complete text, *Flying Saucers Have Landed* walks a curious line between earnest scientific inquiry and junk mysticism—and exhibits the degree to which the latter would continue to rely on the former for legitimacy. Above all, the hybridity of the book suggests how UFO cults sought to occupy the ground between straight science and mainline religion, inhabiting the amorphous middle ground of physics and mysticism, hoping to reach anyone whose concerns went unanswered by more established doctrine.

Adamski's encounter would lead to a flood of similar books that all appeared in quick succession, including Cedric Allingham's *Flying Saucer from Mars*, Truman Bethurum's story, and Daniel Fry's *The White*

Sands Incident. Contactee cults and flying saucer study groups had spread throughout the country, and more and more people had come forward claiming to have interacted with Venusians, Martians, and farther-flung planets. Among the many contactees was Gabriel Green, who founded the Amalgamated Flying Saucer Clubs of America, Inc., which boasted 2,500 members worldwide at its height. Green ran for president in 1960 on the Universal Flying Saucer Party ticket ("The Space People's Choice!"); undaunted by his loss, he ran again for the Senate in California in 1962, and this time did manage to get 113,205 votes.

Dozens of people claimed to have met with visitors from other planets, including Chief Frank Buckshot Standing Horse, who was taken for a ride in 1959 on a spaceship throughout the cosmos by a beautiful woman named Captain Mondraoleeka from Oreon. Mondraoleeka was, like Aura Rhanes and so many other space babes, very beautiful, but unlike those described by white contactees like Bethurum, she did not have blond hair; her hair was "pitch black," according to Standing Horse, and she wore "a belt that looked as if it was jeweled, with a long dress." On their interstellar voyages, they listened to a country radio station out of Little Rock, Arkansas.

For years, these seekers would gather annually in the Southern California desert, the epicenter of the contactee movement. Not far from Joshua Tree National Park is Landers, California, in the Moreno Valley, known for its Giant Rock, a boulder the size of a seven-story building. Formerly the home of a German prospector, Frank Critzer, who dug out a small apartment in the ground beneath the rock and then died in an explosion during a standoff with police in 1942, Giant Rock became a mecca for UFO believers after George Van Tassel bought it. Van Tassel worked as an airline mechanic, then started flight testing for Lockheed, Hughes, and Douglas in 1947. He eventually came out to Landers, building up a tiny strip of dirt into a runway. He took over Critzer's underground apartment, and there began channeling space aliens. In 1951, he contacted the "Council of Twelve," including a figure named Ashtar; eventually Van Tassel would come to claim that a superior race of

Venusians had come to Earth long ago, and while they were here mated with subhuman apes. Their offspring, he claimed, were humans—a more than a little bit racist cosmogony that managed to combine both the Edenic concept of original sin and Darwinian evolution.

Van Tassel's real skill, though, was as an organizer, and in 1954 he held the first Giant Rock Convention, dedicated to those interested in UFOs and life on other planets, along with people who claimed that they'd been contacted. The first convention drew five thousand people, and it was a mainstay of the California desert until Van Tassel's death in 1978. At its peak, it counted more than eleven thousand attendees. (His Integratron, a dome-shaped building some fifty-five feet in diameter, still exists; one can pay to take "sound baths" in it.)

Even despite these minor differences, all contactees took their basic template from Adamski: a beautiful and advanced figure from a planet without war comes to warn us of imminent nuclear destruction, warning us to change our ways. Nuclear Armageddon is in the background of nearly all contactee tales, but there is little doom or overt paranoia. Rather, the Space Brothers (as they became collectively known) offer a benevolent choice: renounce nuclear war and other foibles of humanity, and ascend to a higher plane of peace and universal consciousness.

They took other cues from Adamski as well: his cosmology was heavily influenced by Theosophy, something that also appeared repeatedly in other contactees' stories. Adamski had taught variations on Theosophical principles before he met the Venusians through his "Royal Order of Tibet," in the form of "universal laws" or "universal progressive Christianity." Contactee Calvin Girvin claimed he'd met with two Venusians, Cryxtan and Ashtar, who revealed that long ago Venusians colonized Earth with some ape women they used for manual labor, but then produced offspring with these ape women, creating humanity. This *Homo sapiens* origin story as miscegenation/bestiality also appeared in the writings of George Hunt Williamson: Williamson had been an archaeology student who'd fallen under the sway of American fascist and Hitler admirer William Dudley Pelley, and both men saw in the

UFO contactee story the perfect vehicle for their Theosophically influenced racist worldviews.

Adamski's mysticism, for all its bizarre edicts and nonsensical theology, is at its roots an attempt to bridge the gap between science and religion and restore a sense of order and progress. This, it would seem, was most fundamental: not a belief in God per se, but a belief in *order*, a belief that the world made sense, that there was a plan. One of the most disconcerting aspects of modern science for many was its emphasis on randomness and chaos, that we were not the products of a divine plan so much as a series of unexpectedly successful accidents. Many people simply rejected Darwinian evolution altogether, favoring the ordered, meaning-laden world of biblical literalism. Theosophists tried to have it both ways. Palmer's Shaver Mystery had provided one rationale for the world's order, an attempt at theodicy—an explanation for evil and suffering in the world. The contactee cults likewise were concerned, above all else, with providing a clue to the order of the world, but one that reunited science and religion as mutual expressions of the same thing.

But by concocting an otherworldly, unimpeachable authority for your own personal morality, you instead disenchant the world, rendering it formulaic. Bethurum's aliens represent the meanest possible advancement for humanity: their purpose is not to challenge humanity but to affirm its basest concerns. Rather than encourage more questions, these hoaxes encourage you to accept received wisdom as true.

● ● ●

Truman Bethurum wasn't the only one to receive messages from the planet Clarion. By 1954, a woman in the small suburb of Oak Park, Illinois, named Dorothy Martin began receiving messages from beings she named Guardians. Starting with a strange numbness in her arm, Martin began to write in the handwriting of her dead father—and soon was communicating with beings from Bethurum's Clarion—including the "Elder Brother," and, most important, Sananda, who identified himself as the contemporary incarnation of the historical Jesus.

Martin was instructed to spread the message that atomic testing was upsetting the atmosphere. While attending a Flying Saucer Club lecture by John Otto in April, she was introduced to Charles Laughead, a staff doctor at Michigan State University. He and his wife, Lillian, became her first and most fervent converts; together with the Laugheads, Martin formed a small group of UFO contactees, guided by her automatic writing. Martin's group, for all its futuristic and otherworldly trappings, was the latest version of a century-old movement, Spiritualism, reborn for an atomic age. As with séance mediums from the nineteenth century, Martin would go into trances to receive messages, holding all-night sessions of small groups huddled around (largely) female mystics that could last until six or eight in the morning.

UFO contactee cults were shot through with Christian imagery and mysticism, yet in the case of Martin's group, the usual gender roles of Christianity were reversed, with the women having far more direct access to the mysteries and truth of prophecy. (As the cataclysmic date approached, Martin's husband watched helplessly as her believers moved into their house, fretting over his wife's mental health far more than any impending apocalypse.) Men like Bethurum and Adamski cast themselves as explorers and adventurers, going out into the wilderness to meet the alien as equal, while (mostly) women saw themselves as passive receivers of messages from unseen bodies that invaded them.

By that August, Martin's warnings became more dire, and soon she was predicting an impending cataclysm: an apocalypse in which much of humanity would be wiped out. Martin's group, however, would be saved by a spaceship before the great event that would gather them up and escort them to safety. As Martin's predictions became more grave, Laughead finally contacted the media on August 30 to share the bad news.

Throughout that fall, Martin's group became a minor spectacle; reports of this event began to gain traction, and slowly callers, both in person and on the phone, began to appear, asking for more information about the End of the World. Most were high school students, but there were adults, too, mainly women—along with a fair amount of hecklers. Still, most of those who reached out to the contactees that fall were sincere in wanting to know more, even if at times they were a bit skeptical.

Laughead, continuing to feel it was his duty to warn humanity of its impending doom, spoke at a public event on December 16, where he stated that UFO believers were "in a special category." Such people, he went on, "are people who have had that interest because they had something within themselves that goes back to things they have forgotten. Therefore there is something within you that returned to life." Martin's group remained small, but within her community expectation built to a fever pitch. Martin had warned them that anyone wearing metal would not be taken up when the UFOs came, so the night of December 20 the group removed all change, keys, gum with foil wrappers, and so forth, from their pockets and clothing. At ten minutes to midnight, one member panicked when he realized his pants had a metal zipper; in a hurried surgical operation, Laughead cut the offending zipper out of the man's pants. At a minute to midnight, Martin, ecstatic, exclaimed, "And not a plan has gone astray!"

Midnight arrived. December 21 had come. But there were no UFOs. No cataclysmic floods. No signs of the apocalypse. The world had failed to end on time.

Dorothy Martin became famous under the name a group of researchers gave her—Marian Keech—in the book *When Prophecy Fails* by Leon Festinger, Henry W. Riecken, and Stanley Schachter. Unbeknownst to anyone in the group, several sociologists had infiltrated the cult, hoping to learn what drives a group toward such apocalyptic fantasies. Festinger would go on to coin the term "cognitive dissonance," a key insight into the nature and function of conspiracy theories and apocalyptic beliefs.

When Prophecy Fails sets out to try to understand a simple conundrum: the researchers were surprised to learn that after the saucers failed to arrive, Martin and her group doubled down on their predictions. Why does proselytizing sometimes *increase*, rather than decrease, when a group is presented with unequivocal disconfirmation of their beliefs? Why does a believer in any kind of stigmatized knowledge, when presented with unequivocal evidence to the contrary, reentrench those beliefs further? Festinger, Riecken, and Schachter argue that once you've irrevocably begun down a path, it becomes increasingly harder to admit you're wrong, and you'll increasingly distort the facts and adopt ever more fantastical ideas rather than change course. On the night of December 21, Laughead confessed, "I've had to go a long way. I've given up just about everything. I've cut every tie: I've burned every bridge. I've turned my back on the world. I can't afford to doubt. I have to believe. And there isn't any other truth."

Martin's Clarion cult offers in microcosm a story that would come to define the beliefs of UFOlogists, cryptozoologists, and others: during the initial period of belief, large numbers of believers are attracted to the phenomenon, in part because it has yet to be unequivocally debunked. When the debunking finally arrives (or when positive evidence fails to arrive on schedule), the result is the falling away of many potential believers, and the corresponding strengthening of those who remain.

Faced with the loss of Charles Laughead's job at Michigan State, and the impending loss of custody of their children, the Laugheads retreated from the public spotlight, and the group gradually fell apart. Dorothy Martin went west, to the desert, to be closer to Adamski, Bethurum, and George Hunt Williamson. With Williamson, she would move in 1956 to Lake Titicaca, now calling herself Sister Thedra, to establish the Priory of All Saints, in the northern Peruvian town of Moyobamba, and await more UFOs there. A year later, everyone but Martin had returned to the States; left behind, she was mired in poverty and suffering from ill health, convinced her colleagues had abandoned her. Eventually, she returned to Southern California, and then went north to Mount Shasta, seeking that fabled colony of underground Lemurians, utopia perpetually out of reach.

[18]

GRAY DAYS

Among those seemingly influenced by Adamski's contactee account was a jazz musician originally from Birmingham, Alabama, who was then living in Chicago and, in 1953, began telling his friends that he had been visited by extraterrestrials. Sonny Blount would later recount how he had been contacted in 1936, when he was twenty-two years old and in teachers college, and taken up by friendly aliens to Saturn. There, in a large stadium of some kind, he was invited up on stage by one-antennaed aliens who warned him not to become a teacher and instead advised him to spread their message. "I would speak," he later recalled them telling him, "and the world would listen."

Blount was not yet performing under the name that would make him famous—Sun Ra—but this story of alien visitation would be central to his mythology. Claiming to actually be from Saturn, he became iconic for his mixture of Afrofuturism and Egyptology (something he shared with Theosophists like Harvey Spencer Lewis), creating a mystique rivaled only by his dedication to his music. As his fame grew, he would often repeat his story of meeting aliens, a story that remained remarkably consistent in its details.

Consistent as it was, this story would not enshrine Sun Ra into the usual pantheon of contactees. Though it fits the structure of the contactee story, Sun Ra's experience rarely gets mentioned in the same litany of important stories from the 1950s (and if one accepts his claim that this happened in 1936, he is rarely accorded status as the first contactee). This may be simply because unlike the other contactees, Sun Ra was independently and justly famous for his other talents, as a keyboardist and bandleader who changed the face of jazz and popular music. Or it could be that he was black, and didn't fit in with contactee culture and its emphasis on fair-haired, blue-eyed, jumpsuited Aryans.

John F. Szwed, Sun Ra's biographer, notes that his abduction story, with its emphasis on being chosen and given a message to disseminate to the public, reads like an organic synthesis of two largely incompatible spiritual traditions: the black Baptist tradition of Sun Ra's Alabama youth and the postwar California occultism of Adamski. And while the standard history of UFOs and aliens—at least in the United States—almost entirely involves white people, Sun Ra was not the only black American to commune with aliens.

Barney and Betty Hill's story entirely changed the trajectory of alien contact stories. The Hills' biracial marriage was an unavoidable part of their story; as Christopher Roth noted in his cataloging of alien visitation narratives, it's impossible to avoid the racial connotations in John G. Fuller's book *The Interrupted Journey: Two Lost Hours Aboard a Flying Saucer.* As Fuller recounts the history of the Hills' marriage and their vacation preceding the abduction, it's clear that they two—while they genuinely loved and cared for each other—lived in different worlds; throughout their trip through Canada, Barney is hyperaware of how others perceive him, and on alert both for conflict and for other ethnic minorities who might offer some kind of alliance for him. Betty, meanwhile, though a devoted civil rights worker, seems to share none of this vigilance.

Thus the aliens, when they are finally revealed under hypnosis, are striking. As Barney recounts the moments leading up to seeing the craft through binoculars, he first describes the aliens he sees aboard the ship. At first he notes that one is "friendly-looking," but pressed to describe him, Barney doesn't resort to any of the stereotypes about aliens we're used to. Instead, after struggling a bit, he says: "I think of—I think of—a red-headed Irishman. I don't know why." Still under hypnosis, he pauses for a moment, then clarifies: "I think I know why. Because Irish are usually hostile to Negroes. And when I see a friendly Irish person, I react to him by thinking—*I* will be friendly. And I think this one that is looking over his shoulder is friendly." Aside from this "friendly-looking" Irish-looking alien, Barney continues, there's another, one with an "evil face"; he almost refers to this one as a leader of some sort, then stops himself: "He looks like a German Nazi. He's a Nazi."

Pressed on this, Barney refers to his uniform ("He had a black scarf around his neck, dangling over his left shoulder"), and then continues, this time describing his eyes as "slanted": "But not like a Chinese." Elsewhere in his recollections, Barney recalls a lecture he and Betty attended at Harvard by Carleton S. Coon, the white supremacist Yeti enthusiast: at the lecture, Coon "showed a slide of a group of people who lived around the Magellan Straits," which prompted a reaction from both of the Hills: "This group of Indians, who lived in an extremely cold atmosphere high in the mountains where there was little oxygen, bore a considerably close resemblance to what I'm trying to describe," Barney states. "They had Oriental sort of eyes but the eye socket gave an appearance of being much larger than what it was, because nature had developed a roll of fat around the eye and also around the mouth. So it looked as if the mouth had almost no opening and as if they had practically no nose. They were quite similar, in a general way, to the men I'm trying to describe." Struggling to describe what he's seen, Barney cycles through a number of ethnic and racial stereotypes, looking for some ethnic "other" that best fits what he's seeing. None quite fit, but through his descriptions what becomes clear is that Barney understood these aliens were a threat to him, and they were going to be hostile toward him because he was black.

Betty's descriptions of the aliens, meanwhile, lack these ethnic markers. "Their complexions were of a gray tone," Betty would later state, "like a gray paint with a black base; their lips were of a bluish tint." Martin S. Kottmeyer, a UFO skeptic, has posited that Betty's description of her captors as "gray" was the result of a compromise—unlike the Theosophists before her (or even her husband), she could not easily adopt standard racial categories. "There would be an intimate emotional undertone had Betty conceived of her abductors as either black or white. Choose white and you could be seen as reinforcing racist stereotypes of whites as a master race with superior intellect and technological skill. Choose black and you might reinforce stereotypes of blacks as criminal, evil, and sexually aggressive." Kottmeyer argues instead that her use of "gray" was almost a conscious choice—a way out of the complicated racial politics of the 1960s—and with that word, Betty Hill began a slow shift in how we began to see aliens: no longer just like us but more advanced, they were now increasingly "other," uncanny and foreign. No longer Space Brothers, now they were aliens.

Barney Hill at first resisted his wife's claims of abduction, but gradually came around to agreeing with her. "I feel I was abducted" is how he puts it at the end of *The Interrupted Journey*. He seems to have found himself with two untenable options: embrace an experience he knew would subject him to ridicule from a disbelieving world, or deny the experience his wife had embraced fervently. Either option was bound to alienate him. He chose his wife.

For the Hills, it seems, aliens had been both a cause of a problem and a solution. Betty's insistence that they'd been abducted created a fissure in their marriage, but because aliens were a pure unknown, Barney and Betty could together synthesize the narrative they needed to come back together. Struggling to stay sane, they inadvertently created a far more durable archetype. The contactees' depiction of the alien had been one of human perfection, something unambiguous and worth aspiring to. Which was fine so long as you subscribed to their definition of perfection. As America became more fractured, though, the Aryan Space Brother from Venus would give way to Betty Hill's uncanny other—undefined, and thus whatever the believer needed it to be. Threatening or welcoming, sexual or terrifying. Ultimately amorphous, and, in a word, Gray.

* * *

For the time being, though, the Hills' experience was mostly forgotten—it didn't quite fit the template for contactee narratives, so it gradually faded from popular consciousness. Until, that is, James Earl Jones got ahold of it and optioned it for a TV movie, *The UFO Incident*, which aired in October 1975. The film quickly takes the conflict over the abduction experience and reveals it to be one between a black man and a white woman as they struggle to keep their marriage. "I was brought up to be careful," he tells Betty. "It's like an old scratched broken record playing inside of me. Be careful kid, or they'll kill you." His need for self-preservation in a racist country won't allow him to entertain his wife's beliefs about aliens, lest the white people around him accuse him of being crazy. Betty tells their therapist that her life mainly remained the same after their marriage, but that Barney had moved from a mostly all-black society in Philadelphia to a mostly all-white society in Portsmouth. He made friends easily, she continues, but when Barney finally confesses the UFO experience to one friend, he flat-out calls Barney nuts.

As with Fuller's original book, *The UFO Incident* is clearly less about flying saucers and more about a marriage disintegrating. But if the film had been a means of approaching race in America through an allegory of alien abduction, that's not how it was received. Instead, it set off a new wave of stories. Two weeks after *The UFO Incident* aired, friends of an Arizona brush clearer named Travis Walton reported that he'd gone missing; located five days later, Walton claimed he'd been abducted by aliens. He subsequently failed a lie detector test (the examiner called his responses "gross deception" and the plainest case of lying he'd seen in twenty years), and then demanded another test that he passed. His case won national attention and five thousand dollars from the *National Enquirer* for "1975's Most Extraordinary Encounter with a UFO."

Researcher Philip J. Klass later investigated the events surrounding Walton's abduction, and concluded it likely that Walton's crew—who had been behind schedule on a federal brush clearing contract, had seen *The UFO Incident* and concocted the story as a means of getting out of a contract. But none of that mattered, as more abductees started to tell their stories.

Betty Andreasson, a housewife in South Asburnham, Massachusetts, came forward in early 1977, recounting an experience she'd had ten years prior. On an unseasonably balmy night in January, the lights in the house began to flicker, and a curious pink light shone through the kitchen window. Andreasson would later recall, under hypnosis, how she'd been taken aboard a spaceship by an alien named Quazgaa, and there subjected to a series of probing experiments, including having a long silver needle stuck up her left nostril into her brain, and another probe inserted into her navel to investigate her reproductive organs. With a story uncannily similar to Betty Hill's, a new narrative of alien contact—one of lost memory and probed bodies—had been established.

But this kind of alien narrative was not entirely new. Thirty minutes from South Ashburnham is Lancaster, Massachusetts. A cozy suburb of Boston, it hardly seems on the "frontier" of anything—the deserts of the Wild West are a distant dream here. But in 1675, Lancaster was on the very edge of a dividing line between white settlers and land traditionally inhabited by the Narragansett and the Wampanoag, and as a border town, Lancaster was the site of one of many bloody battles in what became known as King Philip's War. On the morning of February 10, 1675, a raiding party killed thirteen of Lancaster's residents, took an additional twenty-four people hostage, and burned the town to the ground.

Among those taken prisoner was Mary Rowlandson, along with three of her children. For eleven weeks Rowlandson was held captive with a peripatetic band of Indians, moving constantly to keep out of reach of the English militias and continue their raids. The first week, her youngest child, six-year-old Sarah, died from wounds she'd sustained during the original attack, which Rowlandson was unable to properly tend to. Finally, Rowlandson was ransomed for twenty pounds and returned to her family, and a few years later, under the direction of Puritan leader Cotton Mather, wrote a bestselling account of her story, founding a genre of captivity narratives.

The captivity narrative was one of the first authentic Anglo American narratives, one that provided a European culture with its own nascent mythology. Rowlandson's 1682 account was the first, but by 1800 some seven hundred different captivity narratives had been published, many fictional but all adhering to the same core narrative. A white person, from the "civilized world," is forcibly abducted and brought to a strange landscape, in which they're subjected to inspection and humiliation. Often, there's a sexually titillating aspect to the narratives, which allude to torture and rape and emphasize the victim's powerlessness. When the victim is returned to "civilization," they are changed—no longer entirely of the white culture, but not fully "Indian," either.

In the UFO abductee stories of the late 1970s and 1980s, the captivity narrative had been reborn; the Indians had been replaced by aliens, but it was otherwise the same structure: the feeling of powerlessness of the victims (Whitley Strieber, of the blockbuster *Communion*, described feeling "as helpless as a baby, crying like a baby, as frightened as a baby"); sexually tinged anatomical examinations of victims like Betty Andreasson, involving being forced to disrobe and then probed in various orifices by aliens singularly fascinated with human reproductive organs; and a return to the human world feeling vaguely "alienated," for lack of a better term. What one finds in alien abduction narratives, much like with narratives of ritual abuse and recovered memory, is a dislocation of a basic sense of self, an identity in rupture, unmoored and adrift.

It is the same sense of rupture that no doubt Mary Rowlandson felt, a kidnap victim and PTSD survivor—and why it was all the more important that the narrative based on her ordeal be titled *The Sovereignty and Goodness of GOD, Together with the Faithfulness of His Promises Displayed; Being a Narrative of the Captivity and Restoration of Mrs. Mary Rowlandson, Commended by Her, to All That Desires to Know the Lord's*

Doings to, and Dealings with Her. Cotton Mather understood that unless it was couched as redemption, the fissure at the heart of her story would only grow larger.

For the Puritans, there was an all-knowing, all-powerful, and benevolent God to give shape to the trauma of their existence—the Puritans' God was violent and dispensed ready punishment to those who were not already on the path to righteousness. So even something as traumatic as Rowlandson's experience could offer a kind of theodicy: further proof of how even violence and death were part of God's master plan. The alien abduction narrative borrowed heavily from this script, but soon its theology would differ significantly.

[19]

HOST-PLANET REJECTION SYNDROME

Budd Hopkins was a successful but somewhat minor artist—well known within the art world of New York City, but far from a household name. Hopkins was part of the abstract expressionist movement; his work is in the collection of several major museums, including the Museum of Modern Art in New York City, but he'd hardly changed the face of the American art world by the time of his death in 2011. What he did manage to do was change the face of American culture.

His own UFO experience was relatively minor (in 1964 he'd seen a "darkish, elliptical object in the sky" off the coast of Cape Cod), but it had gnawed at him, and primed him to believe. So when he found the owner of the local bodega near his Manhattan apartment pacing the floor uneasily one night, muttering about how things "can come down out of the sky and scare you half to death," Hopkins paid attention. The story he got from the bodega owner, George O'Barski, involved an incident the previous January, when O'Barski had been driving to his home in New Jersey past 2:00 A.M. As he drove through North Hudson Park, his car radio began to sound strange (tinny-sounding static), and he looked over to a field to see that an alien craft had landed. O'Barski watched as small figures descended a ladder. "They looked like kids in snowsuits," he told Hopkins.

Hopkins's article in *The Village Voice*, "Sane Citizen Sees UFO in

New Jersey," would be a turning point for Hopkins, as he began a new stage in his life. While he would continue his art, he would become known as the face of the UFO abduction mythology. Hopkins's status as a midwife of abductee stories—rather than a victim himself—would become a crucial component of this new era. This level of remove afforded a layer of plausibility that first person accounts often lacked. By the 1970s it was easy enough to discount Adamski's narration, of course, and dismiss it as a fraud or a hoax. But the reader can't access O'Barski directly; they must go through Hopkins, who not only can craft the experience but can offer up a level of plausible deniability about holes, gaps, and inconsistencies in the narration. Further, the drama is now not just in the abductee themself, but in Hopkins's reactions and credulity. Jesus had Matthew, Mark, Luke, and John; the Great Gatsby had Nick Carraway. The best stories are written not by the stars, but by their acolytes. Hopkins would be that voice to the UFO abductees.

Hopkins's 1981 book, *Missing Time*, offered sketches of these alien abductors—they had slanted eyes, thin bodies, and gray skin. Most typologies of extraterrestrials will now refer in some form to the Grays (sometimes they're segregated into two groups, the Short Grays and the Tall Grays). These are the abductors—the vaguely humanoid but distinctly inhuman, technologically advanced, and fearsome aliens who probe anuses and wipe memories. The most iconic image of a Gray would appear twenty-five years after the Hills' abduction, on the cover of Whitley Strieber's bestselling book *Communion: A True Story*—the triangular-headed figure with large black eyes, nostrils but no nose, and a thin, barely perceptible mouth.

That the figure on Strieber's book is actually a yellowish green does not make it any less a Gray. Betty Hill had been the first to suggest aliens might be gray, seemingly as a means of escaping the black-white dichotomies of American racial politics. But for Hopkins, "gray" meant "other," and the image struck a chord. The word "gray" is less a color identifier than a proper noun—and, perhaps more important, something more symbolic, something more open-ended. The Grays are gray because they are what you want them to be: not defined by the kinds of symbolic associations we're used to bringing to bear on worldly things.

Hopkins worked with psychiatrists and therapists to use hypnotic memory regression to unearth and discover lost memories. Steve Kilburn, for example, came to Hopkins without a UFO sighting, but with only the vaguest sense about a certain stretch of road—nothing specific, just a feeling that "something happened" to him once while driving home. Despite admitting this "almost ridiculously flimsy pretext for entering into the costly and time-consuming process of hypnotic regression," Hopkins agreed to take Kilburn's case on.

The repressed memory hypnosis sessions became a way to hone and refine a national subconscious, working out the images and motifs that would most likely resonate with an anxious public. Repressed memories were a relatively new concept, and they were promoted by a subset of therapists seeking wider acceptance in the field. They saw institutional norms and professional organizations as barriers to their acceptance, and it's little wonder their methods found a place amid alien abductees.

In the Upper West Side Manhattan brownstone that served as Dr. Girard Franklin's office, Kilburn spoke of a stretch of Route 40 in Maryland between Pikesville and Frederick, and over the course of several sessions, returned to that scene again and again in his memory, until he was narrating a story of some kind of "big wrench," several figures dressed all in black turtlenecks with "funny skin" like putty, chalkish white with a tint of gray—essentially repeating descriptions that had been proffered in various pop culture descriptions since *The UFO Incident*. (The release of Steven Spielberg's *Close Encounters of the Third Kind*, with its child-sized, big-headed aliens, further helped cement a particular kind of physique for extraterrestrials in the mind of the public.)

Pop culture and abduction communities fed off one another in an almost constant feedback loop. The version of aliens described by Hopkins's subjects, perhaps influenced by *The UFO Incident*, would in turn be appropriated by Steven Spielberg's *Close Encounters of the Third Kind*. Production designer Joe Alves interviewed witnesses to get a sense of what aliens might look like, and sketched the film's aliens based on commonalities from witness accounts. (Spielberg did insist, though, that the aliens' look be softened somewhat, so they'd appear more "childlike"— that, plus the fact that ex–Project Blue Book adviser J. Allen Hynek was hired as a consultant for the film would give rise to conspiracy theories that Spielberg's film was government psy-ops, meant to "get the public used to 'odd-looking' aliens that were compassionate, benevolent, and very much our 'space brothers'" in advance of a global reveal of the truth of aliens.) When *Close Encounters* was released in 1977, it grossed more than $300 million, bringing a fringe idea out of the remote margins of culture and square into mainstream consciousness.

Hopkins's hypnotic memory regression was a new technique, startling in its effect and yet entirely untested. Recovered memory therapy had risen to prominence with such books like *Sybil* and Laurence Pazder's *Michelle Remembers*, about a woman who claimed that, under hypnosis, she could remember being physically and sexually abused by a cult of satanists her parents were involved in. These books were pop culture sensations, but in the medical community such practitioners were still fighting to be taken seriously by their peers.

Panics and conspiracies often emerge from moments when there is an acute shift in institutional knowledge. In the case of repressed memory therapy, the narrative was built around the idea that this new treatment had unearthed something that was there all along, hiding in plain sight, that only needed a new approach to be rendered visible. It opened up a new field of inquiry, sending the institution into a crouch position, all by seizing on phenomena where there was scant physical evidence— child abuse, alien abductions—which preyed on the public's basic anxieties. And repressed memory therapy did what all good conspiracy theories do: it gave people a voice for the abstract, inchoate emotions of unease they were feeling.

The problem is that this therapy tends to flatten out experience: in a state of suggestibility, subjects are fed details that come to seem true to them. It seems unlikely that Budd Hopkins was a hoaxer, but that doesn't change the obviousness with which his writings reveal the danger of this kind of hypnotic therapy, in which suggestible individuals are urged to transform their confusion and illness into something extraterrestrial.

In his books, abduction narratives tend to follow the same trajectory: someone contacts Budd Hopkins and her experience, at first, seems anomalous. They undergo a series of hypnosis sessions, and by the time the subject is done, her experience starts to look exactly like every other abductee story. Hopkins's narratives capture the anxiety of the time, while revealing—from the vantage of several decades—many of the same problems.

If there was one alien encounter that certainly did not fit Hopkins's mold, it was the story recounted by Nation of Islam leader Louis Farrakhan, who in a 1989 press conference described an event that had supposedly happened to him four years earlier. On September 17, 1985, Farrakhan and some of his close companions were in Tepoztlan, Mexico, on a tour of religious sites, when they ascended a mountain atop which were the ruins of a temple dedicated to Quetzalcoatl. According to Farrakhan, who revealed all this in a press conference he dubbed "the Announcement," when they reached the top of the mountain, "a Wheel, or what you call an unidentified flying object, appeared at the side of the mountain and called to me to come up into the Wheel." He called back to his companions, but a voice from the Wheel told him, "Not them; just you," and a beam of light appeared from the ship that took him up into the air and on board.

Once on the Wheel, he was given a tour by the pilot (whom he could not see, being only able to "feel his presence"), and in the center of the ship, he heard the voice of Elijah Muhammad, the former leader of the Nation of Islam and Farrakhan's mentor. Taking place firmly in the age of abductees, Farrakhan's narrative borrows much more from the earlier contactee milieu—the occupants of the spaceship are not foreign aliens but transcendental humans. Also, like the contactees, he's given a specific, political message, one concerning the prevention of war. According to

Farrakhan, Elijah Muhammad gave him a message: "President Reagan has met with the Joint Chiefs of Staff to plan a war. I want you to hold a press conference in Washington, D.C., and announce their plan and say to the world that you got the information from me on the Wheel."

Having supposedly received an urgent message about an impending war, Farrakhan waited a full four years to share his experience, claiming it had taken time to decode the meaning of the message. It was only in 1987, when he read a news story that Reagan had indeed been planning a war against Libya, that he understood. In terms of Doomsday prophesies, Farrakhan's is pretty weak, waiting until after the supposed event before even revealing that it had been predicted.

But Farrakhan's Mother Wheel story remains one more example of the malleability of UFO stories. A throwback to the Space Brothers motif of the 1950s with the Wheel inhabitants depicted as a transcendent race, Farrakhan could use his abduction story to validate and vindicate the Nation of Islam and his leadership role. And by coding these superior Space Brothers as black instead of Aryan, Farrakhan preserves the earlier structure while inverting its politics. Maybe this is why, like Sun Ra, Farrakhan is rarely mentioned in collections of other contactees and abductees.

● ● ●

As Hopkins and others expanded their search for abductees, they came to include not just those who'd witnessed something firsthand; but really anyone who had suffered some sort of missed time experience was likely someone who'd been abducted. For that matter, anyone who felt somehow "off," or might have been suffering from some sort of illness they couldn't explain, was a potential candidate to be an abductee.

That sense of an unexplained sense of fatigue, in particular, would become crucial to abductee narratives. Aside from fleeting memories of an abduction or an encounter, Don Donderi notes in *UFOs, ETs, and Alien Abductions: A Scientist Looks at the Evidence*, the main signs of an event are anomalies such as "missing time, damaged clothing, nose-bleeds, or feeling tired or irritable." David M. Jacobs concurs: "Almost all abductees wake up feeling tired, restless, agitated. They feel that they have not had a good night's sleep and that they have been 'through the mill.'"

A twenty-year-old woman named Alison gave the following account on a message board in 2011: "It always happens late at night, I wake up in my room, scared, cold sweating and feeling my heart pumping really fast, I can almost feel it inside my ears. I'm in my room but I feel this presence, like someone is in the room with me . . . or was, cause I've never been able to see anybody." When she was seventeen, she continues, "I started to have trouble at school, headaches and poor sleep quality, so I was feeling tired and weak during the day." Still, she wasn't able to get any answers from therapists or psychiatrists that made sense, which led her ultimately to a forum for alien abductees.

The forum moderator concurred that she was likely a victim of ab-duction. "Most of my experiences with the star people are good and friendly," she wrote back, "but I have also been abducted by aliens who were not so nice." Another user added, "You would find that what you have and is still experiencing most abductees go through the same thing, maybe some difference due to the person him/herself and how the ab-duction happened. I ended up seeing a psychiatrist and have found that while they tend to believe in ghosts and demons aliens are a no no."

Alison, finally finding her concerns validated, responded, "I feel re-lieved now that I've been able to find this community and read your stories, makes me feel not so lonely." Alison, with her unexplained sense of fatigue and her sleep terrors that had no seemingly visible cause, was certainly not alone. Starting in the late 1970s and '80s, we entered a pe-riod when many people seemed to feel tired and physically uneasy in ways they couldn't immediately explain.

Whose experience—and whose pain—are we going to take seriously? This question runs through so many of these stories. Pilots returning from World War II with undiagnosed PTSD, in a culture where they were expected to "man up" and rejoin the workforce. Men hungry for a world of monsters beyond their emasculating desk jobs. Abductees who felt something was off in some fundamental way they could not name, something doctors ignored. The secret behind so many of these unidentified creatures, so many cults and adherents of fringe and stigmatized beliefs, is a desire to be taken seriously one way or another.

We live in the time of what's become known as "contested illnesses," illnesses that, in Joseph Dumit's words, "You have to fight to get." Chronic fatigue syndrome is perhaps the most well known, but there are others, too. A cluster of children in a small town in Connecticut had a high incidence of rheumatoid arthritis, leading to an investigation that ultimately diagnosed the first cases of Lyme disease. But even after the bacteria that causes it was found, children in the northeast continued to complain of a set of symptoms that they blamed on Lyme—now called chronic Lyme—that doctors couldn't explain and tended to dismiss.

Like the town of Lyme, in Woburn, Massachusetts, in the late 1970s became ground zero of another odd disease cluster—this time of leukemia. Citizen activists banded together to map the outbreak, tracing it to two ground wells that provided water to the town. By the 1990s, added to this grim list would be Gulf War related illnesses (GWRI), another set of difficult to diagnose or treat symptoms that were magnified by the government's refusal to come clean about what toxic chemicals veterans may or may not have been exposed to. Anyone seeking to understand the root causes of GWRI was forced to confront a web of chemicals whose interactions are little understood, all of which made understanding, diagnosing, or treating GWRI that much more difficult. One Gulf War vet who spent years trying to untangle the mysteries of his ailment—including the possibility that it was psychosomatic or otherwise unrelated to his service—concluded: "One thing is clear: I am a victim of Gulf War illness, even if my body is not the evidence. I've spent good time worrying about it, days at the hospital, nights arguing with my wife."

These illnesses, taken together with the rise of HIV/AIDS (an epidemic whose hallmarks included a criminal neglect by institutional and government agencies and an epidemiology that confounded traditional science), suggested a slow-boiling crisis in the health-care community of the last few decades. Faith in medicine is dependent not just on a doctor's ability to heal, but on her ability to explain, to narrativize a disease in a way that makes sense to the patient. Even a fatal disease can be made to make sense, but these diseases confounded the usual ways in which medicine explained the body to the patient; they flummoxed doctors, and this tension was immediately compounded by corporations attempting to evade responsibility for toxic dumping, governments stonewalling vets about harms they may have been exposed to, and insurance companies eager to invalidate diagnoses to avoid paying for costly treatment.

Susan Sontag writes of how each of us holds a dual citizenship in the kingdom of the well and the kingdom of the sick. "Although we prefer to use only the good passport, sooner or later each of us is obliged," she writes, "at least for a spell, to identify ourselves as citizens of that other place." Those suffering under this proliferation of new, strange ailments, most of which without a name recognized in the medical community, and none with any clear treatment, found that even when they arrived in the kingdom of the sick they were being refused entry—by their doctors, their insurance companies, their families. Stuck there, they had become illegal aliens.

Hopkins had an answer to that question: alien abduction. For those feeling off, tired, fatigued, Hopkins provided what the medical community could not: a narrative, a story that explained the fatigue. As the alien abduction phenomenon would grow through the 1980s and '90s, more and more abductees would find themselves adopting the language of contested illness, reframing their experience in the rhetoric of chronic fatigue: as one person put it in a chat room in the 1990s, "Come on, people . . . we 'are' the aliens. we seem to be suffering from host-planet rejection syndrome."

PART IV

THE WORLD TURNED SOUR

———————•———————

None of us can go a little way with a theory; when it once possesses us, we are no longer our own masters. It makes us speak its words, and do violence to our natures.

—CARDINAL JOHN HENRY NEWMAN

Southern Nevada is basin and range territory, on the edge between the Mojave Desert and the Great Basin Desert. Driving west to east means an endless pattern of mountain ranges to summit before plummeting down into the next basin. "Each range here," John McPhee says of this landscape, "is like a warship standing on its own, and the Great Basin is an ocean of loose sediment with these mountain ranges standing in it as if they were members of a fleet without precedent, assembled at Guam to assault Japan."

Driving east for forty-five minutes on Highway 6 from Tonopah, Nevada (home to the famous Clown Motel), one reaches Highway 375, which in 1996 the Nevada Department of Transportation renamed the "Extraterrestrial Highway." It runs south toward Las Vegas, along the eastern edge of a range that serves as a wall hiding what lies on the other side—Dreamland, aka Area 51. If the desert here seems mystical sometimes, it may be because its natural barriers make it the perfect place to hold secrets.

Suffused with longing is Rachel, Nevada's Little A'Le'Inn, nestled along the Extraterrestrial Highway, far from everything except the mystery on the other side of the hill. It has become a de rigueur stopping point for those hoping to get close to that mystery, receiving tourists and the curious daily. Outside the Little A'Le'Inn a rusted old wrecker holds aloft a mock flying saucer, a picture of a UFO reads SELF PARKING, and a green humanoid (though, honestly, it looks more like a small green Bigfoot) holds a sign that reads WELCOME EARTHLINGS.

Inside is an otherwise normal diner bedecked with all manner of UFO ephemera. Here kitsch and tchotchkes settle over everything like radioactive dust. Key chains, mouse pads, playing cards, shot glasses, beer cozies, novelty vodka. The same dumb UFO image, the same dumb little green alien, replicated ad infinitum, an exhausting surplus of crapla that drags behind the UFO phenomenon like tin cans attached to the wedding couple's honeymoon car. The ceiling is festooned with signed dollar bills from tourists from all over the world, though every time some supersonic craft overflies the diner and shakes its foundations, a few more dollar bills flutter gently down.

Everyone comes to Rachel; you can't be a serious UFO researcher until you do. The only place more famous for UFOs than Rachel is Roswell, New Mexico. At the time of the Roswell crash, it was just one of many different possible sightings. No one paid much attention to the town that Will Rogers had once called "the prettiest little town in the west," and after the military base closed in 1967 Roswell had little in the way of tourism or industry. Only after Charles Berlitz and William L. Moore published *The Roswell Incident* in 1980 did UFOlogists start to take another look at Roswell. Berlitz and Moore drew attention back to the crash, the contradictory government reports, the confusing stories and unexplained facts.

But equally important, Berlitz and Moore gave UFO lore a place, a home, a location on a map. Roswell became a place of pilgrimage for the faithful, a secular holy site. One rancher, whose property supposedly contained one of the crash sites, opened up his land to tourists, charging them to scoop a handful of dirt from the crash site. In developing these legends around the place, weaving endless tales about these empty spaces in the desert, accreting layers upon layers of meaning like silt in a basin, the UFOlogists have managed to reenchant these desert outposts and forgotten cities, making them wondrous and strange once more.

The pilgrims are as paranoid as the religion. Unlike the majority of UFO sightings that dominated the postwar era through the 1970s, Berlitz and Moore saw in Roswell the importance of a government cover-up, finalizing a change in direction started by Donald Keyhoe. It was not enough to simply watch the skies. One also had to look askance at the official government stories.

In retrospect, the government-involvement axis of the UFO story was almost inevitable. For years, it seemed the world was on the cusp of a major revelation: more and more UFO sightings, more and more photographs, all signs pointing to just a matter of time before we had definitive, irrevocable proof of extraterrestrials. But as that promise failed to materialize, believers went searching for answers. The government cover-up angle became the easiest means for explaining why we didn't have proof of UFOs, by reframing the inquiry: what if there *is* proof, but it's being kept from us?

Paranoia and conspiracy theories are, in a mathematical sense, a function of time over expectation. The longer a narrative continues without delivering on its expected revelation, the more the mind has to look for explanations and justifications for this disconnect. The longer it takes to get that definitive evidence of UFOs, the more elaborate and bizarre the conspiracy theory must evolve, to account for why it's taking so long. If the aliens are already here, then the longer we go without seeing them, the more sinister the government must be.

Our server at the Little A'Le'Inn seemed free of this paranoia. She had worked there for only seven months, and was mostly unmoved by the mystique of Area 51. A pair of French tourists arrived to ask about the Black Mailbox, a location farther down Highway 375 that's long been favored as a prime spot to witness unidentified craft. (The mailbox belonged to rancher Steve Medlin, who eventually got tired of people stuffing it full of letters to aliens, so he first painted it white, and then eventually got rid of it altogether.) She gave them detailed directions, but spoke without emotion one way or another, as if she were guiding them to the airport. Some secrets were more important to national security than others: when I asked her what the "secret alien sauce" on the menu tasted like, she said bluntly it was just Thousand Island dressing.

Despite all these secrets, there's a note of optimism all around you at the Little A'Le'Inn. Everything here is friendly and welcoming—though it feels like a veneer, like we're all trying too hard, overcompensating for the harsh desert environment, and for whatever dangers await on the other side of those mountains.

[20]

THE DISINFORMATION GAME

The temperature was topping 105 degrees outside the Aladdin Hotel and Casino on July 1, 1989, the day Bill Moore had been scheduled to speak to the annual MUFON conference. MUFON, the Mutual UFO Network, had evolved out of NICAP as a civilian-driven UFO investigative body. Since the end of Project Blue Book, MUFON and a few similar organizations had taken on the work of doing serious, sober analyses of sightings, debunking what they could, cataloging what remained unidentified. Moore, the writer who, along with Charles Berlitz, had put Roswell, New Mexico, on the map, was originally to have been followed by famed UFO researcher Stanton Friedman, the evening's headliner.

Bill Moore had first become interested in UFOs as a teenager, after reading Frank Scully's *Behind the Flying Saucers* (Scully's name would later provide the inspiration for *The X-Files'* Agent Dana Scully). Moore joined NICAP in college, and after he graduated he continued work in UFOlogy, developing a reputation for a serious and thorough investigatory style, and his ability to debunk frauds and hoaxes. Then his and Berlitz's book *The Roswell Incident* catapulted Moore to the head of the UFO researching class.

In February 1981, Moore received classified teletypes regarding something called Project Aquarius. Apparently an analysis of some classified photographs of UFOs and indicating that the government (with NASA in the lead) was still actively investigating UFOs (albeit covertly), the Project Aquarius document also made reference to a cryptic organization that would soon become more important. Access to information about Project Aquarius was restricted, the memo stated, to something called MJ TWELVE, though it offered no elaboration on what (or who) that was.

Then on December 11, 1984, a producing partner of Moore's, Jaime Shandera, found a manila envelope in his mailbox containing a roll of undeveloped film. The images on the film would reveal a classified briefing document concerning Operation Majestic 12 (or MJ-12, as it became known). Moore and Shandera, along with Stanton Friedman, spent the next three years trying to authenticate the document, before releasing them to the public.

MJ-12, the document revealed, was a high-level group of military and governmental officials who'd been convened in the wake of the Roswell crash, in order to advise President Truman on the country's intel on aliens. Dated November 18, 1952, this document detailed what the government knew about the Roswell crash: that there had been four entities in the ship that crashed, they'd died on contact, their biology was radically unlike that of humans. The MJ-12 document was the Holy Grail—the proof, finally, that the government knew of, and was actively covering up, the existence of extraterrestrials.

All this was well known to everyone who'd gathered at the Aladdin to hear Moore's talk. It was settled history. All the more shocking, then, when one of the more respected researchers in UFOlogy told his audience that day that everything was fake, and that he had personally been involved in the deception. By the time he was halfway through his talk, Moore was being heckled by the audience. Others sat transfixed. Some stumbled out of the room in a combination of shock, anguish, and tears. By the time he'd finished, Moore had no choice but to escape through the back door, counseling patience, promising that all would be revealed in good time.

• • •

Moore's story mostly involved a man named Paul Bennewitz, with whom many in the room would have been familiar. Bennewitz was a government contractor who owned a company called Thunder Scientific, which made sophisticated weather and temperature gauges for the Air Force. Both his company and his home were on the edge of Kirtland Air Force Base in Albuquerque, a sprawling, top-secret facility that included, among other things, a massive nuclear material storage depot that's been built inside the foothills of the Manzano Mountains.

Bennewitz had been a member of APRO, the Aerial Phenomena Research Organization, a loose group of researchers dedicated to a scientific and rational study of possible UFOs. (In 1969, a portion of the researchers in APRO had split off and formed MUFON.) In 1979, Bennewitz started seeing things: strange lights above the Air Force base, lights that seemed to ascend vertically and could hover motionlessly. He began photographing what he'd seen, climbing up onto his roof in the chill Albuquerque winter nights, photographing and filming distant lights hovering above a top-secret Air Force base. On the borderland between the normal world and an off-limits place of mystery and wonder, Bennewitz was also on the borderland of the scientific institution: a small part of the military-industrial complex, but yet fully aware that he knew little of what truly was going on.

Then on May 5, 1980, Myrna Hansen was driving home with her young son when she saw two huge silent objects "big as two Goodyear blimps," one triangular, the other smaller. After the incident she contacted the local police; when she mentioned that she had seen cattle being killed by these crafts, the cops put her in touch with a deputy sheriff named Gabe Valdez, who in turn suggested she meet with Bennewitz.

By the time she got in touch with Bennewitz, Hansen could no longer remember specific details of that night, so Bennewitz suggested that she undergo hypnosis to attempt to recover the memories. She came to Albuquerque to meet Bennewitz and Leo Sprinkle, a psychologist who specialized in hypnosis and repressed memories, particularly those involving aliens.

Hansen agreed to go under hypnosis to recall memories she couldn't consciously access, but these sessions would not be done in Bennewitz's living room or Sprinkle's office—instead they went to Bennewitz's Lincoln Town Car, the windows of which had been covered in thick sheets of aluminum foil. Both Bennewitz and Hansen believed that aliens were beaming some kind of harmful rays that were preventing her from recalling what had happened. Under hypnosis, she began to repeat a common refrain. *"I'm driving. My son's right there in my ear, talking to me. I'm half tuning him out. The light is so bright. I feel like it's coming in on me."* Hansen claimed that she'd stopped the car and got out to get a closer look, against the wishes of her son; soon a second light was visible. *"They're landing. Oh, God! Cattle are screaming! But I've got to know who it is. . . . The light is so bright. It's orange. I want to see them; I want to go to them. I'm out of the car. Screaming of the cattle, it's horrible, it's horrible! Incredible pain! I still want to go to them, but . . . but they're mad."*

So far, the experience would seem to track with other abduction narratives, with an impressionable witness guided by a therapist and a believer. But Bennewitz was no Budd Hopkins. The next time Leo Sprinkle came to Albuquerque to continue the sessions, a month later, something had changed: "Between May and June," Sprinkle later recalled of Bennewitz, "his demeanor, his reaction to me, and his attitude and take on the whole situation was much different. His attitude toward me as a colleague had changed. Now they were threatening him and might be in his house at any minute. I tried to discuss it with him, but it wasn't discussable." The second session produced more terrifying details, more alarming scenarios, and Sprinkle, deeply concerned, suggested that they go public with Hansen's story. "When I suggested they go public with this information, they looked at me like I was not only weird, but immensely wrong. It was a short session, then a quick good-bye."

Bennewitz began working with a different hypnotist, James Harder (who'd also worked with Travis Walton), finding someone more amenable to his deepening paranoia. Bennewitz and Harder began to move Myrna Hansen around to different locations, looking for the perfect space that would "block the rays" hampering her memory. They subjected Hansen to hypnosis in cars, hotel rooms, basements, even under an aluminum-foil-lined umbrella. Bennewitz wrote to Jim Lorenzen, APRO director, on August 28, 1980, relating that the best technique they'd discovered was using a car in a garage, "use 3 layers of heavy aluminum (barbeque type) foil to cover all windows—grounded to the chrome trim around the windows thoroughly. Masking tape can be used to hold it in place. Precaution: Do not ground the auto. . . ."

From hindsight, the scene feels incredibly bizarre, and more than a little disturbing—whatever trauma Hansen might have felt from the initial experience was now being compounded, it would seem, by two men experimenting with ever more elaborate contraptions and subjecting her to repeated hypnosis sessions in which she was encouraged and rewarded for repeating ever more bizarre narratives about alien abductors, sexually tinged examinations and bodily invasion, and sci-fi horror.

But to Bennewitz, he was getting closer and closer to the truth. Eventually, a narrative emerged that the ships Hansen had seen had come from a secret underground alien base located near Archuleta Mesa on the New Mexico–Colorado border, which Bennewitz and Valdez had glimpsed on their trips up there. These secretive alien crafts were making night forays into the wilderness, murdering and dissecting local cattle for reasons unexplained, and abducting humans for sinister experiments.

The story of Paul Bennewitz ends, in many ways, a story begun with the Shaver Mysteries four decades earlier—and it is perhaps not entirely coincidental that both men told wild stories of alien races inhabiting underground bases, or that both men, to varying degrees, exhibited symptoms consistent with paranoid schizophrenia. Nor is it coincidental, perhaps, that it was precisely these kinds of paranoid stories that took root in the popular imagination, and offered *the* template for how we understand the UFO phenomenon.

Bennewitz, with Hansen as his muse, managed to synthesize various strands of UFO belief—including abductions and government recovery of crashed saucers—into a single conspiracy. Bennewitz had come to believe that the aliens—the "Grays," the more malevolent of the two species he believed were among us—had worked out a secret deal with the government, and had been given an underground base in Dulce, New Mexico, from which they were free to abduct humans and mutilate cattle as part of their gene-splicing experiments.

In a few short decades, the narrative around UFOs had gone from being unexplained objects flitting around, to benevolent Aryan-looking Space Brothers, to malevolent abductors with big eyes and triangular heads. What Bennewitz's revelations cemented was the story of active cooperation with the US military. As public faith in the government plummeted in the wake of Watergate, Vietnam, and revelations about secret CIA projects like MKUltra, protestations by the military that UFOs were nothing to worry about became not only unpersuasive, but active confirmation to many that they were hiding something. The constant revelation of government deception and mistreatment of its own citizens, along with the continued lack of definitive evidence of extraterrestrials, lined up perfectly in suggesting that this, too, could be one more deception perpetrated by the government to the detriment of its own citizens.

The problem was—what to do about this? Between hypnosis sessions with Hansen and photographs he was taking of unidentified aircraft over Kirtland Air Force Base, coupled with his own increasing paranoia, Bennewitz was convinced that something terrible and nefarious was happening, and that the Air Force had to be warned. And so, in the fall of 1980, Bennewitz contacted Kirtland directly, warning of a "serious security problem."

Bennewitz's company, Thunder Scientific, which was then (and still is) in good standing with the Air Force, is close to the Air Force in more ways than one: their headquarters is literally across the street from Kirtland's main entrance. When Bennewitz first contacted them about having recorded possible alien craft above their air space, Kirtland connected him to Sergeant Richard C. Doty, who worked for the Air Force Office of Special Intelligence (AFOSI, basically the Air Force's CIA), who paid Bennewitz a visit at his office. After reviewing Bennewitz's evidence, Doty became alarmed that this civilian contractor might have been intercepting classified communications and coded radio signals from the base.

Bennewitz had been right: there *was* a serious security breach at Kirtland; the problem was that it was not aliens but Bennewitz himself, who'd been photographing whatever top-secret military projects were being tested at Kirtland, and who was now sharing these photographs with a wide network of UFO enthusiasts—a group that many in the government assumed were infiltrated by foreign spies. The Air Force was faced with a conundrum: what to do with Bennewitz and how to keep his story from getting out.

○   ○   ○

That's where Bill Moore came in. In the ballroom of the Aladdin Hotel and Casino, Moore explained to a packed audience how he'd been approached by an AFOSI intelligence officer almost a decade earlier, in early September 1980, who'd promised him classified intelligence in exchange for reports from Moore on what the UFO community was up to. The officer, who gave his code name as "Falcon," offered Moore a deal: in exchange for Moore reporting on the activities of the Aerial Phenomena Research Organization and its members, the government would provide him with what they could about what they actually knew about aliens. Falcon introduced Moore to another officer, Richard Doty (code name "Sparrow"), who would become his primary contact.

Moore, according to his own admission, became the conduit for the government's disinformation campaign: he released the Project Aquarius document, which he knew to be fake, but claimed he did not know that the MJ-12 document was also faked. He also told the audience that he withdrew his participation once he realized the MJ-12 material was faked, and that he'd been tricked into pushing false material out into the community.

According to Moore, the government decided to discredit Bennewitz by feeding him false information. "They were actively trying to defuse him," Moore said, "by pumping as much disinformation through him as he could possibly afford." Moore implied that once the Air Force realized that Bennewitz was a security risk, they decided not simply to shut him up. Instead, they chose to simply push him over the edge. Because of his willingness to accept information from Moore and Doty, information that matched his increasingly paranoid view of the world but which was easily disproved, Bennewitz began to lose credibility. If he was written off as paranoid, his reports of flying technology over Kirtland could likewise be dismissed.

"I know that this whole body of information is false," Moore told the MUFON conference, "because I was in a position to observe much of the disinformation process as it unfolded. And I can tell you it was effective, because I watched Paul become systematically more paranoid and more emotionally unstable as he tried to assimilate what was happening to him." The virus of paranoia had begun to take over its host. "I knew at that time that he was not far from an inevitable nervous collapse. His health had deteriorated, he had lost considerable weight, his hands shook as if from palsy, and he looked terrible. I tried to counsel him to drop the entire UFO thing before his health was completely destroyed. Not long afterward I heard he had been hospitalized and was under psychiatric care."

What Moore was suggesting, in other words, was that he had been complicit in a decade-long plan to sow confusion and paranoia within the already-paranoid UFO community, in an effort to tear the entire culture apart. "Disinformation is a strange and bizarre game," Moore said at one point. "Those who play it are completely aware that an operation's success is dependent upon dropping false information upon a target or 'mark,' in such a way that the person will accept it as truth and will repeat, and even defend it to others as if it were true. One of the key factors in any successful disinformation scheme is that it must contain some elements of truth in order to be credible. Once the information is believed, the work of counterintelligence is complete. They can simply withdraw in the confidence that the dirty work of spreading their poisonous seeds will be done by others."

After Moore's speech at MUFON, there was no going back. Jason Brown, a Los Angeles researcher on conspiracy theories (a conspiracy theorist theorist, if you will), sees MJ-12 and the subsequent revelations surrounding it as a turning point. "The underlying paranoia wasn't new, but the scale, the popular reach of it was. And everything concerning Roswell, UFOs, and aliens is inflected by it afterward." The narrative that the government was covering up knowledge of aliens had always been there, he points out, but "the dominant pop-culture alien prior to MJ12 had a different mood. Both *Close Encounters of the Third Kind* and *E.T.* had sinister government teams covering up the truth, but in both cases, once you got to know them, it turned out they were just hardworking science folk doing their best with a tough situation." MJ-12, on the other hand, not only comes with the evidence that the cover-up story is true, but also that it's been going on for generations, "so it's actually a whole Illuminati-scale cosmic cover-up, and more sinister because everything you know is a lie. And it turns out if you can take people that far, you can take them pretty much as far as you want to go."

The fallout of the MJ-12 debacle among the UFO community was not only a further distrust of the government, but a further distrust of reality itself. It was this increasingly paranoid view of politics and perception that would gradually seep out of this relatively isolated community and into the mainstream public at large, through right-wing talk radio and pop culture entertainment.

[21]

THE PILGRIM'S ROAD

Area 51 was nothing but a blank space on the map until Bob Lazar went on local television to tell the world about it. Lazar was a contractor for Edgerton, Germeshausen, and Grier (EG&G), which had a contract at the top-secret base at Groom Lake; he claimed to hold advanced degrees from both MIT and Caltech, and to be friends with nuclear physicist Edward Teller, whom he said helped him get the job. On November 11, 1989, Nevada television station KLAS ran a program in which Lazar told reporter George Knapp a wild story about the alien technology the government was keeping from the American public.

Knapp's broadcast began by focusing on the Air Force's acquisition of Nevada desert land, part of an ongoing series of disputes that rankled Nevadans then as it still does today. Speculation of alien activity, Knapp said, "was heightened in 1984, when the Air Force seized nearly ninety thousand acres around Groom Lake. The action was, by most accounts, illegal. During congressional hearings about the land grab, Congressman John Siberling grilled the military about the legal authority used in the action and was told the authority was at a much, much higher level than the Air Force." Knapp went on: "In 1987, when the Air Force sought to renew its stranglehold on the Groom range, news articles once again mentioned the talk about alien spacecraft, and subsequent articles in national magazines quoted unnamed sources about things of alien origin flying in Nevada."

This language—*seizure, illegal, stranglehold*—is as central to the story of Area 51 as flying saucers and aliens. Before Lazar's story, Nevadans knew mainly that the government had roped off vast swaths of the desert and wouldn't talk about why. With Lazar, they finally got a story. "It was obvious it came from somewhere else," he told Knapp on the KLAS broadcast, "other than Earth."

Lazar's story has not fared well; he claimed that the UFOs recovered by the military were powered by moscovium (he claimed to have secured a bucket of the element at one point, though it was, he says, stolen from him), except that moscovium decays almost instantaneously to nihonium. No evidence of him having attended MIT or Caltech has ever turned up, though one UFO researcher, Stanton Friedman, discovered he'd taken some classes at Pierce Technical College in the 1970s. But coming only a few months after Bill Moore's infamous MUFON speech, which seemed like it heralded the end of the search for UFOs, Lazar's revelations gave the UFO community a new focus, a place of their own.

It's hard not to detect a whiff of class war in Lazar's story. A man whose only educational records are from Pierce Technical College, who would later claim that he had received advanced degrees from both MIT and Caltech. In Lazar's retelling of his own narrative, he's no longer a blue-collar technician but an advanced scientist whose educational record has been erased because of his revelations. Like cryptid sightings, UFO sightings allowed one to usurp scientists, to claim to have more fundamental and important observational knowledge of the coming scientific paradigms. The wonders of scientific discovery had long ago been institutionalized in the academy, of course, but increasingly they were being further obscured behind the top-secret veil of the military-industrial complex.

But this didn't really matter, since what Lazar had given the UFO community (and the country as a whole) was a new mythology organized around a place: a distant, forbidden Shangri-La, both alluring and terrifying. The perfect desert sublime, a mythical borderland beyond the reach of civilization, dangerous yet alluring.

Like Nessie hunters to Loch Ness, seekers came to the edge of Area 51 to peer into the impenetrable dark—from the Black Mailbox, and from Rachel and its Little A'Le'Inn. In 1993, a two-day convention for Area 51 enthusiasts was held in an army tent just outside the bar, an event described by one participant as quickly devolving into "no-holds-barred Bible-thumping and conspiracy mongering." The disinherited scion of the Lear Jet company, John Lear, gave a speech about a 1954 dental visit by Eisenhower; the dentist story, Lear told an audience, was a cover story for the first top-secret alien-earthling summit: the extraterrestrials gave the American government their alien technology in exchange for "grazing rights," allowing the aliens free rein to abduct humans and cattle for experiments and food. Another speaker railed against the government's then-recent assault on the Branch Davidian compound in Waco, Texas, though it was unclear to many attendees what the relationship to aliens was.

Meanwhile, as the convention approached the "irrepressible atmosphere of an edge-of-town revival meeting," Lazar was the main event, the gospel evangelist who kept everyone in rapt attention. His talk included revelations of a secret meeting between aliens and government scientists that went horribly wrong: a misunderstanding led the aliens to panic and exterminate all forty-four scientists and some additional number of military personnel. None of this leaked to the press, Lazar noted, because the government had only picked scientists who were orphans or lacked strong family ties. (Lazar's formulation helps further reaffirm that sense of the sublime out here: sure, the aliens are terrifying, but their victims are bloodless, nameless, less real in any tangible sense than the aliens themselves. The rest of us, certainly, are not in any real danger.)

The story of Area 51—a fabulously top-secret place where impossible weapons are being developed—is a mirror image of another story, a different desert. The elaborate secrecy around the Manhattan Project marks the turning point in the American desert, when it ceased to be an open land and became a place of secrets and misdirection, when the government turned the land strange and uncanny.

The Trinity Site is open just two days a year—the first Saturdays of April and October—and the line of cars to get inside White Sands spills out onto Highway 380. There are only two locations open: the blast site, with its obelisk, and the McDonald Ranch, two miles away, where the Gadget (as the first bomb was known) was assembled. The ranch house itself is completely uninteresting: The rooms are emptied out, so there's not much to see.

Signs everywhere warn of rattlesnakes, but nowhere will you find any memorial to what happened here on October 13, 1982. That morning, eighty-two-year-old Dave McDonald and his niece Mary set out to reclaim their ranch house, occupying the house with a pair of rifles and an old pistol, erecting a crude barbed-wire fence with signs that read NO TRESPASSING and CLOSED TO THE U. S. ARMY. McDonald had been trying to get his ranch back for decades; to him, it was not a mute, immutable memorial of America's atomic past—it was his family's home, and he wanted it back.

The McDonalds had worked that land long before the Army arrived; they worked the land through the hard droughts of the 1930s, when the government was paying farmers to kill their cows at a dollar a head. When the site was chosen for the Manhattan Project, they were offered compensation, but it was not enough to relocate. The McDonald family was patriotic and understood that sacrifices had to be made during wartime, but they believed once the government was done with their property, it would return it.

"He is in a potential trespassing situation," an Army spokesperson told *The New York Times* at the beginning of the standoff. "We'll have to get him off the range somehow, but not before we find out exactly what his problem is." The military, despite feeling in the right, decided not to let things escalate to violence, and allowed the McDonalds to continue their occupation until they were escorted off government land three days later by New Mexico senator Harrison Schmitt and representative Joseph Skeen. The McDonalds took it as a victory; they'd received national attention for their plight. But Dave McDonald never saw his ranch again; he finally lost his court case in 1988 and he died a few years later.

"They're trying to fool people by calling it a desert," Dave McDonald said. "Last summer the grass was knee high." The tension here has always been one of names as much as anything—to call a place a "desert" is to call it uninhabitable, useless, and worthless. McDonald and the other ranchers who worked the land saw it differently; they saw New Mexico as a vibrant, complex ecosystem.

The McDonalds weren't the only ones contesting the government's definition of "desert." Since 2005, the Tularosa Basin Downwinders Consortium has been trying to educate the population about civilians who were harmed by the fallout from Trinity, as well as to seek answers and compensation from the government. While the official history of Trinity notes that the site was chosen because it was empty, Tina Cordova rejects this. "We know from the census data that there were 40,000 people living in the four counties surrounding Trinity at the time of the test," she said. "That's not remote and uninhabited."

According to Leslie Groves, the general in charge of the Manhattan Project, the site was chosen because it was in the general vicinity of Albuquerque—an ideal location because, in part, "There was good rail service between that city and Chicago, Los Angeles, San Francisco and Washington, and all TWA flights to the Coast stopped there." The idea that it would be in an uninhabited wilderness far from anything is a self-serving lie, one that's disproven by the very obvious proximity to Albuquerque and Socorro. "The desert is empty" is a myth that serves to erase those people who lived downwind. There are, of course, uninhabited deserts, even in the United States, but here convenience for the workers involved won out over those who would suck wind from the bomb for decades afterward.

The Tularosa Basin Downwinders now work on behalf of those suffering from the consequences of these decisions, but theirs was not an isolated experience, of course. From the community at St. George, Utah, who received the brunt of the downwind fallout from the aboveground nuclear tests of the 1940s and '50s, to the community in Hanford, Washington, victims of the "Green Run" (when the government deliberately released nuclear fallout into the atmosphere to track its dispersal), the American postwar military community was cavalier about the safety of its own citizens, who were either insignificant or active guinea pigs.

The prevalence of aboveground tests in the American Southwest, though, coupled with the uncertain effects of exposure and a willful ignorance by government researchers, has created what Joseph Masco calls "the nuclear uncanny": borrowing from Sigmund Freud's definition of the "uncanny" as a psychic process whereby "sensory experience becomes haunted and untrustworthy," the nuclear uncanny is embodied by a fear of radioactive contamination that's "colonized psychic spaces and profoundly shaped individual perceptions of the everyday from the start of the nuclear age, leaving people to wonder if invisible, life-threatening forces intrude upon daily life, bringing cancer, mutation, or death." The nuclear age, coupled with the government's secrecy and its willingness to put its own interests above the health and safety of its own citizens, has turned the land itself strange—we no longer trust it, nor can we rely on our own ability to move through it safely.

Both civilians and the government had a mutually reinforcing stake in the myth of the UFOs, both to enchant the desert once more—citizens, out of a desire to recapture some kind of magic and myth, and the government, to keep us out of their business. Instead of wonder, though, it's only bred distrust. This blurring of secret government operations and UFOs has backfired—now no one trusts the government at all, certainly not when it comes to what's going on in the desert, or what men wearing black suits are up to.

The McDonald Ranch is just one of many places—places once owned by ranchers, farmers, and other settlers that were gradually appropriated by the military. Within the bounds of Area 51 is the Groom Mine, a mining camp that's still owned by the Sheahan family, even though they can no longer legally access it. Founded by Patrick Sheahan in 1889, the mine property originally included four hundred acres and a handful of mining claims; for decades the Sheahan family mined lead, silver, zinc, and copper, passing the mine down from generation to generation. Sheahan picked the area because, unlike the stereotypical image of Nevada desert, there was abundant water and wild game, making homesteading out here feasible.

At the Little A'Le'Inn, next to the gargantuan squat stone monolith commemorating *Independence Day*, is another, smaller plaque, marking "The Groom Mining District": dedicated this 20th day of April, 2008, by the Queho Posse Chapter 19191, of the Ancient and Honorable Order of E Clampus Vitus, a local, somewhat rambunctious historical society dedicated to keeping the West's history alive. The plaque tells the history of the Groom Mine, but claims that it never "proved profitable," and that "no real town ever developed" at the site. Even among local historians and barely noticed commemorative plaques, the Sheahans' story is relegated to a failed business venture. Their connection to this land predates the military, the UFO seekers, and even the aliens themselves—and yet their story, and the real story of the Groom Mine, has been mostly written out of history.

●   ●   ●

We once sought monsters and the unexplained on the edges of far borders, in the empty blank spaces on the map that hadn't yet been filled in. Now, it would seem, we construct those blank spaces within our own territory as secret military bases. Area 51—Dreamland—is a place where dreaming is still possible, a place where we can project our dreams and fears of aliens and of being alienated. This may explain why, in the early months of 1995, a relatively obscure member of the militia movement came out this way, trying to gain access to Area 51—only a few months before he would detonate a massive truck bomb in front of the Alfred P. Murrah Federal Building in Oklahoma City, killing 168 people.

Timothy McVeigh was never a member of the UFO community, per se, and yet he seemed deeply interested in Area 51. After his incarceration, he gave an account of his life to two journalists, Lou Michel and Dan Herbeck, who subsequently published *American Terrorist: Timothy McVeigh and the Oklahoma City Bombing*, based on these interviews. On his way to visit his collaborator Terry Nichols, McVeigh made a side trip to the top-secret government site. He was intrigued by the rumors surrounding the base, but, more importantly, he resented the very idea of a swath of wilderness that was off-limits to civilians.

"McVeigh was outraged by reports that the federal government had posted threatening signs at the site, warning that the use of deadly force had been authorized against people who crossed a certain boundary into the installation," Michel and Herbeck write. He planned to get as close as he could, then park his car and hike up to the mountain ridge, with a canned speech about being on public land ready for any security that might accost him. He was incensed, he later said, at the signs forbidding trespassing and photography. *"You can't tell me on public land I can't take a fuckin' picture*, he thought. *No rent-a-cop can tell me that."* Approached by two guards in an unmarked white jeep, he contemplated murdering them but instead surprised them with a friendly "Hi!" which, he claimed, scared them off. That morning, at dawn, he hiked up to the ridge with his rifle, only to find a Black Hawk helicopter rising up to meet him, swooping low to scare him off; McVeigh stood his ground, took his photographs, and left. He had, Michel and Herbeck write, "accomplished his mission, challenging the government's authority and satisfying his curiosity in one fell swoop."

Ventriloquized through Michel and Herbeck, without independent corroboration, McVeigh's account fairly reeks of self-aggrandizing embellishment; it's hard to know what of his story, if any of it, is true. But McVeigh, awaiting execution for what was then the worst domestic terrorist attack on American soil, felt it important to weave Area 51 into his myth of individual sovereignty over the government. It is not a story about UFOs. Instead it is a story about the secrecy that is enacted around government sites that have become inextricable from UFO narratives. Area 51 was not just any military base; it was *the* place, the place of forbidden secrets, the single greatest metaphor for the government's appropriation of the land.

[22]

ALIENS ON THE LAND

I n a weird way," Greg Valdez would later remember, "I guess some of the best times we had in the police car were responding to reports of cattle mutilations." His father, Gabe Valdez, was an officer with the New Mexico State Police who had become somewhat synonymous with cattle mutilations (or "mutes" for short) in the late 1970s; the more he took an interest in investigating them, the more people called him. It was Valdez who first connected Paul Bennewitz with Myrna Hansen. "For me," Valdez's son Greg recalled, "it was an adventure, driving in the middle of nowhere looking for a dead cow, kind of like a treasure hunt. You never knew what you might find when you arrived."

It began with a three-year-old horse named Lady. On September 9, 1967, Harry King went in search of Lady, who'd hadn't returned to his ranch in three days—after a search, her corpse was found, lying on its side. The horse's head and neck had been stripped clean to the bone, in a cut that was ubiquitously described as "surgical." King noted that there was no blood on the scene, and that there were strange burns and a strong "medicinal" smell.

As news of the strange mutilation spread, Lady was rechristened "Snippy" by the press, and more and more mutilations were discovered, mainly cattle. There were a number of similar traits: the lack of blood, both in the corpse and on the ground, as well as surgical-looking cuts, as though someone or something had removed specific parts of the animals' bodies: eyes, ears, genitals, udders. Both the police and local veterinarians were at a loss: no one, it seemed, had seen anything like this before. Mutilations turned up in Nebraska and Kansas in the fall of 1973, where one witness reported an object that "looked as if it had a little bluish-green light on each side with a glow surrounding it." Some ranchers saw UFOs, while many more saw strange, unmarked, black helicopters that they blamed for the loss of their stock.

Initially the mutes were thought to be the work of rustlers—but rustlers wouldn't have left so much valuable meat behind. Some hypothesized that it might be satanists, killing and dismembering animals as part of some bizarre ritual sacrifice. (Screaming across the front page of the June 13, 1975, issue of the *Colorado Springs Gazette Telegraph* is surely one of the great headlines of the twentieth century: ARE SATAN'S PHANTOM KILLERS MUTILATING CATTLE?) Soon rumors spread that it was some kind of secret military operation out of Fort Riley, Kansas. As the reports snowballed, theories multiplied: journalist Dane Edwards in Brush, Colorado, hypothesized that the government was testing biological weapons to help in Vietnam. Minnesota Alcohol, Tobacco, and Firearms (ATF) agent Donald E. Flickinger investigated reports satanists were somehow mutilating cattle to steal plutonium.

Witnesses in Cripple Creek and Florissant, Colorado, noted a blue helicopter with a strange "V-type tail system and a plain white spot on the side"; others claimed they were green with red fuel tanks. A Honey Creek, Iowa, farmer claimed he'd been shot at by one. A Nebraska farmer near Grand Island shot at and hit a utility helicopter checking on power lines. Afterward, the Nebraska National Guard advised all helicopters to fly at two thousand feet instead of the standard one thousand, to avoid errant fire from irate ranchers.

Rewards were offered to anyone who could stop the mutilations. By 1975, the reports of mutes had gotten so bad that the government needed to get involved. Colorado senator Floyd Haskell sent a letter to the

Denver FBI Office, asking them to open an investigation on cattle muti-lations in the state. "For several months my office has been receiving reports of cattle mutilations throughout Colorado and other western states," he wrote, asking them to investigate.

At the time, it was widely believed that the crisis had a human origin; numerous ranchers reported seeing helicopters in the area before or after discovering a mute, and Haskell was worried that things could escalate out of control. "It appears that ranchers are arming themselves to protect their livestock, as well as their families, because they are frustrated by the unsuccessful investigation," Haskell warned the FBI. "Clearly some-thing must be done before someone gets hurt." In the absence of a clear and plausible explanation from local authorities, it was easy to see how conspiracy theories filled the gap. That's what theories (conspiracy or otherwise) are there for, after all—to make sense of otherwise inexplica-ble phenomenon.

Only gradually did ranchers start to suspect extraterrestrial origins to the cattle mutilations. In 1974, well into the cattle mutilation panic, jour-nalists started making connections between sites of mutilations and un-identified lights in the sky, particularly in Midwest states like Kansas and Nebraska. UFOlogists took the connection and ran with it, believ-ing that the mutilations finally represented physical proof of aliens. In what has since become the enduring explanation, aliens, either in league with the American government or independently, secretly kill and dis-sect cattle throughout the Southwest, leaving behind no trace other than the surgically precise cuts and mysterious corpses.

But one doesn't need extraterrestrial explanations. The cattle indus-try had nearly collapsed in the 1970s due to government interference. In response to worldwide food shortages, the Nixon administration started sending grain to Africa, Asia, and the Soviet Union, which raised the price of grain for feed lots. This in turn increased the price of beef, which led to a consumer boycott, with housewives picketing supermar-kets over high meat prices. Nixon responded by putting a price freeze on beef, but this only made the problem worse—ranchers responded by trying to wait out the government, postponing the slaughter of their cattle. This standoff led to what cattlemen called "the Wreck": slaughtered cattle decreased 19.2 percent, meatpackers were laid off in droves, and when ranchers finally did slaughter their cattle, the animals were past their prime, the resulting beef undesirable and worth far less. When Nixon's price freeze ended finally, beef prices had dropped 33 percent, while grain continued to rise.

The cattle mutilation phenomenon is inextricable from this parallel drama of government interference in the beef industry. With ranchers increasingly anxious over their livestock and livelihood, a stray unexplained death took on heightened significance. Legitimate government distrust due to arbitrary, capricious, or mysterious involvement in the markets became intertwined with fantasies of government helicopters and secret experiments.

When investigators finally did start looking into the mutes, they found, for example, that it was mostly small- and part-time ranchers reporting mutilations; the larger operations didn't report problems. In part, these larger operations were less reliant on each single head of cattle, so a stray death here or there would not result in the same kind of heightened scrutiny. Such larger organizations also could afford lobbyists; if they wanted to fight the government, they could do so in the halls of Washington. Their smaller competition could only fight Uncle Sam with a rifle trained at a helicopter. But larger, longtime operators who had more familiarity with cattle also recognized scavenger activity when they saw it.

And scavenger activity it clearly was. Cattle deaths were common from lightning strikes, diseases like blackleg, or gastrointestinal disease resulting from eating nails, barbed wire, or other pieces of metal. (In 1975, the height of the cattle mutilation scare, overall cattle deaths had actually fallen from the previous years.) Scavengers—coyotes, foxes, vultures, magpies, bobcats, badgers, and flies—tend to go for soft tissue first, including an animal's rectum, udder, and genitalia, along with the eyes and ears. In some cases, a few mutilations may have been the result of vandals or isolated pranksters, but the overwhelming evidence pointed to nature. Try as they might, investigators could find no "classic mutilation" case that wasn't explained by normal, natural processes. Veterinarians and local law enforcement had missed this because neither group is trained in animal pathology (vets work to keep animals alive; they don't often do *CSI*-style crime scene investigations).

The scavenger theory was confirmed in Arkansas in 1979 by the sheriff of Washington County, who'd acquired a dying two-month-old heifer from a rancher, euthanized it, and then placed the carcass in a ravine. Sheriff's deputies kept watch as skunks, vultures, and flies worked on the cow's corpse, and though it was disturbed neither by secret government agents nor by aliens, after thirty hours the corpse looked exactly like a standard cattle mutilation.

What seemed to have happened was that a few unusual cases of animal deaths that lacked immediate explanation led to sudden, heightened scrutiny of an otherwise ignored phenomenon. One can compare the cattle mutilations with another mysterious phenomenon: the rash of windshield pitting in the Pacific Northwest in 1954. In late March of that year, residents of Bellingham, Washington, began to report small pits and dings in their car windshields. The cops, sensing a pattern of some kind, conjectured that it was likely local vandals, using either BB guns or buckshot. They began to prowl the community for the hoodlums, though their searches came up short.

The pitted windshield epidemic spread like wildfire, though, down to Seattle, where used-car lots and even cop cars were hit. No small band of vandals could move that fast, damage that many windshields. Theories abounded. Maybe radioactive fallout, or maybe the Navy's new million-watt radio transmitter at Jim Creek caused the glass to vibrate. Maybe it was cosmic rays or some mysterious atmospheric event, or perhaps sand fleas laying eggs, even a shift in the earth's magnetic fields.

As a panic seized his state, Governor Arthur Langlie convened scientists from the University of Washington, imploring them to solve the problem. Their ultimate verdict was as shocking as it was self-evident: the pits were the result of ordinary wear and tear, mainly from small rocks and gravel thrown up by tires in ordinary road use. They noted that cars had suffered damage only on the front windshield, not on the back, and it was mostly older cars—in car lots, for example, used cars were found to have pitted windshields while new cars did not. The reason the whole thing felt like an epidemic was mainly because most people had simply not paid attention to the condition of their windshields until the story made the news, and when people looked, they found pits that had likely been there for weeks, months, even years (when researching this story, I checked my own windshield and found two pits I'd never previously noticed).

The windshield epidemic died out quickly because it served no compelling narrative—but the mutes could easily serve any number of conspiracy theories. They fed an increasing distrust over federal regulation and policies that affected westerners. Daniel Kagan and Ian Summers, whose book *Mute Evidence* offers a thorough debunking of the phenomenon, suggesting that its outbreak was coterminous with a series of other major events that sapped Americans' belief in government: citing Watergate, Three Mile Island, and the fall of Saigon among others, they conclude that the "mutilation phenomenon can tell you a lot about Americans' loss of faith in institutions that have turned out to be inept, hollow, harmful, and bureaucratically crippled in thought."

But beyond mass hysteria and government paranoia lies a deeper issue, one connected to the land itself. The cattle mutilation phenomenon, rooted in small- and part-time ranchers, revealed an increasing estrangement from the natural world around them, where the habitual and predictable work of coyotes and bottle flies came to be seen as something unearthly and uncanny. And even though the mutes largely faded from public consciousness as the bad ol' days of the 1970s waned, this odd, inchoate sense of feeling estranged from the land has not. Nor has the tendency to shift the blame for this estrangement to the government, or aliens, or both.

• • •

The people that were screwed over first in America were the Native Americans and the blacks," right-wing militia member John Trochmann told journalist David Niewert in 1999. "Now it's our turn. So we better line up with them. They know more about it than we do." In the Sasquatch and the Yeti, believers could see the racial other as inferior, as the uncivilized brute from which we must distinguish ourselves, a caricatured slur directed at colonized people or ethnic minorities. In the Space Brothers contactee myth, this had been reversed: the Venusian as an idealized Aryan perfection, a body to aspire to. Perhaps most bizarre, then, is how many white ranchers out here have adopted the rhetoric of the West's indigenous populations: a formulation in which white men could live out a fantasy of *being* the racial other.

The stories you hear out here are of how *the federal government took our land*: interlopers in the West, the feds came and seized wide blocks of empty desert. Behind the lore of aliens is the history of how the federal government, mainly under the guise of the Defense Department, came out to the West in the first half of the twentieth century and gobbled up vast tracts of western lands. A popular T-shirt features a photo of Sitting Bull with the caption, "Sure you can trust the federal government—*just ask an Indian.*" Settlers were once used as a tool by the federal government to drive Native tribes off their lands, farther and farther west into barely hospitable reservations. Now they in turn feel abandoned by the government, their usefulness expended. They see themselves as the aggrieved victims of the federal government, completely oblivious to the irony and hypocrisy of such a stance.

Here, the government has taken on quasi-occult properties, mystifying and mystical, its agenda unknown and unknowable, except to say it's *against nature*. The government, like the Snowman or something out of Leviticus, has become an abomination. The writer Susan Lepselter spent a season working at the Little A'Le'Inn, gathering stories of aliens and of the land for her book *Evidence of Things Not Seen*. Lepselter, too, finds the idea of the uncanny a useful way of understanding the West; one of the hallmarks of an uncanny sensation is the feeling that "the foundation of the real is here a shifting ground," she writes. "What's real in this story is the conspiracy theory's dense figuring toward meaningfulness among blanched-out histories. *Something is wrong*, but no one knows what." At one point she quotes two white men whose complaints echo Native American loss of land; sitting at the bar, they imagine an "old chief" sitting above them, passing judgment (though they admit they're unsure which people actually lived here—Sioux, maybe?). These white ranchers, themselves feeling alienated from their own culture, incorporated resonances of stories they'd heard about the Native American genocide, adopting them, adapting them into stories about themselves, projecting kinship where none exists. The borders of Area 51 and the McDonald Ranch have spread throughout the entire West.

White people's obsession with seeing themselves as other ethnicities long predates this current moment. Particularly with white Americans imagining themselves as Natives, which Philip Deloria describes in his 1998 book *Playing Indian*, stretches as far back as the Boston Tea Party. Colonists adopted Indian costumes and disguises not because they offered anonymity—surviving records suggest that many of these costumes did little to protect the users' identity. Rather, they were used as a means of embracing a rebellious spirit, as the colonists saw Indian culture as a wild and uncivilized rejection of British rule.

The early colonists saw themselves as not only dressing as Indians, but being reborn as indigenous Americans. Their new government would differ from England's in that it would be sui generis, of America. The Indian, in their eyes, was a potent symbolic mix of both "rebel" and "citizen." Deloria writes that "Indian play was perhaps not so much about a desire to become Indian—or even *American*—as it was a longing for the utopian experience of being in between, of living a paradoxical moment in which absolute liberty coexisted with the absolute." This paradox—one of both freedom and homogeneity—seems to lie at the heart of the far-right American ideology. "Americanness," Deloria writes, "is perhaps not so much the product of a collision of European and Indian as it is a particular working out of a desire to preserve stability and truth while enjoying absolute, anarchic freedom."

The American West has long been that magical, mythical borderland for a specific kind of settler mentality, where one can remain innately "American": a citizen with full-fledged rights who is still an outlaw, a marginal figure on the edge of culture enjoying pure freedom. In such a place, various threads start to intertwine. *Do you have an interest in Native Americans, or maybe some Native American blood?* reads a flyer at a UFO gathering. *It could be a sign that you've been abducted by aliens.* The government has estranged white Americans from what they've come to think of as *their* land, turned the landscape uncanny, has rendered them Indians. The possibility of aliens is one way out. Aliens promise an explanation for why we're feeling so fatigued, and they offer us a kinship in some future humanity, one that transcends the mortal constraints of our bodies. Most of all, though, if aliens are real, they offer a deus ex machina, where the power of the government over us is undone, time and space is finally annihilated, and we finally achieve that apocalyptic redemption.

[23]

A HORSEMAN

At various points in the past two decades, the percentage of Americans who've agreed that the United States government was complicit in the terrorist attacks of September 11 has been staggeringly high. (In a 2018 survey, 53 percent of Americans said they believed the government was covering up inside knowledge about the attacks.) These percentages translate into literally tens of millions of Americans who believe that their government waged open war on its citizens. And yet we have never seen widespread protests, riots, disruptions, boycotts, impeachments, demands for justice, etc., surrounding this belief. Compared to the protests against the Second Iraq War, or protests of police brutality in places like Ferguson, Missouri, there is a conspicuous absence of motivated feeling about this supposed inside job, even though the ramifications of such a conspiracy are hard to overstate. It's yet another version of the sublime: a terrifying idea that is nonetheless curiously abstract.

For the man who first theorized that the terrorist attacks of September 11, 2001, were an inside job, Milton William Cooper, the threat from the government was anything but sublime. He'd been wanted for years by the FBI, and (though he didn't know it at the time) he narrowly escaped arrest on the day that the World Trade Center buildings fell in New York.

But this is all getting ahead of his story. For Cooper's story begins not with 9/11, but with aliens. Cooper appeared on the UFO scene in the mid-1980s, initially just one more colorful figure with a host of theories and hints of secret information he hoped to soon share. He showed up on an early proto-internet user forum, Paranet, in which he claimed that he had witnessed a UFO while serving on the USS *Tiru*, a Navy submarine. The skipper, Cooper claimed, immediately classified the incident, and upon returning to land the witnesses were all debriefed by naval security.

He quickly allied himself with John Lear, the two of them finding common cause in being ostracized for their outlandish claims. Initially, Cooper did little to distinguish himself from his fellow believers; he recycled the same facts and whisperings about MJ-12 and other known conspiracies, and his visions of aliens followed a familiar, thinly veiled racial taxonomy: there were the tall Nordic types called Aryans, and small, gnomelike Grays who had large noses. (It shouldn't be hard to guess which of the two were conceived of as benign and which were evil.)

Cooper's welcome within the UFO community wore out quickly, no doubt due to his extremely paranoid outlook; as one commentator at the time described him: "Raining threats and pronouncements over the UFO field like a continuously firing shotgun, Cooper has recently leveled charges of government spookery against almost every UFOlogist in the field." He turned on Lear, accusing him of being a CIA plant; likewise, in short order he went from praising Bob Lazar's courage in unveiling Area 51 to accusing him, too, of being a disinformation agent. "Cooper is an intelligent man, and the two times I've seen him," Lazar said at one point, "well I hate to call someone a psychopath but he really acts crazy. He seems to believe a lot of what he says to the point he will fight about them and get violent."

In 1991, Cooper published his magnum opus, *Behold a Pale Horse*, a collection of various documents, pamphlets, and other ramblings. In it he wove together all of his various conspiracies into one megaconspiracy, spinning an elaborate story that touched on anything and everything. In his retelling of the MJ-12 document, the government had covered up some twenty-seven UFO crashes (advanced beings they may have been, but apparently they were lousy pilots), resulting in ninety-one alien corpses being recovered along with five living aliens. There were also at least two crashed flying saucers that were found to be filled with human body parts. Truman's secretary of defense, James Forrestal, Cooper contended, had threatened to go public with all of this, leading the CIA to assassinate him and frame his death as a suicide. Afterward, Truman organized a secret group to coordinate against an alien invasion, the Bilderberg Group, which in time became a secret one-world government that now controlled everything. (Cooper went so far as to include *The Protocols of the Elders of Zion*, instructing readers to substitute "the Illuminati" for the Jews.) Having realized that the aliens were, in fact, a threat to humanity, the Bilderberg Group, so Cooper believed, had embarked on developing a series of top-secret weapons projects in the hopes of exterminating them—one of them, Alternative 3, accidentally got out into the human population, where it became known as AIDS.

How could the government possibly fund all this activity? According to Cooper, they did this by dominating the illegal drug trade, and the Bilderberg Group propped up a phony Cold War so they could keep funneling defense spending into secret MJ-12 projects without anyone knowing. Among those who tried to reveal this to the public were John F. Kennedy (assassinated) and Richard Nixon (forced out). Added to all this were a set of dire warnings: that "patriots" must be sure never to be at home on any national holiday, since they will likely be rounded up and gathered into camps, and that in December 1999, the Galileo space probe will detonate in the heart of Jupiter, causing a massive chain reaction that will turn Jupiter into the star Lucifer: "The world will interpret it as a sign of tremendous religious significance. It will fulfill prophecy."

Cooper, in other words, successfully tied traditionally left-wing conspiracies (the CIA running the drug trade, the Kennedy assassination, the ultrarich controlling the world) with right-wing conspiracies (anti-Semitism, Christian apocalyptic fantasies, government paranoia, and so forth) into one strange science fiction fantasy with massive stakes. His ideas found purchase in communities on the right and the left that felt betrayed by America's government and its corporations—including in the black communities of Harlem, where his book was sold by street vendors alongside James Baldwin and *The Autobiography of Malcolm X*. As Wu-Tang Clan member Ol' Dirty Bastard explained, "Everybody gets fucked. William Cooper tells you who's fucking you."

Crucially, though, Cooper was moving away from UFO hypotheses as he was ostracized from the community. "There is always the possibility that I was used," he admits at one point, "that the whole alien scenario is the greatest hoax in history designed to create an alien enemy from outer space in order to expedite the formation of a one-world government. I have found evidence that this could be true. . . . I advise you to consider this scenario as being probable."

By the end of the 1980s, then, UFO mythology had become a crossroads for political extremism of all manners, where disparate fringe groups could meet and exchange ideas. While the left had been targeted by the FBI and CIA in the 1960s, now their paranoia could be taken up by the far right. Tax dodgers, weapons hoarders, frauds, and grifters—they found in this narrative a sense that their illegality was not just common criminality, but evidence of a larger narrative, one in which they could recast themselves—and be seen as—heroes, fighting a cosmic struggle. The UFO story had become a curious mélange of the increasingly specific (and outlandish), while becoming increasingly vague politically, so that anyone could see themselves as a starring figure.

While Cooper was fantasizing about the Illuminati, the rest of America was becoming increasingly obsessed—and enamored—with a different secret society: the FBI. In two landmark television series of the 1990s, *Twin Peaks* and *The X-Files*, the FBI was transformed from a mundane bureaucratic law enforcement organization into a quasi-mystical brotherhood. *Twin Peaks'* Agent Dale Cooper brought with him intuition from transcendental meditation, appearing as a Sherlock-esque savant (unlike Arthur Conan Doyle's creation, often Cooper would not even explain the mechanisms behind his deductions; he just somehow *knew*), while *The X-Files'* Agent Fox Mulder consistently debunked the debunking of his most ardent skeptics.

From the 1950s to the '80s, government secrecy had been thought of as a means to conceal some hidden revelation too important to be known. But by the 1990s, it had become an end unto itself, at least for conspiracists. Decades of intelligence and defense infrastructure had been built up around the Soviet Union as a global foe—when it collapsed, the raison d'etre of that infrastructure underwent a crisis of faith. The pop culture of the 1990s offered a further evolution: no longer was the government hiding anything in particular, it was just hidden, a network of secrets and disinformation. What these shows offered was once again a kind of sublime conspiracy: yes, the government held secrets from us, but the government wasn't monolithic, and there were important freedom fighters on the inside who had our backs. *The X-Files* took the edge off the darker conspiracies that had dominated the alien subculture, allowing the show to transmute the paranoid myths into entertainment.

Gradually these two sides of the same coin built up a feedback loop: writers would pick up strange bits of ephemera from the darkest corners of the fringe movement, using it as grist for the next episode—once broadcast out to the larger public, then, conspiracists would seize upon this raw material and build it out for the next round of theories. As with Ray Palmer's Lemuria, or the *Outer Limits* episode that likely inspired Betty and Barney Hill, the '90s became a zone of osmosis between those interested in entertainment and those interested in scary, dark secrets. In 1997, Chris Carter, the creator of *The X-Files*, told *Rolling Stone* he was reading *Behold a Pale Horse*. "I read these things with fascination. You know, the books that have all those CAPITAL LETTERS."

Cooper was only the most visible vector of this long-simmering convergence of UFO beliefs and antigovernment conspiracies. It was inevitable, and it had far-reaching consequences: it brought antigovernment conspiracism to a much wider audience, who could now follow the rabbit hole from *The X-Files* to internet bulletin boards to Cooper's short-wave broadcasts and *The Protocols of the Elders of Zion*. The mystique and mystery of the possibility of extraterrestrial life, a fantasy of wonderment harmless enough in and of itself, could only be sustained by a belief that there was an active government cover-up involved, which meant accepting that the government was keeping from us something wondrous and strange, the next chapter in human history.

Writing as far back as 2003, Michael Barkun saw UFO belief as the crucial link in mainstreaming any number of conspiratorial beliefs that have since become common and public. "As long as conspiracy theories, such as those that posit a New World Order plot, were strongly linked to antigovernment militants, anti-Semites, and neo-Nazis, the audience for conspiracism was limited," he writes. But this political exile ended, "thanks to the incorporations of New World Order conspiracy into UFO beliefs." UFO belief became the acceptable public face of these deeper fears: seemingly benign, it could be tolerated by polite society in a way that antigovernment conspiracies would not be—while, behind the scenes, the two halves rapidly merged. Cooper made explicit what had always been there, more or less on the surface, unremarked upon but no less remarkable.

What conspiracy theories also shared with the UFO phenomenon was their all-encompassing nature. One may or may not believe in the Loch Ness Monster, but that's as far as the belief goes—Nessie is not pulling the strings of international banking, nor does she bring us utopian technological innovation. But from the beginning aliens were conceived of as beings that could explain everything. In this way, they bore a much closer resemblance to the anti-Semite's paranoid conception of Jews than the cryptozoologist's conception of water beasts.

After all, all this energy had to go somewhere. After the fall of the Soviet Union, American paranoia was suddenly set adrift. For decades, Americans had been taught to see Rosenberg spies and Manchurian candidates everywhere. In the wake of the Cold War's sudden end, this energy might have dissipated, but instead it turned inward.

Cooper's legacy, as the most visible conduit from the UFO commu-

nity to the conspiratorial world, also suggests how, gradually but inexo-
rably, a search for wonder and mystery, for the sublime, for the enchanted
world just out of our grasp, can descend into paranoia. The longer that
sublime remains unknown, unseen, felt but not reached, the more the
mind spins for explanations. In America in particular, those explanations
became the government, and the longer the government kept these sacred secrets from us, the more terrifying that lie became.

In July 1998, Cooper was charged with failing to pay taxes from 1992
to 1994, and for submitting false information for a bank loan. Federal
agents had vowed to arrest him, but promised it would not be like Waco.
They knew he was armed and wouldn't go without a fight, so they bided
their time. "He sits up there isolated and locked in his little world," his
friend Nola Udall said. "The people in town have talked about the situation with him being here but figure it's best just to leave him alone because it really could be another Ruby Ridge." For years they waited, and
then, while he was off his land on November 5, 2001, deputies tried to
arrest him, leading to a firefight in which Cooper was killed.

THE SUBURBAN UNCANNY

onspiracy theorist Linda Thompson's video on the Amtrak repair depot in Beech Grove, Indiana, can still be found on YouTube, and it remains unsettling, consisting mainly of slow, handheld pans of the Beech Grove facility. Nondescript warehouses, stabled trains on sidings, piles of lumber, fenced-in yards. Thompson narrates what you're seeing, coloring your perception of the images, making it clear that this place is anything but benign. The barbed wire lining the fence, she notes, is angled inward rather than outward—"not to keep people out, but to keep people in." The presence of wind socks throughout the yard indicates "expected helicopter activity." Signs taped to fences read simply: RED ZONE. A small brick structure, you're told, is suitable for use as a "processing" building.

Why would the barbed wire be angled inward instead of out? A rational person might offer any number of equally plausible explanations, or simply shrug. Perhaps it was an uncorrected mistake? Indifference toward such seemingly inconsequential mysteries, though, is precisely what differentiates one from a conspiracy theorist. In this simple question of the angled barbed wire, so much is revealed. Thompson warned that the Beech Grove site was one of a number of such facilities spread throughout the country, known collectively as "FEMA camps": these nondescript industrial locations were being kept in a constant state of readiness for a looming, imminent declaration of martial law.

Conspiracy theories are predicated, above all else, on the notion that nothing is innocent or accidental, and important clues can be found in the slightest of details. It is a way of thinking that denies error, errata, and the inexplicable. Like a blond-haired Space Brother in the desert, the conspiracy theorist promises above all a sense of order.

Like any good conspiracy theory, the FEMA camp story has its roots in a kernel of truth. In the wake of various riots and uprisings in the 1960s, the American government began to plan various contingency operations that would involve both the use of covert intelligence gathering on American citizens, and the use of martial law to corral and control civilian populations.

Operation Garden Plot, developed in 1968, focused on preparing for "Sudden and unexpected civil disturbances or other emergencies endangering life or Federal property, disrupting the normal processes of government which require that immediate military action be taken to protect life or Federal property or to prevent disruption of Federal activities." Warning that civil disturbances beyond the control of local and state authorities "may occur at any time," it not only laid out various contingency plans for enforcing martial law, but highlighted various warning signs and contributing factors to civil unrest: "Dissatisfaction with the environmental conditions contributing to racial unrest and civil disturbances and dissatisfaction with national policy as manifested in the anti-draft and anti-Vietnam demonstrations are recognized factors within the political and social structure. As such, they might provide a preconditioned base for a steadily deteriorating situation leading to demonstrations and violent attacks upon the social order."

In assessing the probability for civil unrest, Garden Plot advised looking at "population by race," "presence of large 'blue collar' neighborhoods, presence and degree of activity of militant racial, leftist (anti-war and anti-draft) and extreme right-wing groups, and an assessment of the capabilities of these groups to provoke disturbances," and "existence of wide-spread sense of injustice and real or imagined lack of means of redress." Indicators of potential violence include "high unemployment rate among minority groups," "increased crime rates among minority groups," "protests arising from income disparities between minority and majority groups," "declining rapport between local officials and minority groups," "migrations of large numbers of minority groups," "protests by minority groups to such conditions as slum conditions, segregation in housing and schools, lack of jobs, lack of recreational facilities, police brutality, and local overpricing practices." In other words, what the government found was that inherent social and economic inequality in America would lead naturally to a sense of injustice among those disenfranchised communities, and that this legitimate sense of injustice could in turn lead to civil unrest, including protests against this injustice. Rather than address the roots of this injustice, Garden Plot provided for ways to contain and control protests, riots, and other natural expressions of inequality.

In other words, the roots of the FEMA camp myth are true, but rooted in government suppression of the *left*. The government's long history of targeting civil rights, antiwar, and other left groups was appropriated by the right, particularly those with white supremacist leanings, who made themselves the heroes of this story of government resistance. Houston's William Pabst brought this fear of martial law to the right wing with a pamphlet, *Concentration Camp Plans for U.S. Citizens*, published in 1979. Pabst's pamphlet and subsequent warnings designated a number of potential sites for American concentration camps, in places as far-flung as Mill Point, West Virginia, to Tool Lake, California, from Avon Park, Florida, to Eielson Air Force Base in Alaska. Many of Pabst's suggested sites were various prisons that were under capacity: the penitentiary at Allenwood, Pennsylvania, held three hundred people but could hold up to twelve thousand, he claimed; the federal prison camp in Florence, Arizona, could hold up to thirty-five hundred people, though Pabst claimed it currently had only three hundred prisoners.

It was this tendency to read various government sites as inherently sinister that became a hallmark of right-wing conspiracies, and it made for a heady mix of both specificity and vagueness. Almost all of the sites labeled concentration camps by Pabst were existing federal facilities—either prisons or military installations, both of which were off-limits. Hence, Michael Barkun notes, "nefarious activities can be attributed to them with little likelihood that the claims will be quickly rebutted, and the same security arrangements that shield them from public view may be blamed for the public's supposed ignorance of their true purpose." Conspiracy, in other words, works to turn the government against itself—any secrets the government may hold, legitimately or not, are immediately fodder for malevolent accusations.

Pabst's bête noire was the Law Enforcement Assistance Administration (LEAA), which was active in the 1970s, when FEMA had not yet been established. Almost as soon as it had, though, it became the default demon of government malfeasance. In 1992, *Spotlight*, the newsletter of Christian conspiracist organization Liberty Lobby, claimed that plans for New World Order dictatorship could be found in a top-secret safe in FEMA headquarters; in *The X-Files* movie, one Dr. Kurtzweil claims that FEMA is the principlal agency involved in covering up an alien genesis/ human extermination project. FEMA, the Militia of Montana contended in a 1990s-era pamphlet, "has the power to completely rule over the American people, any time the President should decide to declare Martial law."

Why FEMA? Fear of military occupation, loss of civil rights, surveillance, and control—these anxieties would seem to gather around the Department of Defense, the CIA, and the FBI, and perhaps the National Guard. But FEMA, by definition, deals with emergencies, and emergencies are how you control people. Most constitutional democracies, as it happens, contain various clauses for how and when a government may invoke a state of emergency—in such a situation, any number of normal protocols may be suspended, in deference to some larger crisis. Totalitarian regimes often come to power precisely through invoking states of emergencies; the Nazis, to give one example, never changed the German constitution, they just suspended it for thirteen years. The state of emergency, when the normal lawmaking process is suspended and constitutional protections are unenforced, is the prime means for an abuse of power. FEMA wasn't created for this purpose, of course, but in providing a blueprint for a rapid response to hurricanes or earthquakes, it became the agency most visibly associated with what conspiracists feared might come to pass.

Among Pabst's original locations singled out as future FEMA sites is Camp Minidoka, a Japanese internment camp that now stands as a monument to America's problematic past. Camps like Minidoka were built as distinctly temporary structures, and yet they've achieved a kind of permanence—at first through the exigencies of the war, and then due to the sudden neglect and abandonment (for there was neither appetite nor funding to demolish or repurpose them), and then, finally, as a commemoration. The reason Minidoka persists now is as a reminder to that legacy, and an admonishment: "Never again."

To read such a place as a harbinger of the opposite of that sentiment, to see it as a potential return, is once again a curious rewriting of history. It suggests that the importance of historical, physical reminders of past barbarities is a ruse, that there is no need to commemorate an injustice—either because it is inconsequential, or it was never an injustice in the first place. It casts suspicion on the act of preservation, reducing the purpose of a place like Minidoka to its functional use value: if it could only ever be employed as a camp, then there must be a future camp in mind. Our estrangement to the past is made physical in FEMA camps.

Since Pabst's original sites, mostly military bases and prisons, the numbers of candidate FEMA camps has grown, seeming exponentially. No longer is the desert the locus for estrangement, no longer is it predicated on the edge of the wilderness, the margins. Instead, that enchanted terror has become commonplace, and everywhere is suspect. More and more, as a side effect of late capitalism, things that used to make sense now seem bizarre and inexplicable.

With a landscape that appears chaotic, often purposeless, filled with accidents and errata and detritus, anything can easily appear menacing and directed. The governmental aspect of this theory is almost beside the point: the real focus here is on disused and postindustrial spaces that the conspiracist's mind cannot account for.

∘ ∘ ∘

In a postindustrial landscape, we've left behind all manner of decaying buildings that have, in time, acquired their own aesthetic sheen— resulting in a cottage industry for photographers known as "ruin porn," where dilapidated theaters and factories can be made luminous and eerie through camera filters. The beauty in such images often comes from the aestheticization of abandonment.

And based on Thompson's video, one might expect that the Amtrak facility in Beech Grove would be one such place: derelict, abandoned, or rarely used. But Beech Grove is no ruin: its parking lot full, it hums with activity throughout the week. The FEMA camp story is more about our own sense of estrangement from the things that surround us. FEMA camps emerge as something like the antithesis of ruin porn: things that should be derelict but that aren't, that still have life even after the viewer has decided that they should be abandoned.

It's a question of perspective. Anyone familiar with Amtrak and its workings could look at the Beech Grove depot and see nothing out of the ordinary, but for someone who has never worked on the railroads, any aspect of the work here might be anomalous, anything can be a rea- son to fear. Estranged from this kind of work, the conspiracist sees it all as fundamentally suspicious. Beech Grove is 1,800 miles from Area 51, but the two places share a kinship with each other, and a thousand other places across the country: a sinister and strange wilderness composed of warehouses and big-box stores, hulking structures that surrounds us on every side, an uncanny borderland that has moved out of the deserts and forests and into our backyard.

Into this landscape enters Walmart. When Walmart moves on, they leave behind massive, hulking box stores in their wake, and often these will leave gaping holes in a small town's commercial centers, an eyesore of waste that can neither be ignored nor done away with. These remains, it would seem, have recently become yet another target for FEMA camps.

FEMA camp conspiracists see in their hulking mystique further government malevolence. Emptied out but not torn down, underutilized but not abandoned, they've become prime locations of FEMA camps speculation. In 2017, a YouTube user uploaded a video titled "Closed Walmart FEMA Camp San Jose Sept 2017 Footage," consisting of nothing but a handheld camera shot of the building's exterior. As one user put it in the comments, "The place really does look closed down and RUN down. But those security cameras and what looks to be a future prison camp . . . now THAT is worrisome." When I went to investigate the site myself, the property manager happened to be on site, and he explained that Walmart had wanted a larger building so they could add groceries; the so-called prison camp was currently in the process of being renovated for a fitness center. But it is the combination of a currently disused building and security cameras that seems to trigger conspiracy theorists, who maintain a perfectly ordinary facet of the building has become immediately sinister after the building closed. But the locus for this particular paranoia is a crumbling infrastructure, a decaying industrialization, and the Rust Beltification of America.

This is the new wilderness, the new uncanny. "Big box structures are ephemeral in their usage, and their aesthetic is designed to convey temporality," architecture critic Julia Christensen writes. "Big box buildings exist in our attention's blind spot and also in the blind spot of memory. 'When was this building constructed?' and 'How long has this building been here empty in the middle of your town?' are questions I must have asked three hundred times in the last few years. And usually the reply is, 'I don't know. I can't remember when it was built. I can't remember when it was vacated.' Despite its sheer hulk and centrality, people apparently do not notice big box buildings in their direct line of attention or memory. Perhaps the designers of big box buildings hope that the featureless structures will just fade into the landscape, so that communities will not express concern over their appearance or their vacancy."

One of the way conspiracies function is by taking the ordinary and suddenly devoting an inordinate amount of attention to it. Just as taking an ordinary word and repeating it endlessly will make it sound strange and foreign, so too will focusing intently on the mundane often make it feel sinister, haunted, conspicuous. Big-box stores are designed not to be noticed, to fade into the background; by consciously noticing them, they became strange and terrifying.

Most conspiracy theories are nothing but theories—paranoid fantasies, anxieties given shape. But every so often, the strangeness of the world catches up to them—and overtakes them. In 2018, whistleblowers and journalists revealed that hundreds of immigrant children were being forcibly separated from their parents and housed in mass detention camps, in an effort (according to President Trump's then chief of staff John Kelly and then attorney general Jeff Sessions) to discourage refugees seeking asylum in the United States. Under harsh fluorescents kept on twenty-four hours a day, children were at times administered psychotropic drugs without their consent.

One of the sites that received widespread attention was located in Brownsville, Texas, where migrant children slept on cots without word of their parents or when they would see release. Here some 1,500 children lived in a nightmare dystopia, the closest thing to a concentration camp on US soil since World War II. And the Brownsville detention center, the press later revealed, was a repurposed Walmart.

PART V

THE POSTAPOCALYPTIC HANGOVER

———————◆———————

Reality denied comes back to haunt.

—PHILIP K. DICK,
FLOW MY TEARS, THE POLICEMAN SAID

[25]

THE COMFORTS OF LEMURIA

Before I'm out of the car, Conrad is walking out to meet me. A member of the board of directors of the Lemurian Fellowship, he's been here for almost fifty years. A kindly, easygoing man, he takes me over to a patio set underneath the shade of a pine tree, where we talk of ancient civilizations and lost continents.

In the early years of the twenty-first century, the popularity of fringe theories regarding aliens, cryptids, and lost continents all seemed to be in decline. Taken less and less seriously, they all started to feel a bit quaint. Reporting at a scantly attended MUFON conference in 2014, Mark Jacobson declared the movement all but over. (His *New York Magazine* dispatch was titled simply "The End of UFOs.") But lately this trend is reversing, fueled by basic cable television shows and new waves of anxiety. I wanted to find out why, which meant more traveling.

I'd traveled from Mount Shasta in California to Darien, Georgia, from New England to Nevada, searching for some kind of tangible evidence, and I'd mostly come up empty-handed. The Sasquatch has retreated into burned and blackened forests, the Lemurians deign not to show themselves to me, and the meat, it seems, has all decayed. But what about the beliefs themselves? Do they remain? I came to Ramona, California, where the last vestiges of the Lemurians are waiting with an outstretched hand, to try to find out.

When the Lemurian Fellowship first came here, there were barely six hundred people living in Ramona. About thirty miles northeast of San Diego, it's a community nestled amid a rocky landscape of chaparral-dotted gulleys and boulder-strewn hillsides. Here a small group inspired by the teachings of a physician and author Robert D. Stelle acquired some land and built a small compound. Stelle claimed he'd received tele-pathic communications about the lost civilization of Lemuria. His wis-dom is now contained primarily in a 1952 book *The Sun Rises*, a bible of sorts for the movement, which tells a *Clan of the Cave Bear*–esque fan-tasy story of primitive humans living on the continent of Lemuria who receive wisdom from an advanced civilization (imagine if it took the ape in *2001: A Space Odyssey* four hundred extremely tedious pages to throw the femur in the air).

The heady smell of red pine needles at our feet, Conrad explains to me the essence of Lemurian teachings: balance. He pulls a small, wooden triangle from his pocket, worn smooth, and tracing his finger along each edge, explains the three essential aspects of humanity: mentality, ideality, and materiality. Lemurian society, he explains, worked out a balance of these three forces, but after Lemuria began to decline, "some of its people went to Atlantis, and they were more materialistic, so Atlantis was the more materialistic civilization. The mental group wound up in Egypt, so that was more of a mentalist society. And India was the more idealistic, spiritualist society." The Lemurian Fellowship now focuses on these three civilizations: each was out of balance in a different way, they reason, so by studying each they might be better able to rediscover that perfect Lemurian balance. Through correspondence courses, the fellowship promises to teach you the skills and wisdom to achieve "a happier outlook on life, with steadily improving mental alertness and the ability to create finer living conditions," a greatly increased "knowledge that will help you know how to handle any situation, the growing ability to be of help to others," a better ability to manage one's health and finances, greater "peace of mind as fears and worries are replaced by knowledge and con-fidence, and a sense of security infiltrates every phase of your life."

What happened to Lemuria? "It declined," Conrad explains, "because in the very early years they brought in people who did not study with the elders. Those people eventually became an element that wasn't interested in really learning anything; they were interested in criticizing things." And then, he notes, "Human problems raised their heads, and other people started down the wrong path, too." All this was revealed to Stelle in the 1930s during the Depression, and it's not lost on me that even in Conrad's gentle version of events there's a legacy of antimigrant labor rhetoric in the fall of Lemuria: a utopian civilization of advanced thinkers brought down by foreign laborers.

It's a small movement—Conrad estimates there are a few dozen in the San Diego area, with hundreds spread out across the globe. He learned about Lemuria from his parents, who were among the first generation of the Lemurian Fellowship. It took him seventeen years to fully become a member of the order (now, he estimates, it takes most people closer to five to seven years). The movement survives by donations from members, fees from their instructional courses, and a woodworking shop that makes and sells housewares and musical supplies. As we walk through the compound, he's pleased to highlight the craftsmanship of the Lemurians: the handmade wooden stands with brass collars and fittings that do look quite handsome.

In the office, I ask about a framed picture of the Last Supper, and Conrad (now joined by a few other Lemurians) explains how they take the best from various world religions and "enhance" them. Then he shows me two framed maps: one, a sonar relief map of the Pacific Ocean floor; the other, the revealed outline of the original continent of Lemuria. That fabled continent contained California, British Columbia, and Alaska on its northeast edge and Australia in its southwest. The mountain ridges that covered the center of Lemuria, Conrad points out, resemble the topography of the ocean floor, though before I can suggest that they do not, in fact, look that much alike, he's quick to add that there's been some shifting in the last twenty-five thousand years, so it's not exact.

The goal is to get me to sign up for the courses, my first step down the path to becoming a Fellow. I'm given some literature and a free CD "for my drive home," and I'm talked into buying a paperback copy of *The Sun Rises*. On top of that, I spend a few bucks on a small key chain trinket like Conrad's.

I've always been partial to fine woodworking, and regardless of one's beliefs the Lemurians make really exemplary products. I'm happy to slide the acacia triangle into my pocket, where it gives me a vague sense of reassurance. But I can't find a way into their religion. I do my best to be polite, which is easy given their unfailingly generous and easygoing nature, but the notion that one must believe in a sunken continent and ancient civilization for these ideas of generosity and benevolence to take hold seems a bridge too far. I can't help thinking of Truman Bethurum's Venusian friend, Aura Rhanes, traveling all this way to tell us the most straightforward moralities.

It's not that the teachings of the Lemurian Fellowship are problematic—in fact, the doctrine seems pretty good, all things considered. But its edifice rests on a clairvoyant revelation from the elders of a lost civilization that never existed. Why, I found myself wondering, does one need to accept the sunken continent hypothesis to accept Stelle's ideas? In trying to make the leap out of straightforward self-help, Stelle relied on what he saw as a transcendental source that could not be questioned. It seems less about sunken geology than it does about the reassurance of an unimpeachable source of authority.

● ● ●

I f the Lemurian Fellowship itself seems a dying, vestigial remnant of a passé cosmology, many of those original ideas continue to be wildly popular. Indeed, if one is seeking the descendants of Madame Blavatsky, look not to remote cults in the California wilds, but to the History Channel and its most popular and long-running show, *Ancient Aliens*.

"Could alien beings really be living on planet Earth hidden inside mountains?" the narrator Robert Clotworthy breathlessly wonders. "And, if so, might they have built advanced civilizations, not only within Mount Shasta but in mountains across the world?" Since launching in 2010, *Ancient Aliens* has become a phenomenon and Giorgio Tsoulakos an icon, with his towering hair and a well-known meme of him midsentence with the caption, "I'm not saying it was aliens . . . but it was aliens." At a June 2018 AlienCon, a convention for fans of the show, Tsoulakos was feted as a celebrity: people lined up for photographs and autographs while vendors hawked bobblehead dolls of Tsoulakos and his stratospherically teased hair.

It took *Ancient Aliens* until season 6 in 2013 to turn its attention to Mount Shasta, in an episode titled "Aliens and Mysterious Mountains," but when it finally got there, it tackled the question with gusto. Author Nick Redfern was just one among many talking heads recruited to hypothesize about the mountain's Lemurian possibilities. "Over the years, there have been a number of very significant U. F. O. sightings around Mount Shasta," Redfern tells us. Kathleen McGowan, a mystic who's claimed to be descended from Jesus and Mary Magdalene, refers to Frederick Spencer Oliver's *A Dweller in Two Planets*: "A book came out in the 1890s proposing the idea that there was a culture that lived within subterranean chambers in Mount Shasta." Another talking head, conspiracy theorist Tim Swartz, predictably ties these ideas to "local Native American" beliefs.

What draws people to *Ancient Aliens* is the sense that there's wonder and mystery in ancient history, that the past—a foreign continent that can never be reached—can be whatever we dream it to be. Behind a lot of this belief is something archaeologist David S. Anderson called a "Golden Age Story." "The past is a mythic landscape," he told me. "People can paint what they want to on the past, because it's far enough away that people can make it look whatever they like. People always want to believe that things used to be better, so it resonates for people who want to believe that there was a golden time"—a time-tested message in

American politics, as Anderson noted, quoting Donald Trump's ubiquitous campaign slogan: Make America Great Again.

Anderson has focused much of his research and scholarship on debunking pseudo archaeology. "In general the professional field has dismissed it until the last few years," he told me. "But if we never talk about it we cede the territory, and if no one's out there talking about it we lose the ground." At the same time Erich von Däniken's *Chariot of the Gods?* was first taking hold in a public consciousness, the profession of archaeology was changing—the introduction of radiocarbon dating radically affected the work of archaeologists, who could now more definitively date past civilizations. What became known as processual archaeology stopped focusing on merely digging up artifacts and describing them, and instead turned to making archaeology into more of a hard science, focusing on laws and models that could determine facts about the past beyond a shadow of a doubt.

This shift came at the same time that universities as a whole were transitioning to a more insular, professionalized model. Academics were rewarded professionally for contributions to their disciplines, but not for work that reached a broader public. All of these developments, like a perfect storm, combined to more or less cede the popular understanding of archaeology to amateurs like Tsoulakos (who boasts of not having an archaeology degree) and his mystical alien gods.

Ancient Aliens traffics in the notion that ancient creation myths and stories from literature represent not the religions or art of these earlier cultures, but literal fact. In an age when we ourselves are surrounded by such a flourishing of art and literature of all kinds, how can it be that all their art and culture was nothing but documentary? The sheer abundance of our own imaginative endeavors ought to give us pause before assuming our ancestors lacked any creativity, as John Napier pointed out. "Will H. G. Wells's dreams of interplanetary travel be taken, in the future, as evidence of their reality in the early twentieth century?" he asks, when presented with theories that ancient civilizations depicted literal Bigfoots. "And will the paintings of Salvador Dalí be paraded as proof that even in those far-off days the ancients knew how to make flexible watches?" The desire to *prove* a thing exists, in other words, is also a desire to circumscribe human imagination, a refusal to accept that we make the world as we are made by it. It is a rejection of the creativity inherent in human culture. When we seek proof of aliens in the human cultural imagination, we may be enchanting the world, but we do so at the cost of disenchanting our own humanity.

In a companion book to the *Ancient Aliens* series entitled *The Search for Alien Life: Who Shaped Our World?* a sidebar titled "Monkeys *Not* in the Middle" makes clear the stakes here, with the none-too-subtle nod to creationism and the Scopes Monkey Trial. After rehashing a quick summary of how we went from a geocentric model of the universe to first a heliocentric model, and then one of multiple solar systems, galaxies, and even universes, the text concludes: "This fact that we are less special than previously believed has been a hard pill to swallow for many, but on the flip side, it makes the odds that we are alone in the universe seem to be very slim indeed. And that is exciting news to those searching for extra-terrestrial life." Motivated by anxiety over the vastness of the universe and the potential randomness of humanity's existence, ancient aliens proponents respond by positing some external, mythical force behind our origin and our civilizations' development—beliefs that restore a sense of order and meaning in the world.

As Kevin Burns, *Ancient Aliens'* creator and producer, puts it, the show isn't "about little green men in outer space. That's the three-headed snake lady that gets you into the tent. It's really a show about looking for God. Science would have you believe we are the result of nothing more than a chance assemblage of matter. The real truth is we don't know." The sleight of hand in that final assertion is what archaeologists and scientists like Anderson find so galling: why must these vital metaphysical questions ne-cessitate the denial of the very real facts that scientists do know?

There is no amount of fact-checking, no litany of scientific assertions, that can directly confront this anxiety, this fear that some have that science has pushed us off an existential cliff of nihilism. Like all conspiracy theories, ancient-aliens theories can't be combated with just fact because they are products of belief.

*   *   *

Like a repressed memory, Lemuria continues to rise up out of the murky waters of popular consciousness in odd ways. Take Sean David Morton, for example, who offered tours of Area 51 during the early years of this millennium while peddling instant debt relief via a workshop called "The Sovereign Factor: The Revolution Starts with You." Morton encouraged people to simply declare their emancipation from the government, and that with the right amount of forms filed, one's student loans, tax bills, and property mortgages would simply be erased. As a member of what's become known as the sovereign citizen movement, a fringe community that argues that they are not bound by traffic laws, tax bills, or court decisions, Morton filed four years of fraudulent tax returns from 2005 to 2008, in the process claiming $4 million in tax refunds. The scheme worked well enough at first: in April of 2007, the IRS deposited more than $480,000 in his and his wife's bank account. Morton went on to peddle a mutual fund based on his psychic abilities, and attracted some one hundred investors who gave him more than $6 million, which finally got the attention of the government, who won an $11.5 million judgment against him in 2013. He responded with a series of phony legal filings and further attempts to bilk his followers out of money, all the while maintaining that the government had no legal sovereignty over him.

At least one of the reasons he argued this was that he was not a United States national, but was, in fact, an ambassador from the Republic of New Lemuria. In a legal filing from 2013, he told the judge that he was afforded all the legal protection due any ambassador, based on the Vienna Convention on Diplomatic Relations of 1961; as such, he

claimed, he was not under the jurisdiction of any US court. The Republic of New Lemuria, it turns out, is not much more than a post office box
in the San Fernando Valley of Los Angeles. It claims possession of the
Bokak Atoll, the most remote atoll in the Marshall Islands, but this is
bogus and the judge in Morton's case was notably unimpressed with his
claims of diplomatic immunity.

Meanwhile, while all this pseudoscience and wish fulfillment was
continuing to proliferate over the past few years, in a quiet bit of news
that was hardly noticed, Lemuria was found.

In 2013, geologists announced the island of Mauritius bore the geologic traces of an earlier continent that had since broken up. Despite the
fact that Mauritius is only a few million years old, geologist Bjorn Jamtveit and his team, examining microscopic soil samples, found evidence
of zircon dating back 3 billion years, suggesting that Mauritius may be
the remnant of a larger continent that separated during a shift in plate
tectonics. Jamtveit and his fellow researchers called their discovery Mau-
ritia, but it would, if real, vaguely map onto the rough area where Sclater
had predicted Lemuria to be. That being said, Jamtveit's hypothesis
wouldn't validate Sclater's lemur theory, since this proposed landmass
would have disintegrated long before lemurs evolved. The researchers
also estimated that their sunken continent was about a quarter of the
size of Madagascar—so hardly a continent at all. In fact, it might have
been part of a larger continent that also included both Madagascar and
India, called Rodinia. Nonetheless, news outlets ran with various sensational headlines, including LEMURIA: THE FABLED LOST CONTINENT THAT
TURNED OUT TO BE REAL—ALMOST, writing up Jamtveit's findings while
relying heavily on the history of Sclater's Lemuria.

But the revelations about this actual (sort of) Lemuria are a reminder
of how much wonder there is left in the natural world, how much we're
still discovering about our planet, and how much mystery remains in the
actual landscape and soil. For many of us, this is enough: the wonders of
the natural world fascinate and inspire in a myriad of ways. Many more,
though, will look and turn away disappointed, finding no proof of utopia

or God in fragments of zircon. The main and central difference hinges on the question of what you expect out of the natural world: do you see it as a wondrous and strange thing unto itself, or do you expect it to reveal humanity back to itself? The problem with geologic samples is that the place revealed by them has no direct symbolic value. The crime of mainstream science, for too many, is the revelation that the world owes us nothing.

The need for imagined marginal worlds populated with monsters and enlightened humans is a deep-seated one that's going to persist, but it's at odds with the world of strange wonder that's all around us. Like Atlantis, the geologic underpinnings of Lemuria have always been beside the point. Lemuria is a perpetual edgeworld—a place to exist in the mind and on the map but never to be glimpsed or realized. It's a vast unknown onto which you can project your own theories, biases, beliefs, anxieties, and hopes—all without fear that you'll ever have to provide evidence one way or another. Lemuria, if it exists at all, exists now in my pocket, in a small triangle of wood polished with belief.

[26]

UNDER THE SIGN OF THE COELACANTH

A rainy, early spring day in Gloucester, Massachusetts. The whole town seems to be holding its breath for the tourist season, just about to begin. For months the town has sheltered in place through the winter, like any seaside town—half the houses empty, the businesses with reduced hours. Any weekend now, though, the tourists will be back, breathing life once more into Cape Ann.

Down on Cressy Beach, on a shoal of rocks beneath a promontory, there is a mural of the sea serpent. On a large boulder that marks the end of the beach, a long, loosely coiled creature that looks a bit like the ampersand on the Dungeons and Dragons logo. It has four stubby legs, each with ferocious claws, and a long jaw and red sliver of a tongue. Robert Stephenson had only graduated from high school when he painted the beast in 1955, before joining the Army. After he retired, he returned to Gloucester and formally began his training as a painter, and became a local fixture until his death in 2013. Stephenson's sea serpent mural, likewise, has become a fixture of the community, perhaps more so than the monster itself. And truth be told, it looks very little like the descriptions recorded during that 1817 summer, whose dominating feature was the humps rising out of the water. This serpent, its long body spilling onto itself like a pile of rigging, lacks that simple elegance—though it has its own dragonlike charm.

No one here wants to talk about the sea serpent. The docent at the Maritime Museum has heard about it, of course—everyone has—but it's just some local legend. It doesn't mean anything. At two different bookstores I stop into, nobody knows much about the sea serpent, but they both point me to the book Wayne Soini's *The Gloucester Sea Serpent*. It is everywhere books are sold. It seems to be all Gloucester wants to say about their sea serpent. Soini refers to the botched taxonomy job by the New England Linnaean Society as a "flop": "because a Loblolly Cove snake distracted and confused" the committee, they "lost their chance at scientific acclaim." The story of the sea serpent has become a story of a committee duped by a rickety snake and the limitations of taxonomy.

But the sea serpent's tale is more than just a failure, and any serious discussion of cryptozoology should have the Gloucester sea serpent front and center. It may not have the pull of Nessie, or Bigfoot, or even Lake Champlain's Champ. It doesn't even have a diminutive nickname. It's just the sea serpent. But it is, I think it's fair to say, special.

Most cryptid sightings are one-on-one occurrences: someone alone at night, on a backcountry road or in an isolated woods. Sometimes it's a small group. Maybe there's a fuzzy photograph, but soon enough the creature vanishes, never to return. But the Gloucester sea serpent was different. Scores of people saw it—people came from all over, gathered on the shore to gawk, and there it was. Visible from shore or from a boat, exactly as expected. Different people on different days, all independently, all with more or less the same basic descriptions. No other cryptid in the long history of such beasts can boast such visibility—not Bigfoot, not Nessie.

Whatever it was, it was not a hoax or a hallucination. The Gloucester sea serpent faded from memory because the New England Linnaean Society got it wrong, creating a new species based on a snake plagued by rickets. When their error was exposed, the original sightings, it seems, were forgotten. But while Jacob Bigelow's analysis of the rickety snake disproved the holotype specimen, Bigelow didn't disprove the sightings themselves. The people who saw the sea serpent all agreed it was much bigger than a normal snake anyway.

The sightings defy all of the modern tropes for cryptid sightings, and yet the sea serpent has none of the cachet that other cryptids do. It seems possible, a rationalist could argue, that it was an oarfish, or some other animal that's since been cataloged. It would be impossible to know for sure, of course, since we have nothing but those eyewitness reports. But this is as good a story as cryptozoologists are likely to find, in terms of the preponderance of evidence. Why doesn't it get more love? Two hundred miles north of here, there might be an answer.

∘ ∘ ∘

Loren Coleman's International Cryptozoology Museum in Portland, Maine, remains the hub for all things Sasquatch and Nessie, as it has since 2003. It's moved locations over the years, but is now situated in a relatively new development called Thompson's Point—there's a wine bar and a taco joint, and a pretty busy brunch spot, along with an adjacent concert venue. It feels like one of those shopping/nightlife destinations that hasn't quite materialized yet. Inside, the narrow museum doesn't occupy much square footage, but is crammed to the gills with stuff. The Jersey Devil, New England's water monsters, and all manner of Wild Men are represented here.

Disappointingly, though, a good deal of the exhibits are pop culture ephemera—action figures, lunch boxes, movie posters—which tend to overwhelm the newspaper clippings and other "evidence." At times it feels like one is in a comic-book store rather than a museum—there are a few cast footprints and grainy photos here and there, but it's best not to visit the International Cryptozoology Museum hoping to be convinced by the preponderance of documentation.

That doesn't mean that Coleman himself isn't serious about his work. Indeed, Coleman is the last of a long legacy—he got interested in cryptozoology in his teens, and now is the last living remnant of that earlier age of heroic adventurers like Tom Slick, who plunged into the wilderness in hopes of glory. He's published dozens of books on crypto-zoology, and while his writings often veer toward the speculative, he nonetheless has maintained credibility as residing on the scientific end of cryptozoology. In a disreputable field, Coleman remains among the most reputable.

I've come to the Third Annual International Cryptozoology Confer-ence to see where the future of monster hunting lies. There are a good fifty or so attendees this Labor Day weekend; more than you can find at some other venues, but less so than you might expect. The vendors' ta-bles are a bit sparse—not more than two dozen in all. If this was once a major destination, it is no longer. During the breaks between the talks, a surf rock band obliterates any chance of conversation, their riffs echo-ing through the open hall, ricocheting off the concrete and steel at deafening levels.

The logo of the conference this year is a giant panda. Thought by zoologists in the West to be mythical until 1869, its story mirrors that of the mascot of the Cryptozoology Museum itself: *Latimeria chalum-nae*, the coelacanth. When Marjorie Courtenay-Latimer, curator of the East London Museum in South Africa, discovered one in a fisherman's trawling net in 1938, the animal had long been presumed extinct—the fossil record indicated it had last been seen on Earth some 70 million years ago.

Coelacanths and pandas are enticing mascots for cryptozoology, be-cause they remind us that the animal kingdom still holds mystery for us, and there are still creatures—even large, charismatic megafauna—that might be waiting to be found. But they also raise problems, precisely because their circumstances are so different from most cryptid stories. Rather than a blurry photograph or a dubious eyewitness account, the coelacanth appeared in the twentieth century as a corpse, an actual spec-imen that could be studied, documented, preserved. Once scientists went looking for more, they found them. Any potential for a hoax was dispelled as more and more specimens were retrieved, including living specimens, and the animal was documented on film. In other words, unlike cryptids, the panda and the coelacanth refused to remain hidden.

The talks at the conference seem almost of a different time. They don't break much new ground: there's a short film on the Florida skunk ape, a talk on the Beast of Gévaudan, and a lecture by Dawn Prince-Hughes titled "Songs of the Ape People." Most of the speakers rely on the same data set that cryptozoologists have been working for decades: eyewitness accounts, interpolated folklore, occasionally a bent tree or a weird-looking footprint, and some blurry photographs.

Then Todd Disotell gets up. A primatologist at Columbia University, he's a popular figure in the cryptozoology world because, in addition to being a gregarious speaker and all-around genial guy, he seems more willing than many of his colleagues to take amateur cryptozoologists seriously. In 2014, he cohosted the reality show *10 Million Dollar Bigfoot Bounty*, in which Bigfoot hunters sought evidence of the cryptid's existence that would stand up to scientific scrutiny. (None did.)

Still, the audience is friendly toward Disotell, who shares their sense of adventure and their love of the undiscovered. He starts by discussing the Tapanuli orangutan, an extremely rare species that lives in a single forest in Sumatra; only in the past ten years was this species identified as distinct from other orangutans, and though their numbers are small (critically endangered, their population is estimated at eight hundred), they are nonetheless a newly discovered species. In other words, Disotell tells the audience that there are still unknown primates waiting to be found. We haven't fully exhausted the world's largesse.

But it's also a not so subtle rebuke of the way Bigfoot hunters continue to go about their work. Building to an exasperated crescendo, Disotell tells the audience, "Stop sending me hair samples and grainy photographs!" If Bigfoot hunters want to be taken seriously, he exclaims, they need quality video, a body (or at least a body part), a live specimen. Plaster casts of footprints simply won't cut it.

What Disotell's talk makes plain is that the tried-and-true methods

of documentation among cryptozoologists—footprint casts, blurry photographs, lone eyewitness accounts, shaky video—are not only unaccept-
able as proof of a new species, but increasingly anachronistic in a world
of high-definition cell-phone cameras. If a Bigfoot—or a sea serpent, or
a giant bird, or Nessie—is really out there, there's simply no excuse anymore for not being able to get a good, clear video of the dang thing.
Cryptozoology, in many ways, seems stuck at an impasse—mainstream
science has repeatedly evaluated the kinds of evidence that cryptozoologists have offered, and rejected it as insufficient. Cryptozoologists,
meanwhile, have doubled down.

How do you bring together the antiscience cryptid hunters with folks
like Disotell, who are trying to remain open-minded while continuing
to insist on some kind of actual evidence? The fact remains that there
are new species being discovered every day, things that would in another
context easily fall under the heading of cryptozoology, and yet these
things remain outside the sphere of interest for cryptid enthusiasts. At
the same time, those things proffered by Sasquatch hunters as incontrovertible evidence remain uninteresting for scientists, precisely because
they're anything but incontrovertible. The two communities remain at
odds, talking past each other.

◦ ◦ ◦

Meanwhile, a new creature has been seen stalking the woods of
North America. Dogman gets described in multiple ways: either
as a canine-looking creature walking upright or a Bigfoot type with an
elongated snout. Though Dogman believers claim that evidence of the
creature may go back to ancient Egypt (the dog-faced god Anubis, some
claim, is actually a literal cryptid), in the cryptid lore it's a far more recent
development. Most contemporary Dogman legends can be traced back
to a Michigan DJ, Steve Cook of WTCM-FM in Traverse City. For
April Fool's Day 1987, Cook recorded a song about the Dogman called
"The Legend," basing it on Native American accounts he'd come across.

Cook received calls from listeners who'd claimed to actually have seen the thing, and after an appearance in 2010 on an episode of *Monster-Quest*, the Dogman broke out of Michigan and began to appear throughout North America.

It's described as significantly more dangerous than Bigfoot—whereas the latter is a gentle, silent, solitary figure, Dogman seems threatening and aggressive. A report from Broome County, New York, collected on the website Dogman Encounters, comes from a woman who came home with her two children to an eerie silence, creeping her out and prompting her to grab her children and bolt for the door. While she fumbled to get her house key in the door, she heard a low growl coming from her left: "As the growl continued," she recounted, "it seemed to melt into audible words, spoken in a very deep and gruff tone, that seemed to have a rough sort of reverberation quality to them. What I heard as clear as day was, 'You can't get in.' The only word that I'm unsure of is the first, 'You,' as the sound of growl transitioned to English words and it sounded more like 'Yyyyhhh.'"

Until I started talking to contemporary cryptozoologists, I'd never heard of Dogman before—it doesn't show up in the traditional accounts and doesn't have the storied history of a water monster or the Jersey Devil. But Dogman's popularity is on the rise these days. For Blake Smith, cohost of the skeptic podcast *MonsterTalk,* it's a noteworthy shift, because, as he notes, "There is no evolutionary basis for bipedal canids and the whole Dogman thing feels a lot more like a supernatural or magical (or folklore) type of event." Descriptions of a menacing figure that can speak English certainly departs far from the standard cryptid description, and Dogman's rising popularity suggests that cryptozoology may be veering toward what Smith calls "magical and ultraterrestrial thinking" in cryptozoology. "I see that as bad for anybody who wants to really bag one of these things for scientific study because it's hard enough to get people with scientific credentials interested in doing fieldwork around cryptids. Nobody's getting grant money to study werewolves—which is basically what Dogman seems to be."

The Dogman appears to blend into the supernatural rather than merely the untaxonomized. It is as if the impasse that defined cryptozoology—between the blue-collar adventurers and the would-be scientists—has finally given way; those who now pronounce the Dogman as a viable cryptid are no longer seeking to prove science. They're now closer to paranormal investigators than scientists. This is a shame for those hanging on and trying to do serious scientific work outside the academy, but it's also possible that this may be for the best—particularly if you look at someone like Henry H. Bauer.

● ● ●

A belief in the reality of Nessies is not harmful," Bauer wrote in 1986 in his book *The Enigma of Loch Ness*. Bauer, who at the time was a professor of chemistry at Virginia Tech and would go on to be the dean of its College of Arts and Sciences, worked hard in his early career to distinguish between harmless speculation and dangerous conspiracy. Questions of "quackery in medical matters (psychic surgery, extreme forms of faith healing, laetrile, and so forth) or of cults led by fanatics or impostors," are one thing, he notes, but belief "in cryptozoological phenomena—Loch Ness monsters, sea serpents, Bigfoot, Mokele-Mbembe (dinosaurs in Africa)—seems to me singularly harmless."

But the problem with fringe beliefs is that often one conspiracy begets another: once you've decided that the consensus is wrong about a given arena of scientific knowledge, it's easier to cast suspicion on other consensus beliefs as well, and once you've made the choice to doubt mainstream science, it can be hard to pick and choose which orthodoxies to discard.

It's true that Bauer's interest in Nessiedom is itself fairly harmless (as is the interest of anyone else who spends their days taking sonar readings in the Loch), but since he began his fascination with the mysterious water beast, Bauer has himself ventured into murkier waters. After retiring from Virginia Tech, Bauer became the editor of the *Journal of Scientific*

Exploration, which focused on various fringe studies, including paranormal activity, UFOs, ESP, and so forth. Under Bauer's direction the journal also began to publish pseudoscientific critiques of AIDS research, and Bauer ultimately published his own AIDS denialist hypothesis. Though Bauer has never done any research on AIDS or HIV, his book became a major citation by AIDS denialists, who used it to bolster their unfounded claims that "many of the epidemiological aspects of HIV . . . are literally incompatible with the hypothesis that it causes AIDS." Bauer's credentials and his ability to mimic the pose and rhetoric of serious scholarship while not engaging in any direct research on AIDS have had a devastating effect.

In Loch Ness Bauer found what he perceived to be the arrogance of the scientific edifice: "The Loch Ness affair well illustrates, I believe, some general and important aspects of the interaction of science with the wider society; for example, that science generally dismisses (at first, at least) claims by laymen of unusual events, phenomena, or theories; that outsiders can rarely induce scientists to take such things seriously; and that the interested observer finds it difficult to make sense of the ensuing argument and to reach a reasonable judgment." It didn't matter that this was an institution that he himself had once been a part of as a notable chemist; the refusal of mainstream science to take the possibility of Nessie seriously was a glaring act of hubris, one that cast into doubt much of scientific orthodoxy.

"To find a circumstantially made case compelling," Bauer admits, "one must be prepared to see coherence, a pattern of relationship, among phenomena that are not incontrovertibly related." Taking as his truth the existence of Nessie forced an entirely new mode of inquiry, one based on circumstantial evidence and blurred photographs, one that required discounting the scientific method and ignoring the absence of evidence. Once down that road, Bauer was prone to allow his homophobic views to guide his skepticism toward the AIDS narrative, to the detriment of science.

So long as fringe belief is engaged with mainstream, institutionalized science, there is a tension that threatens to spill over past shadowy water creatures and bipedal apes. The further divorced cryptozoology becomes from science, perhaps the less likely it will be to actively disrupt scientific consensus.

It's not that there aren't cryptids out there to be found—but they won't be mythical monsters. The Gloucester sea serpent has lost its fascination for us because it's been bested by even weirder things we've since found in the ocean: deep-sea isopods, colossal squids, feathered lobsters—things that are beautiful and strange but that still belong in the realms of taxonomy. These creatures do not exist for our own symbolic matrix. Just as geologic evidence of the real "Lemuria" has little to do with the mythical civilizations of Lemuria, the new species discovered constantly by scientists have no symbolic meaning for ourselves, as the natural world once did.

Our disappointment with the natural world has to do with the fact that it no longer serves to reflect back our values and fears to us. Moving away from cryptids involves more than just a reaffirmation of objective science and verifiable evidence—it will take reconceptualizing the world away from a sense that Man and his God are at the center of all things, and that all things exist to reflect us back to ourselves.

[27]

ELEGIES

Temperatures were pushing one hundred when I arrived in Albuquerque, but by that night a storm had moved across northern New Mexico, and Santa Fe was cool and rainy throughout the weekend. The high deserts of northern New Mexico and Arizona don't require much imagination to make them feel foreign—the light here feels neon, electrified somehow, and the rows of adobe-bunker houses could be alien as well as anything else. Add to this the fact that the American Southwest, even in its population centers like Albuquerque, is infused at every level with a highly secretive military-industrial complex that, over the course of decades, has resulted in a quasi-mystical component that runs through the entire land.

It was mid-June, and the Dulce Base Conspiracy Symposium was taking place, down by the farmers' market. An all-day affair dedicated to a serious question of what was happening under the Archuleta Mesa and what had happened to Paul Bennewitz, it featured three speakers: Greg Valdez, whose father Gabe Valdez had investigated cattle mutilations with Bennewitz; Greg Bishop, who's written perhaps the most comprehensive account of Bennewitz's story, *Project Beta*; and Christian Lambright, whose book *X Descending* tries to explain what it might have been that Bennewitz was really photographing over Kirtland.

"If all you know is what someone else told you," Lambright says at one point, "you don't know anything." It's a statement that both rings true and seems to undermine the entire day. After all, we've been sitting for six hours listening to other people tell us things. It's a paradox that runs through the entire community: a dogged insistence on empirical, firsthand evidence, combined with a willingness to believe others' interpretations.

A recurrent thread is the notion that there's always *more* to the story, there's always another rabbit hole to go down. The cattle mutilations aren't being discussed here, but they're an important part of the story, Valdez reiterates, and you should do your own research on them. The National Institute for Discovery Science (NIDS) is important, but we're not going to dwell on it here—you should go do your own research about that. Information is like an underground base, a rabbit warren of tunnels that lead ever onward, a labyrinth of ideas.

Among the more fascinating elements of the day is the level of disagreement among the speakers—"We have things we disagree with, but that's okay because we're all looking for the same thing," Bishop says at one point, though he'll later suggest that anything involving aliens and the government is worth ignoring, something Lambright will more or less discount in his own talk.

People have different ideas as to who's responsible—for some, it's the Air Force, for others, it's the CIA. Bishop notes in his book that several of the early, faked memos by the Air Force mentioned NASA involvement: "The AFOSI trick had the effect of deflecting inquiries away from Kirtland and to an agency (NASA) who could plausibly and rightfully deny that they had any interest." The longer, stranger, and more convoluted this narrative has become, the more of a need there is to point fingers. Any good conspiracy theory is like a shark: it can never stop moving, and it's always on the hunt for new targets. Myrna Hansen is suggested by multiple speakers to have been a plant of the government, part of the same disinformation campaign involving Doty and eventually Moore. ("I will go out on a limb here and say that the story of Myrna Hansen was probably a well-orchestrated hoax," Greg Valdez writes in his book about his father, *Dulce Base: The Truth and Evidence from the Case Files of Gabe Valdez*.)

Overall, a great deal of the day is also given over to wild speculation. Photos of a hunting tower on the edge of a clearing are described as having bulletproof windows. (How do you identify that glass is or isn't bulletproof from fifty feet away?) There is a consistent demeanor of sober paranoia: a sense that everything is wrong and nothing is innocent, but that the best way to approach this creeping dread is with the dispassion of a scientist.

At some point the talks devolved into repeated scrutiny of grainy, empty photographs by Paul Bennewitz taken in 1979 and 1980. Two photographs taken in Dulce had ghostly blurs swiping across the frame, diagonally downward, as though they might be some kind of craft caught on camera, but in both cases the blurs not only streak through the background, but also the foreground, cutting across a pine trunk— an impossibility if this was a craft of some kind, but perfectly consistent with some kind of chemical error or smudge on the negative. Other photos are fed through endless Photoshop filters, changing shape and color until some kind of new meaning can be tortured out of them.

Mostly, though, the entire day is something of an elegy for Paul Bennewitz, the figure around whom the entire axis of UFO history rotates. No matter how wild the theories get, how knowing the looks, no one here ever loses sight of the very human tragedy at the heart of all of this. As Valdez writes in his book, "The tragic part of this story is the fact that many people dismiss or forget about what happened to Paul," not to mention the ranchers who lost cattle. "There was no reason the Air Force and the other agencies involved had to ruin anyone's life because of an aircraft or a science experiment that most Americans could not care about." We never get so far down the rabbit hole that we forget that these were human beings whose lives were changed—in some cases ruined—by the very work that we've all gathered here to do. Even as we peer ever closer at Bennewitz's photographs, you can't shake the fact that he looked too closely into the abyss, and the abyss looked back.

At one point in the documentary *Mirage Men*, Richard Doty says of Bennewitz, "He was a veteran, and people like that are easy to fool." It is perhaps the most naked display of Doty's cynicism—and, by extension, the government's cynicism toward its own service members. It also, though, hints at the connection between post-traumatic stress disorder and conspiracy, since both involve a hypervigilance that can't be shut off, and an uncontrollable assumption that nothing is innocent, that threats are everywhere, and that everything has heightened meaning. The post-Watergate era, the post-AIDS era, the post-9/11 era: we have become a nation of PTSD, a nation that cannot shut off the hunt for meaning and terror in each and every thing.

There was a time when the story of UFOs and aliens followed a relatively static timeline: there were the acknowledged greatest hits, from Kenneth Arnold to Roswell to Thomas Mantell to the Hills to Whitley Strieber and on and on. Each version both built on what had come before and altered the story ever so slightly. But since the 1990s, without the core of prominent, seemingly objective researchers in groups like MUFON, aliens have become something different. According to the website Locklip.com, devoted to news of aliens and UFOs, there are at least six different alien species currently living among us. The Short Grays are the most well known, responsible for the majority of abductions of humans. They are the subordinates to the Tall Grays, who are "always present at any diplomatic agreements with the global shadow government," Locklip reports. Far more dangerous are the Alpha Draconians, a race of giant lizardlike humanoids with sinister plans for the human race, and their minions, the Annunaki and the Native Reptilians. Only the Sirians seem to pose no threat to humanity, having not only gifted us with their technology but also having been responsible for directing the rescue operations during the sinking of Atlantis. The main questions these days are which ones are friendly and which ones are hostile—and exactly how dangerous this latter group is.

There's no attempt to verify any of this, of course—this kind of belief has become self-selecting, a venue for those who've adapted the wide variety of mythology and conspiracy to fit their own purposes. Alien conspiracy theories have branched into hundreds of directions over the past few decades, taking all possible shapes and casts.

Aliens, after all, still manage to fill psychological needs. They can offer the threat of an apocalyptic ending (*War of the Worlds*), a superintelligent force indicting humanity's failures (*This Island Earth*), or the simple reassurance that we are not alone out there (*Contact*). For abductees, aliens offer something else: a sense of specialness, a uniqueness that sets them apart from those around them. Aliens, in short, are a black box (or perhaps a black obelisk) whose identity and definition can be tailored to different conceptions and fantasies. If you tend toward the dystopian, they are aggressive world-destroyers; if you need solace in knowing you're not alone, they're there for you, too. Cryptids fill a sense of wonder in the natural world, but aliens are far more adaptable, and much more ready to fulfill our yearnings for the sublime.

The increasingly complex taxonomy that has come to define the various extraterrestrial races supposedly warring for the soul of the planet suggests the various ways in which the fantastical, the bizarre, and the wondrous have tried to leapfrog over our dogged attempt to see everything as manifestations of ourselves. To the Theosophists' cosmos, in which every alien looked like a Nazi poster boy, the Hills added something strange and upsetting—but something that could transcend how we understood humanity and racial classifications. No sooner had we seized on this possibility, though, than did the Grays become ourselves once more, with their technology and parasitism. So more and more creatures had to be added to the cosmology, one by one, until we had a panoply of races and warring factions, always trying to get out of the limitations of ourselves.

Back in Albuquerque with an hour to kill before my flight home, I stopped at the nearby National Museum of Nuclear Science and History. Chartered by the US Congress and designated as a repository for America's nuclear history, there is a lot of technical information about the size and shape of various bombs, and a lot of quirky tidbits about life at Los Alamos. In addition to the bomb and missile casings, there are a few radioactive artifacts (including Fiesta's orange-red glazed dinnerware, made with uranium oxide). But there is extremely little about downwind radiation effects or any legacy of the fallout of subsequent nuclear testing throughout the Southwest.

The museum's motto is "Reactions welcome," but it quickly becomes clear that there's a strict kind of reaction they're looking for. The museum is set up with a defined path that tells the story of America's nuclear history, and it begins with Nazi and Japanese attempts to build their own atomic weapons, along with recitations of their cruelty and barbarism. From there the Manhattan Project is depicted in its heroic, noble pursuit of scientific achievement, alongside anodyne artifacts and dioramas. There is a small space devoted to the victims of Hiroshima and Nagasaki, but then the viewer is whisked along to a room full of bomb and missile types, replete with specs and factoids. There's no mention of the lingering effects of aboveground testing, or the problems with nuclear waste disposal. The only acknowledgment of problems with nuclear power are in two panels devoted to Chernobyl and Fukushima—neither, notably, in the United States.

If this is how we choose to write our "official" history—deliberately self-serving, actively erasing our faults in favor of our triumphs—is it truly any wonder that so many of us look elsewhere, to fringe beliefs and conspiracies? Even if we should no longer use cryptids, lost continents, or UFOs as a wedge against mainstream science, that doesn't necessarily mean that science has nothing to answer for. The world of paranoid distrust did not arise out of a vacuum. The Tuskegee syphilis experiment, the *Challenger* disaster, the AIDS crisis—again and again science and government have revealed not only their failure to deliver on basic health and safety, but their steadfast refusal to take ownership. Until they do, conspiracies about government cover-ups will continue, and distrust of the scientific establishment will be widespread and often warranted. When there is evidence of a cover-up to spread opioids among the population, it's that much harder to dispel conspiracies about chemtrails.

The story told in the National Museum of Nuclear Science and History—a story of harmless nuclear power, of just and uncomplicated war, of good guys and bad guys—was far, far more ludicrous, bizarre, and unbelievable than anything I'd heard in that small theater in Santa Fe. A country that tells its citizens lies is powerless to defend against competing lies, and the desert of the Southwest has become a territory of endless lies. As Norio Hayakawa said during the symposium: "We just don't know what reality is yet."

[28]

CREATIVE MYTHOLOGY

The UFO Festival of Pine Bush, New York, is filled with the kinds of things you'd find at any street festival: fried food kiosks, local tchotchke sellers, the smell of sunscreen and sweat. Bakeries sell cupcakes, Girl Scouts sell cookies, and a local Baptist church is trying to win converts. But there's also the mounds and mounds of alien-related toys and crapla: ubiquitous green alien balloons, coffee mugs, mouse pads. Vendors include someone selling crystals and another selling light sabers, debating continuity errors in the latest *Star Wars* film with other fans. The street musician is playing themed music, including Elton John's "Rocket Man." The sign on the organic grocery store reads WE COME IN PEAS. One person's T-shirt features a traditional alien face with the words HUMANS AREN'T REAL. Another T-shirt has a very advanced and enlightened-looking alien holding a sign that reads STOP DRONE ATTACKS.

How did this tiny town of less than two thousand, twenty miles from the Hudson River, nestled in a dense forest, become the UFO capital of the East Coast? While it's far from the deserts of New Mexico and Nevada, the Hudson Valley has had its own share of UFO intrigue: in the 1980s, a strange object was repeatedly sighted floating through the night sky. It came to be known as the Hudson Valley Boomerang or the Westchester Triangle, after its general shape and the county where it was most frequently sighted.

In their book *Night Siege*, J. Allen Hynek, Philip J. Imbrogno, and Bob Pratt chronicle the history of the Hudson Valley sightings throughout the 1980s (the authors change the names of the various eyewitnesses in the book, making independent verification a bit difficult; the reproduced stills from various home videos of the supposed craft are likewise barely legible as anything more than VHS scan lines). A retired police officer living in Kent, outside on New Year's Eve, 1982, saw a group of lights—some red, some green, some white—in the sky to the south of him. More sightings followed. A woman living in nearby Lake Carmel had an incident on February 26 of the following year, her car radio turning to static as she came over a low rise, seeing ahead of her a grouping of some fifty lights hovering slowly but deliberately over the hills in the distance.

On March 24, 1983, more than three hundred sightings were recorded, most in Westchester and Putnam counties, and mostly of a large, triangular or boomerang-shaped object, hovering slowly over the towns east of the Hudson River. One witness stated, "I'm a pilot and I'm familiar with all kinds of prop-driven aircraft, and this was not any type of aircraft I'm familiar with, I'm sure of that."

Police in Danbury, Connecticut, knew of similar sightings, *Night Siege*'s authors claimed, but would not speak to them about it. ("Stable people do not report UFOs," the police told them.) Eventually Hynek and his coauthors would find reports of strange occurrences stretching back into the 1950s: "Like the legend of Sleepy Hollow, which lies near the heart of the Hudson Valley sightings, the boomerang-shaped UFO was becoming local history."

No official explanation was ever offered, and it remains unclear what—if anything—was being spotted over the skies of the mid-Hudson region. But one thing is abundantly clear: the sightings were all clustered on the east side of the river, in Putnam and Westchester counties, stretching at times north into Dutchess County and east into Connecticut. Almost no sightings were reported west of the river itself.

Pine Bush isn't in Westchester County; it's in Orange County, west of the Hudson River, on the border of Ulster, and a good hour's drive to Westchester on the interstate. In other words, no matter what one makes of the Westchester Triangle, its story does not involve Pine Bush—at least it didn't, until the sightings had all died down and the region had moved on. Then, in the late 1980s, paranormal researcher Ellen Crystall began coming to Pine Bush, gathering up her photographs and sightings into her 1991 book, *Silent Invasion*, arguing that Pine Bush was the epicenter of something new and disturbing.

Silent Invasion brought Crystall to Joan Rivers, Geraldo, and other talk shows, but failed to make the splash she'd intended; the photographs were too blurry to be taken seriously, and there wasn't much else to substantiate her accounts. She explained away blurry photographs as being tainted by "intentional magnetic or microwave disruptions" by the aliens in order to "camouflage" their craft, but many of the more serious UFO researchers dismissed her book and moved on from the Hudson Valley. One of the few people who took her seriously, geologist Bruce Cornet, would end up further damaging the seriousness of Pine Bush's claim; after taking up Crystall's mantle, Cornet began proclaiming that the region where Pine Bush was located, Wallkill Valley, was an exact replica of the Martian landscape's Cydonia, where the supposed "face" of Mars is located. He dubbed Pine Bush "Cydonia II."

Still, Pine Bush's location—deeply rural yet within an easy drive of a major city—made it an appealing tourist destination. Pine Bush sightings slowly began to grow, even after the Westchester Triangle enthusiasm had died down, and today the people of Pine Bush definitely have their stories. One woman named Kerry who grew up there in the 1990s and 2000s told me one story of when she was a teenager, sleeping over at the house of a friend who lived deep in the woods. In the middle of the night, Kerry says, they were both awakened by "a weird green light" coming from the forest behind them. When I asked if it could have been headlights from a truck or something, she explained that there were no roads back there, no way for a car to get there—plus, she added, "I've never seen anything illuminated in green." After she told her father, he advised her to downplay it and not mention it; her teachers in school likewise tended to tamp down any talk of aliens among the students.

Now the town has begun to embrace its legacy: the Cup and Saucer Diner changed its sign, swapping out the original plate for a UFO pouring light into a coffee cup, and Pine Bush became New York's ground central for extraterrestrials.

On this weekend in June there's no downplaying any of it. In addition to the vendors hoping to cash in on the weirdness, there's a parade of cosplayers and a roster of speakers (the year before Travis Walton was a featured speaker on his experiences). This year Rosemary Ellen Guiley is speaking on "Psychic Protection," Bill Wiand is discussing recent local UFO encounters, MUFON's chief video analyst Marc D'antonio is talking about exoplanets and alien life, and a professor of esoteric studies, Nathan Rosenblum, a Theosophist, is discussing "Orion and Its Inhabitants: Their Role on Earth."

"We can see numerous monuments across the surface of the Earth that reflect knowledge of Orion and its inhabitants on Earth in ancient times," Rosenblum is saying. He's talking about how the pyramids in Egypt and Mexico follow a "belt" pattern—which is to say, any time you see three buildings in a row, there's a tendency by some to take this as evidence that they were built by people in contact with space aliens from Orion. In the speaker's tent people come and go, dropping in for five minutes of this, ten minutes of that, mostly polite and curious but without a real look of engagement. Attendees are offered a variety of beliefs, many of which conflict with one another, but all of which are laid out like a buffet: the great thing about mysticism—as opposed to science or religion—is that believers are free to pick and choose from among the variety of theories and decide which they like and which they discard.

"This is exactly like a powwow for white people," one member of the Bigfoot Researchers of the Hudson Valley says. They're perhaps the most interesting group here at the Pine Bush UFO Fair; the BRHV grew out of a fascination Gayle Beatty had, eventually becoming a small group. They explore the wilds of the Hudson Valley and the Catskills, documenting what they claim to be evidence of Bigfoot, but which is often hard to make out. They note that there are no extant remains of any dead Bigfoot because they bury their dead. They are sometimes contacted by residents who worry that a creature may be disturbing their backyard; the BRHV will come out and leave some kind of peace offering for them.

The BRHV is unusual in that its members are all women; most similar cryptid-hunting groups (or, for that matter, ghost-hunting groups) are male dominated; the emphasis is on the "hunting," even if they don't aim to kill their quarry. As "researchers," perhaps, the BRHV envisions themselves as having a different aim, though in many ways their actual work looks much the same.

But what are these things? According to Debbie Ray, another member of the BHRV, they're aliens. They are slowly making their presence known to humans, though, she says, they're waiting for three crucial steps before they announce their presence. First, complete denuclearization, and second, an end to global warming. Third, they will only communicate with one person, requiring an ambassador who, Ray believes, is the Malaysian astrophysicist Mazlan Othman, formerly the director of the United Nations Office for Outer Space Affairs, though she was replaced in 2014 by the Italian astrophysicist Simonetta di Pippo—presumably the current ambassador to our hirsute alien friends.

This mythology recycles a bit of the 1950s nuclear anxiety for a new age when tensions between the United States and Iran and North Korea run high, but the new twist is, of course, global warming.. Perhaps a limited nuclear exchange between North Korea and the United States doesn't feel as apocalyptic as the full-blown mutually assured destruction of the Cold War, and so it's been paired with another apocalyptic scenario. Or perhaps climate change has simply spiraled so out of control since the halcyon days of the Cold War that our extraterrestrial guests are obligated to point it out to us.

What I found at Pine Bush is what happens when a community has given up on any pretense of science; there is none of the rigor of a crypto-zoologist like Loren Coleman, and none of the kind of investigatory zeal of MUFON. The days of treating Bigfoot and aliens as verifiable, demonstrable figures seem to be fading, and in the wake of the absence of evidence, these concepts are collapsing into each other. No more are cryptids and aliens distinct creatures; now everything is dumped into the same hopper, and believers are free to pick and choose whatever they want.

Pine Bush was not to be the last time I would hear the theory that Bigfoots are actually aliens. At the Dulce Base Conspiracy Symposium, there was an unannounced speaker, a woman named Geraldine from the Jicarilla Apache tribe of Dulce. She and a few other tribal members had come to Santa Fe to help promote another conference about the base beneath Archuleta Mesa, one that was actually taking place on Apache land a few weeks later. Norio Hayakawa invited her up to speak in the afternoon, interrupting the focus on Paul Bennewitz to share her own experiences. Geraldine took the stage, sitting in a chair under the lights wearing a baseball hat with a silhouette of Bigfoot underneath the word OREGON.

She explained how her husband had seen a flying saucer in the 1970s, and from there had developed a cosmology: the gray aliens, she averred, are bad, since they kill cows, but the blue ones want to get together with Indians because they're very religious. Ever since then, she'd seen UFOs—as well as Bigfoot.

Why are all these things happening on the reservation, she wondered aloud. It's because, she went on, the Bigfoot were Apache elders who were finally returning for the end-times. She described her surprise on hearing two Bigfoots speak in Apache. The world is coming to an end soon, Geraldine said, which is why there's no more rain. The hidden government base was responsible for the springs drying up on Apache land, responsible for the poisoning of the rivers. The aliens, she said, would save the Indians—"I don't know how."

Geraldine's vision of Bigfoot was a new twist on the traditional version of Wild Man lore: an apocalyptic vision that promised a redemption and an end to history. Her eschatology was different from Debbie Ray's, but the form was the same: the appearance of the Bigfoot aliens signaled a quickening, heralding the End of Days.

If cryptids and aliens once had distinct lineages and meanings, they've collapsed now; no longer are aliens just the hairless, big-eyed, physically weak but psychically superior beings—they're now just as likely to be reborn Native American deities. This collapse has enabled new possibilities to create whatever belief system you want—resulting in a free-form, constantly mutable mythology that's adaptable to the believer's cosmology. Believers have found ways to hybridize beliefs about cryptids and UFOs to construct various self-serving mythologies. For both Debbie and Geraldine, the image of Bigfoot is no longer a fragment of the natural world, hidden and misunderstood; instead, it's a vision of the future, a handmaiden-in-waiting for the next chapter in human history.

What unites them is the belief in a presence that is waiting just off in the wings, just out of sight, *waiting* for the right time. As the millennial Christian fever that surrounded the year 2000 has dispersed into popular consciousness, everyone believes that something is *just about to happen*, and these Bigfoot sightings have become, for many, further signs and portents.

After the event, I spoke to various other people at the symposium, including another member of the Jicarilla Apache tribe, Brian. When I asked Brian if he'd ever seen a Bigfoot, he replied soberly, "I wish I hadn't." He went on to explain: "Before, I used to enjoy walking in the woods. But now that I know I'm no longer the top of the food chain, no longer the apex predator, it doesn't feel safe anymore." When I asked Brian where he thought the Bigfoot had come from, he explained how they used to live in the wilds of Wyoming, but, "as white people built houses up in the hills," they'd started migrating south, and now lived among the Apache in northern New Mexico.

Then I asked if he agreed with Geraldine's theory that they were Apache elders. "Geraldine?" He looked at me. "Everybody thinks she's crazy."

A PHILOSOPHY OF NON-FACTS

When you sift through all of the thousands of UFO sightings, filtering out the wish fulfillment and confirmation bias, discounting the recovered memories and outright paranoia, the vast majority of what you have left boils down to some variation on *someone saw some weird light in the sky*. A light that didn't seem to move like a plane or a satellite, that was too close or too far away, but that was otherwise unremarkable. There are few sightings that, like the Gloucester sea serpent or the Shipton footprint, continue to mystify or openly defy explanation. One of them occurred on April 24, 1964, in Socorro, New Mexico, and on the first Saturday of October—the same day that the nearby Trinity Site is open to the public—I took my friend Jason Brown, the "conspiracy theorist's theorist," down there to poke around.

In the long history of UFO sightings, the Socorro Incident stands out: not only is it one of the strongest accounts on record, but it also has escaped much of the hype and tourist industries that have defined Area 51, Roswell, or Pine Bush. It happened at about 5:50 on that April evening. Patrolman Lonnie Zamora was in pursuit of a speeding car—a black Chevrolet—when he heard a roar and saw some kind of flame shooting up in the sky about a half mile away to the southwest. Zamora's first thought was that a dynamite shack might have exploded, so he broke off his chase to investigate.

He would later describe the flame he saw as a bluish-orange, seemingly motionless but descending slightly. It was difficult to see for sure, since he was still driving and the sun was in his eyes, but the flame seemed a sort of narrow funnel—not what you'd expect from an explosion. He turned off onto a rough gravel road that ran alongside an arroyo, as the roar and flame both cut out.

Ahead, Zamora saw what he initially took to be an overturned car. The vehicle, he'd later explained, stood out against the desert backdrop—it was whitish, like aluminum, though definitely not chrome. Beside it stood two figures dressed in white coveralls. He stopped the car and radioed in that he was going to investigate. As he got out, the thing had begun to take off again. Zamora heard that same loud roar, and watched as the vehicle rose straight up into the air.

Fearing it might explode, Zamora fled, though he kept his eye on the thing, which now appeared oval—smooth without windows or doors, but with some kind of red lettering on its side. He ran past his car, banging his leg against the fender and knocking off his glasses, but he didn't stop for them and kept running until he had crested a small hill. He would've kept on running but the noise had stopped; when he turned he saw the object moving silently away from him. Hovering about ten to fifteen feet off the ground, it moved quickly, and he watched it until it disappeared out of sight. Zamora got back to his car and called in for assistance, but by the time his fellow officers arrived, the only sign of anything at the landing site was some charred dirt and a few burning bushes.

Zamora had been a member of the Socorro Police Department for about five years; he was well liked, well respected, and trusted. This is part of what makes Zamora's account so compelling: he did not drink, was not given to wild tales, and in Socorro his word counted for something. Add to that the rigorous detail and narrative clarity. The Project Blue Book investigators who interviewed him decided that there was "no doubt that Lonnie Zamora saw an object which left quite an impression on him," going on further to say that there was also "no question about Zamora's reliability. He is a serious police officer, a pillar of his church, and a man well versed in recognizing airborne vehicles in his area. He is puzzled by what he saw, and frankly, so are we." It was, they concluded, "the best-documented case on record," and despite thorough subsequent investigations, they were unable "to find the vehicle or other stimulus that scared Zamora to the point of panic."

We set out to find the location of the Lonnie Zamora sighting. Unlike other famous UFO locations, there were no overt markers, no road signs, no conglomeration of kitsch to suggest we were on the right trail. The people of Socorro seem to have made a decision not to capitalize on their town's extraterrestrial fame, allowing no indication that anything out of the ordinary had ever happened in this sleepy town. On the Saturday that the Trinity Test Site was open, surely one of the biggest days for tourism in the area, the Socorro Tourist Office itself was closed.

Which is not to say that the people of Socorro don't have thoughts about UFOs. In the Los Alamos Gallery and Gift Shop—a large room filled with small kiosks of various local artists, an indoor crafts fair—a woman named Georgia had numerous stories for me or anyone who'd listen. She had been in high school when the Zamora incident happened, and while she didn't see the crash site, several of her friends did—they described to her black circles in the ground, not only burnt but sort of pressed down into the earth.

When I asked her if it might have been a secret military aircraft, she responded, "I'm not sure of anything, but I wouldn't put it past the military." She could recall nights when she was in high school, lying in the grass with her friends, seeing fields of lights in the sky that would all move together in formation, and then scatter suddenly as if they'd hit some invisible thing above her head. "If you look up in the night sky," she said, "there are *incredible* things."

It was easier to see things in the 1960s and '70s, before the area was built up as much as it is now. But, she said, "everybody here has their stories, everybody here has seen something." Then she leaned close to me and in a conspiratorial tone said, "All Roswell had was a *balloon*."

Georgia, though, for all her stories, couldn't direct us to the crash site.

The internet was more helpful, but it still took an hour of driving, checking websites, and more driving, trying to find something that matched the location's description. Despite being the only occupant sighting in Project Blue Book's history still listed as "unknown," its importance to UFO believers seems to have long been eclipsed by the more sensational stories.

It's bizarre, Brown notes, how difficult it is to locate directions to the Zamora site on the internet. "I knew it was going to be physically unmarked and unremarkable," he says, "but it is a very precisely located spot. In town, right off the highway, down the road from a significant city, easy parking at the church, freaky military shit in all directions. I don't know how many agencies ended up mapping and documenting the location of the incident. They recovered hard physical evidence, for Chrissakes!

"And the skeptics came in waves! Years apart, trying different theories—" He lists various theories that were put forth to debunk Zamora's account: perhaps the sun was in his eyes, maybe it was a lunar probe being tested by NASA, or perhaps it was high school kids pulling an elaborate prank. "But in the end, the eyewitness account remained the most plausible version of events based on available evidence, even though it's totally implausible."

It's striking, Brown admits, "how unfetishized the spot itself is, and how relatively obscure its extremely well-documented location is in an era of ubiquitous locatability. That obscurity feels significant. I mean, we got pamphlets with the bus stops of the Area 51 commuters. There're multiple tours to the various Roswell 'sites.' Yet one of the best documented UFO *landing* locations is somehow a minor pain to get an address?"

But one website eventually pointed us to an arroyo behind a Korean church, and another confirmed it with GPS coordinates. The road alongside the arroyo is still mostly dirt, though it's now ringed with houses. We parked and wandered into the scrub, vaguely alert for rattlesnakes. Eventually, we found a small ring of stones, two feet in diameter, which was the only marker of where the event had supposedly taken place.

The lore of UFOs is ultimately not much more than this, the elevation of non-space into something resonant, something mystical. There would be no weeping statue of Mary, no relics of Lourdes prompting spontaneous miracles. There is just the desert. We took a couple of photos and then headed back to the car. Later, we stopped at a bar in Albuquerque before Brown's flight back home, where, punctuated by interjections from an overly friendly bartender, we talked about Socorro, UFOs, and Jacques Vallée.

A computer scientist by training and a venture capitalist, Vallée has long been one of the more well-known UFOlogists. He had initially sought out physical evidence of extraterrestrials, but by the 1960s had begun to revise his theories, leading to his 1969 book, *Passport to Magonia: From Folklore to Flying Saucers.* Of all the hundreds of theories about UFOs, Vallée's ideas (what commonly get called the "interdimensional hypothesis," as opposed to the "extraterrestrial hypothesis") are perhaps the only ones that continued to make sense after the MJ-12 government conspiracy days, the only ones managing to remain plausible after so many decades.

Vallée calls his book a "philosophical book, if there were a philosophy of non-facts." His goal is to suggest "a possible parallel between the rumors of today and the beliefs that were held by our ancestors, beliefs of stupendous fights with mysterious supermen, of rings where magic lingered, of dwarfish races haunting the land." In other words, what if the legends, myths, and religious stories that date back centuries are the same as the modern UFO sightings? Vallée's argument suggests that whatever it is we started seeing after 1947, it was part of a longer trajectory, and that UFOs, flying saucers, and aliens were only the latest names we gave to a phenomenon other people have, at other times, called fairies, elves, angels, or demons.

For Vallée, the mechanisms that generate all of these various beliefs— the mystical and the religious, the anomalous and the unexplained, are all identical. "Their human context and their effect on humans are constant." Which means, he argues, "*It has little to do with the problem of knowing whether UFOs are physical objects or not.* Attempting to understand the meaning, the purpose of the so-called flying saucers, as many people are doing today, is just as futile as was the pursuit of the fairies, if one makes the mistake of confusing appearance as reality." Rather, all of these phenomena have "stable, invariant features," rendering them identical, despite the "chameleonlike character of the secondary attributes of the sightings: the shapes of the objects, the appearances of their occupants, their reported statements," all of which, Vallée suggests, "vary as a function of the cultural environment into which they are projected."

But, of course, people still see (or claim to see) angels, and miracles are still thought by many to occur. Those who want the magic of angels and demons can find many communities in which such phenomena exist. So the believers of UFOs, if you believe Vallée, are a different kind of religious cult, one in which the traditional hierarchy of God is rejected.

What Vallée sees behind all of this is some incomprehensible alien (in the most fundamental sense of the word) presence, one that we are incapable of understanding as it is, and which as such gets filtered through our religious motifs, our scientific principles, our biases and fears— always distorted from whatever it actually may be to something that we can give a name to: angels, fairies, UFOs. Perhaps this intelligence, whatever it is, is attempting to communicate with us, appearing to us in motifs that we recognize to help prepare our understanding. But it's just as likely, according to this hypothesis, that they're indifferent to us— they may simply be passing by on the way to somewhere else, engaged in whatever business they have that concerns none of us.

Ken Layne told me at one point that the "worst thing about UFO people" is their constant need to come up with some theory to explain what they're seeing: "Ah, you know, they'll say, it's the Venusians, or the gondola-heads, or whatever." Whatever all this anomalous phenomena is, he counters, we'll likely never know what it is or be able to understand it. Layne offers a *2001: A Space Odyssey* model of understanding: some other intelligence that has, through time, given us "these little evolutionary kicks from something ultimately inexplicable to us at this phase." It's a difficult thing, he concludes, "to think that there's something we may never ever understand, that may have some subtle control over the development of our species."

Back at the bar, Brown brought up the Fermi Paradox once again: "If you start with the premise, a scientific premise, that life is likely to exist elsewhere, far more evolved than we are, but we aren't finding it, then one possibility is that complex life is a failure. A complete and utter failure, doomed to fail beyond a certain point that we are either approaching but haven't quite reached yet, and ultimately no civilization continues beyond"—he gestures at the wood-paneled brew pub with thirty or so microbrews on tap, a scattering of patrons, some of whom have their dog on a leash sleeping beneath their table, a server delivering fries and jalapeño poppers—"this."

The alternative, he suggests, is that somewhere some civilization has progressed beyond us, and "we don't understand WHAT it is. It's like ants approaching an interstate: We don't get it. It's all around us, but we don't even perceive it." There are, as he sees it, the two options: "The death of everything, once Walmart has achieved dominance? Some people believe that. But the more—let's call it—optimistic hypothesis, is that we're simply slime molds compared to monkeys, that we can't comprehend what form life has taken."

Is it fair, I ask, that what we're calling aliens changes through the centuries because the only way we have to access them is through our own cultural preoccupations? "That is accurate!" Brown agrees. "I find it persuasive in ways that other ideas are not. And I find it charming."

I'll confess I find it charming, too—but I'm not sure I find it persuasive. While it's compelling, it's equally problematic, since it posits a hypothesis that can't be tested one way or another. Vallée's hypothesis has survived the test of time in part because, like so many other fringe theories, there's no way to prove or disprove it conclusively.

Another way of saying this is that after decades of exhaustive, serious, and sometimes expensive research and inquiry into UFOs and aliens, the most persuasive and most likely hypothesis—the *best we can come up with*—is something that can't be tested, something that is on its face utterly unscientific. To say that all these eyewitness accounts are the emanations of some kind of force beyond our comprehension, and that we'll never know or be able to test or prove this theory, is no different from religion—an article of faith. Nor, though, is it all that different from the only other alternative I can think of: that the human mind is complex in ways we'll never understand, and there will never be good reasons to explain why someone like Lonnie Zamora—clearheaded and clearly not crazy—said he saw what he said he saw.

Strange things still hover in the sky. In November 2004, two F/A-18F Super Hornets were on a training mission a hundred miles out from San Diego over the Pacific Ocean when a radio operator informed them of a "real-world vector" they were tracking. The jets headed to investigate, only to find a forty-foot-long oval of some kind, hovering fifty feet off the water. One of the pilots, Commander David Fravor, circled down to investigate, only to have the craft come up to meet him halfway before taking off. "It accelerated like nothing I've ever seen," he later recalled. He admitted he was "pretty weirded out."

The pilots' accounts and some footage of a gray blur was made public in 2017 by *The New York Times*, which also revealed that the US Department of Defense was still very much interested in such things. While Project Blue Book wrapped up at the end of 1969, the *Times* reported that there was still work being done in the Pentagon to track unidentified objects in the sky, a project funded by three US senators: Harry Reid of Nevada, Daniel Inouye of Hawaii, and Ted Stevens of Alaska. The money—$22 million—went to pay a contractor and longtime friend of Reid's, NASA contractor Robert Bigelow. Reid had taken care to ensure that the project was kept out of the public eye, part of the Pentagon's so-called black money, but when he was reached for comment, he was far from apologetic. "I'm not embarrassed or ashamed or sorry I got this thing going," he said. "I think it's one of the good things I did in my congressional service."

Twenty-two million dollars is a curious number. In terms of the

Pentagon's overall budget, it's nothing, just a speck in the limitless sky. For an independent contractor, though, it's a generous kickback for a project with little expectation of actually turning up anything. If, however, the military indisputably has evidence of extraterrestrial craft—surely one of the most important discoveries in the history of humanity—then $22 million seems a woefully paltry sum. It's hard to tell whether or not this is a legitimate government program or simply graft, but Occam's razor suggests simple corruption.

For many who read the *Times* story, it was difficult to deny that it offered proof of alien craft. But what, really, is new here? Once again, a blurry video of a indistinct blob, combined with first-person testimony that's difficult to verify. As Donald Keyhoe could have told you, it's always been possible to find a half dozen mid-ranking Air Force officers to go on record and say they've seen something they can't explain. And it has always been possible to film blurry blobs. The sky has always been filled with unexplainable sights. That doesn't mean that there are aliens or extraterrestrial craft flying about. It just means that Edward Ruppelt's original term for these things remains the best, and most apt: they may be objects, they may be flying, but above all they are simply as yet unidentified.

By then it was time to get Brown to the airport, so I took him to catch his flight, then spent the night in Albuquerque. The next morning, eager to get back on the road, I left Albuquerque just before dawn—as I drove out on the highway, the sky was covered in strange, black objects against the oranges and reds of sunrise. It took a minute to adjust before I realized they were hot-air balloons. It's always balloons.

CONCLUSION: WHAT REMAINS

It is difficult to imagine what can't be described.
—CRISTINA RIVERA GARZA, *THE TAIGA SYNDROME*

After half a century of UFOs and Bigfoot, of varying degrees of serious inquiry, it's harder and harder to find whatever once was the serious scientific pursuit of any of this. The days of cryptozoologists and MUFON are over; anything remotely approaching serious science has given way to this improvisational millenarianism. Through the course of investigating cryptids, UFOs, and aliens, I kept coming back to the conclusion that they were mostly a sideshow, mostly a distraction from the real event, which was a longer-term history of the institutionalization of the modern scientific edifice and our need to push back on this, as well as an attempt to claim the middle ground between science and mainstream religion. I found time and time again people latching on to these theories not because of any direct proof of any of it, but because they distrusted scientists or the government, or were seeking some way to salve their anxieties of modernity. Is there anything beyond mystic wish fulfillment, any serious attempt to understand what all of these anomalous experiences are? If you strip away all the kitsch, all the mythologizing and pop culture, what's left?

The website for the Rosicrucian Museum features a paraphrase of a quote from Francis Bacon, "If one will begin with certainties, one will end in doubts; however if one were content to begin with doubts, one will end in certainties." It's a mantra for so many in various fringe communities, since it offers a strong rebuke to received wisdom, and its aphoristic construction makes for a pithy rejoinder. What I found time and time again, though, is how quickly those who start from doubts jump to certainties. Doubting the American government is fully forthcoming with its citizens is one thing; certainty that it is hiding aliens is another. Doubting that science knows everything is fine; certainty that a bent tree in a forest is empirical evidence of Bigfoot is another. The only worthwhile way to investigate any of this phenomenon, it seems, is to be aware of one's biases and strive to eliminate them. To be free of a preconceived certainty, to be willing to admit the unexplained without that automatic obsession to explain it.

The goal of this book has been to trace how two different, but related, shocks hit the industrialized world in the nineteenth century, causing a rift in how we understood it, and how a number of fringe beliefs emerged from that rift. The bargain made here is that, in exchange for giving up scientific consensus or objective rationality, the believer gets something in exchange: a little bit of wonder, a world reenchanted, a sense we're not alone, or perhaps another way of finding meaning in a difficult world. It can seem innocuous enough, particularly if one is careful to stay away from some of the darker conspiracy theories that shade out of these beliefs. But how harmless is it?

This clarity of thinking—while it can be difficult to maintain— nonetheless allows you to sift out the obvious hoaxes, delusions, and false positives. The Fort Bragg home invasion, the Maury Island Incident, Bob Lazar's Area 51 tales. Theosophical contactee narratives of fair-haired, blue-eyed space neighbors strain all credulity, as do stories of an evolutionarily impossible and English-speaking Dogman. The countless stories of inexplicable lights in the sky are tantalizing, but don't offer much to go on; the lack of any physical evidence of cryptids—particularly those being actively hunted—is likewise discouraging. Attempting to sort judiciously through all this evidence turns up few events or sightings that hold up to any sort of scrutiny.

But there are still some that do. I'm drawn back to those stories that consistently resist an easy and final explanation. If you believe that this world is truly bereft of wonder, then there are countless events that will challenge those beliefs, things not easily explained, things weird and wild that hover all around us.

What did Kenneth Arnold see over Mount Rainier? What happened to Ruth Lowe's child that 1977 evening in Lawndale? What explains the bizarre story Lonnie Zamora told about what he saw in that arroyo? And what the heck did all those people see in Gloucester Bay that August two hundred years ago? Even for the most arduous skeptic, there are events that are not easily discarded. There are explanations, sure, but they're not that much better than the eyewitness accounts.

The problem is that these intriguing stories are quickly buried beneath an avalanche of subsequent nonsense. With any credible eyewitness accounts, believers arrive immediately, heralding the new discovery. They're followed by the skeptics, looking for a reason to doubt them. Then come the cranks, the hoaxers, the frauds. Copycat sightings are announced and then quickly debunked. After the Lawndale incident, for example, Norma and Kenneth Knollenberg of New Holland, Illinois, reported another strange bird—this was one had been photographed on their farm on July 22, predating the incident with Ruth Lowe. Examining the photograph, though, it was clear that they had managed to glimpse a relatively unremarkable peahen. Meanwhile, on July 28, several "vulture-like birds" in the area around Lawndale were reported that evening by various witnesses, but a bird reported in Logan County described as "cranelike" suggested something unrelated to the central Lawndale mystery. One James Majors described a bird carrying off on July 29 a small pig weighing forty to sixty pounds, a physical impossibility that was not taken seriously; then, by August, the sightings and media attention had mostly stopped.

At some point, whatever that original sighting might have been disappears from our sight entirely. The original event is laid over with so many competing narratives—narratives of belief and of doubt—that it becomes impossible to get back to the initial account. Witnesses recant rather than face the withering scorn of their community or to save their marriages, or they embrace fringe groups of cranks entirely, further sapping their credibility.

No matter how credible those eyewitness accounts might have been, they're lost to us now. The stories of Kenneth Arnold and Ruth Lowe come to us now only as urban legend and folklore. As our record keeping keeps getting better, we've come to believe that our recent past at least is largely knowable. We may dispute the causes of history's wars, second-guess decisions made by past leaders, or revise the historical record in light of new discoveries—but we generally agree on the basic facts. Not only that, we generally agree that the basic facts are knowable. But even a cursory dip into the world of anomalies reveals countless incidents in which the basic facts are simply unknowable. This is maybe the hardest pill to swallow.

This, despite the ubiquity of means of recording events that we now have—print, film and photography, online archives. What then, about the recordings, the videos, the photographs? These would seem to be more durable, more reliable, than simply eyewitness reports, and yet they're even more dubious. The Surgeon's Photograph was hoaxed, as was the Gimlin-Patterson film. No photograph of a UFO has held up to any kind of scrutiny.

In fact, it's not only that this surplus of records doesn't guarantee that the facts will be preserved, but that the opposite is true: the more we strive to document and record, the more likely the truth is to slip away. Supposedly objective media like photography and wire reports has led not to proof but to a breakdown in consensus altogether. The rise of the idea of "fake news," after all, is itself a phenomenon of too much information rather than not enough. Our zeal for record keeping without methodology has quickly eclipsed our ability to process it.

There's a reason, in other words, why despite our technological capacities having increased exponentially, cryptid and UFO technology remains mired in the pre-internet age. We have incredibly powerful cameras built into our phones, and yet Bigfoot photos continue to be blurry,

UFO videos continue to be just blinking lights in the sky. Despite the rapid increase in satellite and mapping capabilities, cryptozoologists continue to insist that the beasts they hunt are too canny to be caught up in these webs. In the love of these creatures hides a nostalgia for a moment in time when recording technology was good but not great, when a fleeting glimpse was the best you could get.

But they also call up in us a nostalgia for those empty spaces on the map, exactly the spaces that have disappeared in the wake of these advanced technologies and other aspects of our modern age. Despite incredibly detailed maps of every inch of the world, we insist there are unexplored spaces. With the seafloor's contours well established, we continue to believe that somewhere down there might be a sunken utopia. Off-limits to everything but our imagination, we insist that military bases hold unspeakable secrets. Climate change is denuding our forests of their density, but we insist that strange hairy beasts can still hide in the wastelands the fires leave behind. As the internet age and the twenty-first century shrunk our world smaller and smaller, we found ourselves imagining that there were still places left unexplored.

Ultimately, we don't want to know what happened over Mount Rainier. We don't want to know what was in the skies over Lawndale. Like *The X-Files'* Fox Mulder, we want to believe, but it's more than that. We want to be right. We want to find, in these anomalous events, proof of our own worldview, reassurance of our preconceived ideas. We're not looking for the truth; we're looking for confirmation.

In the absence of something tangible, something concrete, something definitive, we don't have anything. Which is why I had to go to Transylvania University.

o o o

Kurt Gohde, an art professor at Transylvania University in Lexington, Kentucky, was cleaning out closets in 2002 when he first came across the jar. The thirteenth oldest university in the country,

Transylvania (whose fortunes have ebbed and flowed through the years) developed a large, eclectic collection of curiosities and forgotten art through the years. Working with the librarian to catalog some of it, Gohde began going through various storage closets and attics around the campus, looking for misplaced treasures and interesting ephemera. In the closet used by the theater department to store props, he found a box filled with various specimen jars. Most of them were empty, their contents long evaporated or lost, but there was one, still sealed, with one word written on it: *Olympia*.

And inside, what looked like a chunk of meat.

"I desperately wanted to believe it was meat rain," he said of his discovery. "I didn't think that at first, because it was just a box of stuff." But another professor, Jamie Day, who shares Gohde's interest in the lost miscellany of Transylvania University, was able to date the bottle to two to three years prior to 1876, suggesting a very strong possibility that Gohde had found the last known remnant of the Kentucky Meat Shower.

Gohde had agreed to meet me at a local coffee shop on the edge of campus to discuss inexplicable rains and other things Fortean. As we talked of aliens, cryptids, and other assorted weirdnesses, he reflected that, usually in science, "the burden of proof is on the outlandish idea, but somehow with cryptozoology and that sort of thing, there's a shift of the burden of proof away from the outlandish idea." Historically, the meat rain incident at Olympia Springs came at a time when science didn't *need* to solve everything, when people were more or less okay with some things being just pure wonder. "But now science has to explain *everything*, and so now the only way," Gohde said, to continue to maintain that sense of wonder, "is to shift the burden of proof" to scientific understanding.

That's why we haven't seen another shower of meat like the 1876 event: "if any similar thing happened now, it would be solved," and we wouldn't still be sitting around trying to figure out the answer a hundred and fifty years later. The anomalous nature of the event had as much to do with its moment in time and the very specific circumstances of how it was received by the media and the scientific community as it does with anomalous weather or bizarre phenomena. "In 1876, it was interesting to the scientific community for a month maybe, and then something else happened and they forgot it."

When I asked him what he believed, Gohde admitted: "I'm most convinced by the vulture vomit, but the problem with that is that it's directly contradicted by Mrs. Crouch's direct testimony. . . . I feel like if it was a flock of vultures vomiting, she might have mentioned it. I do feel like that is the most reasonable explanation, but it actually doesn't seem to hold water with the one person who's telling the story." We finished our coffees, and it was time to see the meat itself.

The last remaining chunk of the Kentucky Meat Shower is normally kept in a cabinet of the Monroe Moosnick Museum, in the basement of the university's science building. Maintained primarily by Jamie Day, the physics professor who's collaborated with Gohde in collecting and cataloging Transylvania's treasures, it's a vast repository of fascinating and forgotten objects. Among the objects in the collection are a wax anatomical Venus—a full-sized model of a woman's head and torso sculpted in lifelike wax and used for medical teaching prior to the heavy use of cadavers. Though Transylvania's Venus—the only one in North America that's of the same quality as the collections in La Specola in Florence or Austria's Josephinium—was long ago burned in a fire, and now her face is hideously blackened, her formerly serene expression replaced by something terrifying and garish. They also have what's known as a madstone—one of the largest, perhaps the largest, in existence (almost two feet in diameter). Essentially a hairball removed from a cow's stomach, madstones were considered to have magical healing powers, and were thought to cure rabies: by pressing one against a dog bite, it was thought, the madstone would draw out the sickness (a version of this folk belief has been passed down in the hangover idiom, "Hair of the dog that bit you").

But I was there, first and foremost, to see the meat. It resides in a squat jar about eight inches high, stopped up with a fat cork. The label is brown with age and nearly worn away; the liquid inside (whatever it is, it's not formaldehyde) is a murky yellow—out of which, rising like a miniature albino Loch Ness Monster, is the meat sample. It doesn't, to be honest, look anything like meat, not after so many years—it's vaguely gelatinous in appearance, a buckle of organic matter a few inches long. Had I come across it without any context, with no understanding of what I was looking at, I doubt I'd be able to identify it as anything at all. But after reading so much about it, I found it eerily beautiful—the meat hums with its own enigma. It speaks of a world beyond our understanding, a world we can glimpse here and there but never fully see.

Like Gohde, I tend to agree that the vulture story is the most plausible, but also like him, I remain unconvinced that it answers all the questions. When I asked him how he reckons with the admittedly problematic vulture narrative, he replied, "I use it to just continue to tell all the other stories. My interest in the meat rain—and the reason that I'm totally okay with exposing the problems with the vulture story without having a better answer—is that I like that there are a lot of bad answers. To me that is more interesting than having a solution." Gohde's comfort with the origin of the meat rain being unanswered is, he says at last, "all part of a feeling that we can do our best to explain things, and sometimes that's all we can say: 'I've done my best, there's not enough for me to do more.'"

The most compelling anomalies that turned up in researching this book, like the Kentucky Meat Shower, exist out of the reach of confirmation or debunking; the evidence we have is compelling but not sufficient, which works against both definitive solutions and definitive attempts to dispel them.

They linger in our consciousness for a reason. When I asked him why the story of the meat shower persisted, Gohde concurred: "I think it's our need to know," he said, "that there are things slightly beyond our understanding." For some of us, those things slightly beyond our understanding are string theory, black holes, or the life cycle of the *Vampyroteuthis infernalis*. For others, they're the intricacies of the human mind, or the unplumbed depths of *King Lear* or *Mrs. Dalloway*. For others, though, it's a small plug of meat in a liquid-filled jar.

A bigger question, to my mind, is not whether or not there are anomalous incidents out there like Arnold's Mount Rainier sighting or the Lawndale Incident, but rather, what do we do with such knowledge? There is a repeated danger—one incredibly tempting and all but impossible to avoid—to use such stories to affirm our previously held beliefs. What Charles Fort offered was a means of looking at these strange events that militated against ideology seeping in, which remains, a hundred years later, his most valuable gift. But it's easy to forget how that gift is supposed to work.

The crank view of the world swaps out the splendor and dynamism of everything around us for pat, one-size-fits-all explanations that flatter our perceptions and prejudices. It chases order and reassurance at the expense of wonder and variety, and it too easily defaults to paranoia and conspiracy as a defense against being wrong.

It is a view of nature that is one of fundamental meanness: it reduces everything around us to its lowest common denominator. If there is a lesson here, it is to cling to the wonder, to the possibilities, without allowing your doubt to become its own certainty. The goal should never be to narrow the world, but to enlarge it.

ACKNOWLEDGMENTS

This book owes its life and existence primarily to two singular people whom I'm lucky enough to call colleagues and friends. Jason Brown started me down this particular path of the weird many years ago, and I remain indebted to his insights and his feedback. And Michelle Legro was there with her uncommon wisdom at key moments throughout the writing process, helping me turn this project from a random free-flowing association of ideas into an actual book.

In addition, numerous people offered their ideas, recommendations, expertise, and time. I'm grateful to David S. Anderson, Kurt Gohde, Jamie Day, Aaron Bady, Elissa Washuta, Erin Chapman, Blake Smith, Karen Stollznow, Clyde Tallio, Asa S. Mittman, Ken Layne, Gayle Beatty, Meaghan Walsh Gerard, Jack Womack, Lauren Oliver, Troy Taylor, Emily Hughes, Liberty Hardy, Kerry Soeller, Mark McAdams, Karl Erickson, and Gretchen Larsen. That said, any errors of fact and judgment are mine alone.

I'm beyond fortunate to have as an agent Anna Sproul-Latimer, who has been a relentless advocate of my work for many years. One could not ask for a better partner in crime. Thank you also to everyone at Ross-Yoon, especially Gail Ross, Howard Yoon, and Dara Kaye, for all of their hard work.

Thank you to Melanie Tortoroli, who acquired this manuscript and gave it life, and to Emily Wunderlich for seeing it through with her editorial wisdom and perennial patience. Thanks to Jane Cavolina, whose copy editing went above and beyond. Thanks to everyone else at Viking, past and present, for their support.

Thanks to the Order of the Good Death—particularly Caitlin Doughty, Sarah Chavez, Elizabeth Harper, Louise Hung, and Megan Rosenbloom—for their constant friendship. Thanks to everyone at Betalevel, my home away from home. Special thanks to the editorial team at *Sucks Magazine*—Ben Armintor, Rob Fellman, Karen Gregory, Matthew Harrison, Joe Howley, Tim Maughan, Vimala Pasupathi, Sava Singh, and Karl Steel—for keeping me sane. Thank you to Patricia Matthew for reasons I'll never quite be able to put into words.

Thanks to Nicole, and to Alistair for sticking around.

During the writing of this book I lost my mother, Audrey. It was she who taught me to love books and reading, and it is to her memory that this book is dedicated.

NOTES

INTRODUCTION: THE FIRE

2 **"glowing in twenty-four hours"**: Joe Mathews, "Long Island's UFO Plot Trial: A Flying Saucer True Believer Must Answer Charges That He Intended to Kill Three People He Believed Were Covering Up Alien Landings," *Baltimore Sun*, August 4, 1997.

3 **"our worst nightmares come true"**: Press conference, News 12 Live, June 12, 1996, archived at www.youtube.com/watch?v=Q3zYbR3nIwE&list =PLcAKygvTqGnUtKyujOXp8UNrhnj_0zlhd&index=1.

3 **from 39 percent in 2016 to 57 percent in 2018**: Chapman University, "Survey of American Fears 2018," www.chapman.edu/wilkinson/research-centers /babbie-center/survey-american-fears.aspx.

4 **"humanity that defies definition"**: John T. McQuiston, "Plot Against L.I. Leaders Is Tied to Fear of U.F.O.'s," *New York Times*, June 22, 1996, Section 1, 24.

5 **"at least once during historical times"**: Carl Sagan, "Direct Contact Among Galactic Civilizations by Relativistic Interstellar Spaceflight," *Planetary Space Science* 11 (1963): 496. See also: Michael Shermer, *The Skeptic Encyclopedia of Pseudoscience, Volume 1* (Santa Barbara: ABC-CLIO, 2002), 17–18.

6 **humanity and alien civilization**: Erich von Däniken, *Chariots of the Gods* (New York: Berkley Books, 1999).

6 **an ever-expanding grand scheme**: As Susan Lepselter explains, conspiracy theories and fringe beliefs are the product of "an endless bricolage, but rather than building something concrete from the 'odds and ends' at hand, here the product is never finished; you select the part for the rush of its echo to another part. Here each found or revealed sign leads on to other resemblances, other openings." Susan Lepselter, *The Resonance of Unseen Things: Poetics, Power,*

Captivity, and UFOs in the American Uncanny (Ann Arbor: University of Michigan Press, 2016), 4.

7 **and those who hadn't:** Kenneth L. Feder, *American Antiquity* 49, no. 3 (July 1984): 525–41.

9 **"master all things by calculation":** Max Weber, "Science as a Vocation," in *From Max Weber: Essays in Sociology*, trans. and ed. H. H. Gerth and C. Wright Mills (Abington, UK: Routledge, 1991), 139.

9 **"straight road of progress":** Svetlana Boym, *The Future of Nostalgia* (New York: Basic Books, 2001), xvii.

PART I: SUNKEN LANDS AND FALLING MEAT

FIELD NOTES: MOUNT SHASTA, CALIFORNIA

15 **"You can't improve it":** "Mt. Shasta: Desecration of Panther Spring, Our Genesis Place," Winnemem Wintu website, www.winnememwintu.us/mount-shasta/.

CHAPTER I: THE MAN WHO COULD NOT BE TURNED

19 **"the rest of my life":** Quoted in John D. Hicks, "The Political Career of Ignatius Donnelly," *Mississippi Valley Historical Review* 8, no. 1/2 (June–Sept. 1921): 81.

20 **"great drama of human advancement":** Quoted in Ralph L. Harmon, "Ignatius Donnelly and His Faded Metropolis," *Minnesota History* 17, no. 2 (September 1936), 265.

20 **"will rise upon their site":** Harmon, "Ignatius Donnelly and His Faded Metropolis."

21 **"the unmastered continent":** Quoted in Kerwin Lee Klein, *Frontiers of Historical Imagination: Narrating the European Conquest of Native America, 1890–1990* (Berkeley: University of California Press, 1999), 81.

21 **dominion over the wilds:** Klein, *Frontiers of Historical Imagination.*

22 **the Nile Delta region:** Plato, *Timaeus and Critias*, trans. Desmond Lee (New York: Penguin Classics, 2008).

22 **the lost city of Troy:** Mark Adams, *Meet Me in Atlantis: Across Three Continents in Search of the Legendary Sunken City* (New York: Dutton, 2016), 41–43.

23 **"the presence of that island":** Ignatius Donnelly, *Atlantis: The Antediluvian World* (New York: Gramercy Publishing Company, 1985), 50.

23 **"the thinkers of our day?":** Donnelly, *Atlantis*, 35.

24 **as a compliment:** Various reactions to Donnelly's book can be found in Donald H. DeMeules, "Ignatius Donnelly: A Don Quixote in the World of Science," *Minnesota History* 37, no. 6 (June 1961), 231.

24 **"from their source areas":** Quoted in Adams, *Meet Me in Atlantis*, 47.

25 **"examination to the archaeologist"**: Lewis Spence, *The History of Atlantis* (New York: Bell Publishing Company, 1968), 1.

26 **"the machinery of the world go round"**: Oliver Wendell Holmes, *Over the Teacups* (Cambridge, MA: Riverside Press, 1891), 161.

26 **"they have been unable to understand"**: J. P., "Science and Folly," *Nature* 75, no. 1931 (November 8, 1906), 25.

CHAPTER 2: ABANDONED GEOGRAPHY

28 **"geography of a bygone age"**: Quoted in Sumathi Ramaswamy, *The Lost Land of Lemuria: Fabulous Geographies, Catastrophic Histories* (Berkeley: University of California Press, 2004), 28.

29 **"the probable cradle of the human race"**: Quoted in Ramaswamy, *The Lost Land of Lemuria*, 35.

29 **"Founding Mother of the Occult"**: Quoted in Gary Lachman, *Madame Blavatsky: The Mother of Modern Spirituality* (New York: Jeremy P. Tarcher/Penguin, 2012), x.

30 **"creators of the twentieth century"**: Quoted in Lachman, *Madame Blavatsky*, xi.

31 **"tyranny of that Usurper, Authority"**: Walter Charleton, *Physiologia Epicuro-Gassendo-Charletoniana, or, A Fabrick of Science Natural, upon the Hypothesis of Atoms Founded by Epicurus, Repaired by Petrus Gassendus, Augmented by Walter Charleton* (New York: Johnson Reprint Corp., 1966), 94.

31 **complement the Bible**: Peter Harrison, *The Territories of Science and Religion* (Chicago: University of Chicago Press, 2015), 57–59.

31 **"but not His image"**: Quoted in Harrison, *The Territories of Science and Religion*, 76.

31 **crystallized into the word "science"**: Harrison, *The Territories of Science and Religion*, 95.

33 **and wrote "occultist"**: Lachman, *Madame Blavatsky*, 106.

35 **"therefore to be believed in"**: Helena Petrovna Blavatsky, *The Secret Doctrine: The Synthesis of Science, Religion, and Philosophy, Volume II: Anthropogenesis* (London: Theosophical Publishing House, 1893), 120.

CHAPTER 3: THE CREDULITY OF INCREDULITY

37 **"self-evident and indisputable facts"**: Wishar S. Cervé (H. Spencer Lewis), *Lemuria: The Lost Continent of the Pacific* (San Jose, CA: Supreme Grand Lodge of AMORC, 1931), 13.

38 **founding its great ancient civilization**: Augustus Le Plongeon, *Queen M'oo and the Egyptian Sphinx* (New York: published by the author, 1896).

38 **"the country of California":** Cervé (Lewis), *Lemuria*, 209.

39 **"These hidden Lemurians":** Cervé (Lewis), *Lemuria*, 178.

40 **race of telepathic superbeings:** Michael Zanger, *Mt. Shasta: History, Legend & Lore* (Berkeley: Celestial Arts, 1992), 100.

CHAPTER 4: DISPATCHES FROM THE DESERT OF BLOOD

41 **"when meat which looked like":** "Flesh Descending in a Shower," *The New York Times*, March 10, 1876.

41 **learn more about this "carnal rain":** "The Carnal Rain," *New York Herald*, March 21, 1876, 4.

43 **"entirely in harmony with natural laws":** "The Kentucky Shower of Flesh," *Scientific American Supplement* no. 2 (July 1, 1876), 426.

43 **"doubtless of the frog":** "The Shower of Flesh," *The Friend* XLIX, no. 32 (1876): 253.

44 **arrived at the *Scientific American:*** A. Mead Edwards, "The Kentucky Meat-Shower," *Scientific American Supplement* no. 2 (July 22, 1876), 473.

44 **described it as "dried":** Charles Fort, *The Complete Books of Charles Fort* (New York: Dover, 1974), 45.

45 **"a great thick cloud":** Fort, *The Complete Books of Charles Fort*, 81.

45 **"precise picking out of frogs or toads":** Fort, *The Complete Books of Charles Fort*, 82.

46 **"ever seen produced in America":** Jim Steinmeyer, *Charles Fort: The Man Who Invented the Supernatural* (New York: Jeremy P. Tarcher/Penguin, 2008), 84.

47 **"he became a crank":** Damon Knight, *Charles Fort: Prophet of the Unexplained* (New York: Doubleday & Company, Inc., 1970), 55.

47 **not just a book but a "religion":** Steinmeyer, *Charles Fort*, 165–66.

48 **"data that Science has excluded":** Fort, *The Complete Books of Charles Fort*, 3.

48 **"If you don't publish it, you'll lose me":** Steinmeyer, *Charles Fort*, 166.

CHAPTER 5: BELIEVE NOTHING

50 **"for its own sake":** Patricia J. Gumport, "Graduate Education and Research: Interdependence and Strain," in *American Higher Education in the Twenty-First Century: Social, Political and Economic Challenges.* ed. Phillip G. Altbach and Robert O. Berdahl (Baltimore: Johns Hopkins University Press, 2005), 430–35.

50 **"does not include such phenomena":** Charles Fort, *The Complete Books of Charles Fort* (New York: Dover, 1974), 45.

51 **"as a beneficent being"**: Fort, *The Complete Books of Charles Fort*, 558.

52 **"our sciences and understandings are haunted"**: Jim Steinmeyer, *Charles Fort: The Man Who Invented the Supernatural* (New York: Jeremy P. Tarcher/Penguin, 2008), 162.

52 **"started a band"**: Kristine McKenna, "Lots of Aura, No Air Play," *Los Angeles Times*, May 23, 1982, L6.

54 **"Italy is nearest to it—or them"**: Fort, *The Complete Books of Charles Fort*, 300.

54 **about the origins of fossils**: Fort, *The Complete Books of Charles Fort*, 165.

54 **"either oppose or do not encourage them"**: Damon Knight, *Charles Fort: Prophet of the Unexplained* (New York: Doubleday & Company, Inc., 1970), 172.

55 **"the same way that atheism requires faith"**: Steinmeyer, *Charles Fort*, 289.

56 **"truth outdoes fiction every time"**: Interview with Jack Womack, August 18, 2018.

PART II: THE END OF MONSTERS

FIELD NOTES: DARIEN, GEORGIA

60 **water monster of Darien, Georgia**: Jacqueline Berlin, "Mythical Creature Sparking Interest," *Brunswick News,* January 31, 2001, thebrunswicknews.com /news/local_news/mythical-creature-sparking-interest/article_ad9a9e79-0e91 -5215-b7a9-d255a2181622.html.

CHAPTER 6: THE LINNAEAN SOCIETY OF NEW ENGLAND VERSUS THE GLOUCESTER SEA SERPENT

64 **close to a mile a minute**: Eyewitness accounts are documented in "Report of a Committee of the Linnaean Society of New England Relative to a Large Marine Animal, Supposed to Be a Serpent, Seen Near Cape Ann, Massachusetts, in August 1817" (Boston: Cummings and Hilliard, 1817).

68 **likely a case of rickets**: William Sturgis Bigelow, *A Memoir of Henry Jacob Bigelow* (Boston: Little, Brown, and Company, 1900), 153–54.

68 **"and at others, 100 feet long"**: David Humphreys, *Letters from the Hon. David Humphreys, F. R. S., to the Right Hon. Sir Joseph Banks, President of the Royal Society, London, Containing Some Account of the Serpent of the Ocean Frequently Seen in Gloucester Bay* (New York: Kirk & Mercein, 1817), 18.

CHAPTER 7: SPECTACULAR TAXONOMY

69 **"it could not have been a salmon"**: Gareth Williams, *A Monstrous Commotion: The Mysteries of Loch Ness* (London: Orion Books, 2015), 13.

71 **"one-eighth of it being above water"**: Ernest Hemingway, *Death in the Afternoon* (New York: Scribner Classics, 1960), 154.

71 **tradition and superstition:** *Proceedings of the Linnean Society of London* (One Hundred and Forty-Seventh Session, 1934–35), 7–12.

72 **"the makeup of most established zoologists":** Constance Whyte, *More Than a Legend* (London: Hamish Hamilton, 1961), xi.

72 **"a hunch to go out and follow it up":** Whyte, *More Than a Legend*, x.

73 **"as mere incompetence on our part":** Quoted in Williams, *A Monstrous Commotion*, 88.

73 **claimed its first victim:** Williams, *A Monstrous Commotion*, 90.

74 **"and all definitely mentally retarded":** Quoted in Williams, *A Monstrous Commotion*, 247.

75 **guided by an open-minded skepticism:** George Gaylord Simpson, "Mammals and Cryptozoology," *Proceedings of the American Philosophical Society* 128, no. 1 (March 30, 1984): 1–2.

75 **"I couldn't care less about science":** Quoted in Joshua Blu Buhs, *Bigfoot: The Life and Times of a Legend* (Chicago: University of Chicago Press, 2009), 135.

76 **"thus capable of mythification":** Bernard Huevalmans, "How Many Animal Species Remain to Be Discovered?," *Cryptozoology* 2 (1983): 5.

76 **"from which the myth developed":** Simpson, "Mammals and Cryptozoology," 3.

77 **they rightly assumed, would confer legitimacy:** Williams, *A Monstrous Commotion*, 235.

77 **"It was, of course, pure hokum":** Henry A. Bauer, *The Enigma of Loch Ness: Making Sense of a Mystery* (Urbana, IL: University of Chicago Press, 1988), 3.

77 **"and always has been":** Quoted in David Martin and Alastair Boyd, *Nessie: The Surgeon's Photograph Exposed* (London: Thorne, 1999), 20.

CHAPTER 8: THE EDGE OF THE MAP

79 **the left side colored black:** Herbert C. Kraft, *The Lenape: Archaeology, History, and Ethnography* (Newark: New Jersey Historical Society, 1986), 169–70.

80 **"who bears the brunt of the blame":** Brian Regal and Frank J. Esposito, *The Secret History of the Jersey Devil: How Quakers, Hucksters, and Benjamin Franklin Created a Monster* (Baltimore: Johns Hopkins University Press, 2018), 5.

80 **"bore little resemblance to a child":** Regal and Esposito, *The Secret History of the Jersey Devil*, 15.

80 **"who has sex with the devil":** Regal and Esposito, *The Secret History of the Jersey Devil*, 5.

81 **"a chupacabra is a dog":** "Mythical Chupacabra Found in Texas?," *Los Angeles Times,* September 1, 2007.

82 **"ears are so big that they hang down to their knees":** C W. R. D. Moseley, trans., *The Travels of Sir John Mandeville* (London: Penguin Books, 1983), 137.

82 **"the weirder things get":** Interview with Karl Steel, February 6, 2018.

85 **"Conveniently to paint them":** "The Mississippi Voyage of Jolliet and Marquette," in *Early Narratives of the Northwest, 1634–1699,* ed. Louis Phelps Kellogg (New York: Scribner and Sons, 1917), 249.

85 **"some Enchantment in their Faces":** Louis Hennepin, *A New Discovery of a Vast Country in America: Extending Above Four Thousand Miles, Between New France and New Mexico* (London: Henry Bonwicke, 1699), 130.

86 **"being covered with a long beard or mane":** Quoted in Mark A. Hall, *Thunderbirds: America's Living Legends of Giant Birds* (New York: Paraview Press, 1984), 50.

86 **"not yet classified by scientist or nature-faker":** Regal and Esposito, *The Secret History of the Jersey Devil,* 75.

87 **"survivors of those prehistoric animals and fossilized remains":** Curtis D. MacDougall, *Hoaxes* (New York: Dover, 1958), 33.

88 **he's eminently adaptable:** Molly Fitzpatrick, "Who's Afraid of the Jersey Devil? How New Jersey Tamed Its Most Terrifying Legend," Thrillist, October 18, 2017, www.thrillist.com/entertainment/nation/new-jersey-devil-urban-legend -history.

88 **and the two creatures flew off:** Hall, *Thunderbirds,* 14–16.

89 **"I don't think the child was picked up":** Hall, *Thunderbirds,* 17.

90 **"more of us would be devils out there":** Emily Eppig, "The Hunt for the Jersey Devil: An Interview with Laura Leuter of the Devil Hunters," *Paranormal Society,* www.theparanormalsociety.org/library/articles/cryptozoology/789-the -hunt-for-the-jersey-devil.

CHAPTER 9: THE HOME INVASION

91 **"perfectly round eyes":** "Fabled 'Bigfoot' Reported Seen; Chased Two Men, Woman into House," *Madera Tribune,* February 15, 1962, 2.

92 **"mountain goblin" or "snow goblin":** Bacil F. Kirtley, "Notes upon a Central Asian Legend," *Folklore* 74, no. 1 (Spring 1963): 318–20.

93 **ZZ-Top-esque beards:** See Sherry C. M. Lindquist and Asa Simon Mittman, *Medieval Monsters: Terrors, Aliens, Wonders* (New York: Morgan Library & Museum, 2018), 118.

93 **felt similarly about Nessie:** Richard J. Greenwell and James E. King, "Attitudes of Physical Anthropologists Toward Reports of Bigfoot and Nessie," *Current Anthropology* 22, no. 1 (February 1981).

94 **"the Abominable Snowman":** Joshua Blu Buhs, *Bigfoot: The Life and Times of a Legend* (Chicago: University of Chicago Press, 2009), 13.

94 **"of an atom bomb":** Buhs, *Bigfoot*, 13.

95 **"They are incompatible with holiness and blessing":** Mary Douglas, *Purity and Danger: An Analysis of the Concepts of Pollution and Taboo* (London: Routledge, 1995), 96.

CHAPTER 10: LOST IN TRANSLATIONS

96 **as "killing dragons":** see Peter H. Hansen, *The Summits of Modern Man: Mountaineering After the Enlightenment* (Cambridge: Harvard University Press, 2013), 7.

97 **"as in the case of other four-footed animals":** Henry Balfour, H. W. Tilman, J. B. Auden, Francis Younghusband, and K. Mason, "The Shaksgam Expedition, 1937: Discussion," *Geographical Journal* 91, no. 4 (April 1938): 337.

98 **"over snow-covered glaciers with naked feet":** Eric Shipton, *That Untravelled World: An Autobiography* (Seattle: Mountaineers Books, 2015), 111.

98 **"bear or Yeti, monkey or man":** Gardner Soule, "Everest's Conqueror Tracks Abominable Snowman," *Popular Science*, September 1960, 258.

99 **together to further this goal:** Loren Coleman, *Tom Slick: True Life Encounters in Cryptozoology* (Fresno, CA: Craven Street Books, 2002).

100 **"Today the revolutionaries need encouragement":** Coleman, *Tom Slick*, 39–40.

100 **"The fingers were hooked and curled":** "Tracing the Origins of a 'Yeti's Finger,'" BBC, December 27, 2011, www.bbc.com/news/science-environment -16264752.

101 **"I never asked him where he got it from":** "Tracing the Origins of a 'Yeti's Finger.'"

101 **back to England unnoticed:** "Tracing the Origins of a 'Yeti's Finger.'"

102 **supernatural license for the theft:** Patrick J. Geary, *Furta Sacra: Thefts of Relics in the Central Middle Ages* (Princeton: Princeton University Press, 1990).

102 **"find the origins of human behavior":** Quoted in Brian Regal, *Searching for Sasquatch: Crackpots, Eggheads, and Cryptozoology* (New York: Palgrave Macmillan, 2011), 39.

103 **his chance to hunt the Yeti:** Regal, *Searching for Sasquatch*, 39–41.

103 **in Slick's papers:** Catherine Nixon Cooke, *Tom Slick: Mystery Hunter* (New York: Paraview, 2000).

104 "U.S. support of Nepal sovereignty": Jessie Kratz, "On Exhibit: The 'Yeti Memo,'" *National Archives Pieces of History*, September 28, 2017, prologue .blogs.archives.gov/2017/09/28/on-exhibit-the-yeti-memo/.

104 "Soviet Sees Espionage in U.S. Snowman Hunt": "Soviet Sees Espionage in U.S. Snowman Hunt," *New York Times*, April 27, 1957, 8.

104 somewhere on the mountain: Robert Beckhusen, "Inside the CIA Mission to Haul Plutonium Up the Himalayas," *Wired*, April 29, 2013, www.wired.com /2013/04/cia-himalayan-spies/.

CHAPTER 11: MEN, AND WILD MEN

106 the legend began to grow: Andrew Genzoli, "Giant Footprints Puzzle Residents Along Trinity River," *Humboldt Times*, October 5, 1958.

107 "the fear was made to seem absurd, too": Joshua Blu Buhs, *Bigfoot: The Life and Times of a Legend* (Chicago: University of Chicago Press, 2009), 70–71.

107 "so the Indians left them alone": Marian T. Place, *On the Track of Bigfoot* (New York: Dodd Mead, 1974), 67–68.

107 masculinity itself was undergoing a crisis: Buhs, *Bigfoot*, 95–96.

109 a proper name: John W. Burns, "Introducing B.C.'s Hairy Giants," *MacLean's*, April 1, 1929, 9.

110 "does get annoying.": Interview with Snxakila (Clyde Tallio), August 14, 2019.

111 "difficult to confirm his story": Henry S. Sharp, *The Transformation of Bigfoot: Maleness, Power, and Belief Among the Chipewyan* (Washington, DC: Smithsonian Institution Press, 1988).

112 "One of these ideas was Bigfoot or Sasquatch": Sharp, *The Transformation of Bigfoot*, 94–95.

112 "I've never seen one": Sharp, *The Transformation of Bigfoot*, 97.

CHAPTER 12: BELIEVING IS SEEING

114 face-to-face with a Wild Man: Warren Smith, "America's Terrifying Woodland Monster-men," *Saga Magazine*, July 1969, reprinted at www.bigfootencounters .com/articles/saga1969.htm.

117 "it started to look like an impossibility": Joshua Blu Buhs, *Bigfoot: The Life and Times of a Legend* (Chicago: University of Chicago Press, 2009), 141.

118 "argument about the nature of film itself": Don DeLillo, *Underworld* (New York: Scribner, 1997), 495–96.

118 "to admit such a creature really lives": Quoted in Buhs, *Bigfoot*, 140.

118 he told *Outside* magazine in 2016, "ruined me": Leah Sottile, "The Man Who Created Bigfoot," *Outside*, July 5, 2016, www.outsideonline.com/2095096/man-who -created-bigfoot.

118 "Hoaxes prove that believing in seeing": Kevin Young, *Bunk: The Rise of Hoaxes, Humbug, Plagiarists, Phonies, Post-Facts, and Fake News* (Minneapolis, MN: Graywolf, 2017), 58.

118 "that add up to a ritual": Young, *Bunk*, 96.

119 described it as "negro black": Quoted in *Bigfoot*, 52.

119 among white society: John P. Jackson, "'In Ways Unacademical': The Reception of Carleton S. Coon's 'The Origin of Races,'" *Journal of the History of Biology* 34, no. 2 (Summer 2001).

120 "conspiracy of Mafia-like ramifications": John Napier, *Bigfoot: The Yeti and Sasquatch in Myth and Reality* (New York: E. P. Dutton, 1973), 117.

120 "on imaginative speculation": Napier, *Bigfoot*, 132–33.

121 "is part of human culture": Napier, *Bigfoot*, 17.

121 "the more remote and unapproachable they are, the better": Napier, *Bigfoot*, 193.

PART III: IN THESE PERILOUS TIMES

FIELD NOTES: THE WHITE MOUNTAINS, NEW HAMPSHIRE

127 It was 5:00 A.M.: John G. Fuller, *The Interrupted Journey: Two Lost Hours "Aboard a Flying Saucer"* (New York: Dial Press, 1966).

127 "barren hostility of the wooden area": Fuller, *The Interrupted Journey*, 83.

127 "What took you so long to get home": Fuller, *The Interrupted Journey*, 44.

128 "Not lights, just one huge light": Fuller, *The Interrupted Journey*, 88.

128 "*What do they want*": Fuller, *The Interrupted Journey*, 89.

CHAPTER 13: FRAGMENTS

131 disappearing into a thundercloud: Curtis Peebles, *Watch the Skies: A Chronicle of the Flying Saucer Myth* (Washington, DC: Smithsonian Institution Press, 1994), 13.

132 "In fact, I had never seen him before": Kenneth Arnold, "The Mystery of the Flying Disks," *Fate* 1. no. 1 (1946), accessed at https://www.saturdaynightuforia .com/html/articles/articlehtml/saucsum2.html.

133 "with a gun in our possession": Kenneth Arnold and Ray Palmer, *The Coming of the Saucers: A Documentary Report on Sky Objects That Have Mystified the World* (N.p.: Global Grey, 2018), 39.

CHAPTER 14: AN UNIMPEACHABLE WITNESS

135 **unknown to the majority of the American public:** Ross Coen, *Fu-Go: The Curious History of Japan's Balloon Bomb Attack on America* (Lincoln: University of Nebraska Press, 2014).

135 **higher and higher into the air:** Theresa L. Kraus, "The CAA Helps America Prepare for World War II," Federal Aviation Administration, www.faa.gov /about/history/milestones/media/The_CAA_Helps_America_Prepare_for _World_WarII.pdf.

135 **the more they found there:** On Foo Fighters, see, for example, "Balls of Fire Stalk U.S. Fighters in Night Assaults Over Germany," *New York Times,* January 2, 1945, 1.

136 **"like saucers skipped over water":** Robert E. Bartholomew, "From Airships to Flying Saucers: Oregon's Place in the Evolution of UFO Lore," *Oregon Historical Quarterly* 101, no. 2 (Summer 2000): 201.

136 **"'I must believe my eyes'":** Bartholomew, "From Airships to Flying Saucers," 201.

136 **for use in local news stories:** Bartholomew, "From Airships to Flying Saucers," 203.

136 **news could be "objective":** See Richard A. Schwarzlose, *The Nation's Newsbrokers, Volume 1: The Formative Years: From Pretelegraph to 1865* (Evanston, IL: Northwestern University Press, 1989), 181.

137 **"the prestige of a newspaper printing them":** Curtis D. MacDougall, *Hoaxes* (New York: Dover, 1958), 4.

137 **"a guess as to what they were":** Bartholomew, "From Airships to Flying Saucers," 203.

CHAPTER 15: WELDING

139 **run over by a milk truck:** Fred Nadis, *The Man from Mars: Ray Palmer's Amazing Pulp Journey* (New York: Jeremy P. Tarcher/Penguin, 2013), 7.

140 **"Be a follower":** Quoted in Richard Toronto, *War Over Lemuria: Richard Shaver, Ray Palmer and the Strangest Chapter of 1940s Science Fiction* (Jefferson, NC: McFarland & Company, Inc., 2013), 145.

141 **"every word of it was true":** John A. Keel, "The Man Who Invented Flying Saucers," in *Searching for the String: Selected Writings of John A. Keel* (Point Pleasant, WV: New Saucerian Books, 2014), 119.

141 **"a fly buzzing by your ear":** Toronto, *War Over Lemuria*, 89.

142 **"definite proof of the Atlantean legend":** Quoted in Nadis, *The Man from Mars*, 58.

142 **"fear of public ridicule":** Quoted in Nadis, *The Man from Mars*, 119.

144 would be "racial memory": Quoted in Nadis, *The Man from Mars*, 70.

145 "you just don't think the way we do": Quoted in Nadis, *The Man from Mars*, 152.

145 "For heaven's sake, drop the whole thing": Keel, "The Man Who Invented Flying Saucers," 121.

CHAPTER 16: A JITTERY AGE

147 sketchy on what exactly it was: Curtis Peebles, *Watch the Skies: A Chronicle of the Flying Saucer Myth* (Washington, DC: Smithsonian Institution Press, 1994), 10–11.

147 "as large as man-made aircraft": Peebles, *Watch the Skies*, 15.

148 "concern to the national security": Peebles, *Watch the Skies*, 16.

148 "he found the Air Force had already been there": Peebles, *Watch the Skies*, 17.

148 "from a metallic object": Peebles, *Watch the Skies*, 19.

148 "close in for a better look": Peebles, *Watch the Skies*.

149 other readily explainable phenomena: George Gallup, "Nine Out of Ten Heard of Flying Saucers," Public Opinion News Service, August 15, 1947.

149 seen the flying craft: Peebles, *Watch the Skies*, 21.

150 weren't necessarily shaped like disks: Edward J. Ruppelt, *The Report on Unidentified Flying Objects: The Original 1956 Edition* (New York: Cosimo Books, 2011), 1.

150 "the strict brush-off attitude to the UFO problem": J. Allen Hynek, *The UFO Experience: A Scientific Inquiry* (New York: Marlowe & Company, 1998), 174.

150 infamous 1835 moon hoax: "A Rash of Flying Discs Breaks Out Over the U.S.," *Life,* July 21, 1947, 14–16.

151 a "jittery age": Sidney Shalett, "What You Can Believe About Flying Saucers," *Saturday Evening Post*, May 7, 1949, 185.

151 "for the secret of the disks": Donald Keyhoe, *The Flying Saucers Are Real* (New York: Fawcett Publications, 1950), 6.

151 "wholly nonexistent 'flying saucers'": Bob Considine, "The Disgraceful Flying Saucer Hoax!," *Cosmopolitan*, January 1951, 33.

153 "revision of current scientific concepts": Peebles, *Watch the Skies*, 84.

153 "protective organs of the body politic": Peebles, *Watch the Skies*, 84.

155 "take the place of news": "They Are Balloons," *New York Times,* February 14, 1951, 28.

CHAPTER 17: THE CALL FROM CLARION

157 **"in small flat pleats":** Truman Bethurum, *Aboard a Flying Saucer* (Los Angeles: DeVorss & Company, 1954), 40.

157 **"they put them in chains":** Bethurum, *Aboard a Flying Saucer*, 123–24.

158 **"you get Christianity and Islam":** Interview with Ken Layne, March 18, 2018.

158 HAVE WE VISITORS FROM OUTER SPACE?: H. B. Darrach and Robert Ginna, "Have We Visitors from Outer Space?," *Life*, April 7, 1952.

159 *Flying Saucers Have Landed:* Desmond Leslie and George Adamski, *Flying Saucers Have Landed* (New York: British Book Centre, 1953).

160 **to get 113,205 votes:** Adam Gorightly and Greg Bishop, *"A" Is for Adamski: The Golden Age of the UFO Contactees* (N.p.: Gorightly Press, 2018), 115.

160 **"with a long dress":** Gorightly and Bishop, *"A" Is for Adamski*, 303.

161 **counted more than eleven thousand attendees:** Curtis Peebles, *Watch the Skies: A Chronicle of the Flying Saucer Myth* (Washington, DC: Smithsonian Institution Press, 1994), 157.

161 **these ape women, creating humanity:** Calvin C. Girvin, *The Night Has a Thousand Saucers* (Clarksburg, WV: Saucerian Press, 1967).

162 **Theosophically influenced racist worldviews:** Scott Beekman, *William Dudley Pelley: A Life in Right-Wing Extremism and the Occult* (Syracuse, NY: Syracuse University Press, 2005).

163 **the contemporary incarnation of the historical Jesus:** Leon Festinger, Henry W. Riecken, and Stanley Schachter, *When Prophecy Fails: A Social and Psychological Study of a Modern Group That Predicted the Destruction of the World* (New York: Harper Torchbooks, 1956), 38.

164 **"something within you that returned to life":** Festinger, Riecken, and Schachter, *When Prophecy Fails*, 136.

164 **"And not a plan has gone astray":** Festinger, Riecken, and Schachter, *When Prophecy Fails*, 153.

165 **"And there isn't any other truth":** Festinger, Riecken, and Schachter, *When Prophecy Fails*, 170.

165 **perpetually out of reach:** Michael Barkun, *A Culture of Conspiracy: Apocalyptic Visions in Contemporary America* (Berkeley: University of California Press, 2003), 157.

CHAPTER 18: GRAY DAYS

166 **"and the world would listen":** Quoted in John F. Szwed, *Space Is the Place: The Lives and Times of Sun Ra* (Edinburgh: Mojo Books, 2000), 30.

166 **"pantheon of contactees"**: Adam Gorightly and Greg Bishop's *"A" Is for Adamski* is one of the few sources I've found that includes Sun Ra among the usual roster of contactees.

167 **and the postwar California occultism of Adamski**: Szwed, *Space Is the Place*, 31.

167 **alien visitation narratives**: Christopher F. Roth, "Ufology as Anthropology: Race, Extraterrestrials, and the Occult," in Deborah Battaglia, *E.T. Culture: Anthropology in Outerspaces* (Durham, NC: Duke University Press, 2005).

168 **"He's a Nazi"**: John G. Fuller, *The Interrupted Journey: Two Lost Hours "Aboard a Flying Saucer"* (New York: Dial Press, 1966), 90.

168 **"But not like a Chinese"**: Fuller, *The Interrupted Journey*, 91.

168 **"the men I'm trying to describe"**: Fuller, *The Interrupted Journey*, 262.

169 **"their lips were of a bluish tint"**: Fuller, *The Interrupted Journey*, 297.

169 **"blacks as criminal, evil, and sexually aggressive"**: Martin S Kottmeyer, "Why Are the Grays Gray?," *MUFON UFO Journal*, no. 319 (November 1994), 9.

169 **"I feel I was abducted"**: Fuller, *The Interrupted Journey*, 252.

170 **"Be careful kid, or they'll kill you"**: Richard A. Colla, *The UFO Incident*, NBC, October 20, 1975.

170 **"Most Extraordinary Encounter with a UFO"**: Curtis Peebles, *Watch the Skies: A Chronicle of the Flying Saucer Myth* (Washington, DC: Smithsonian Institution Press, 1994), 231.

171 **getting out of a contract**: Peebles, *Watch the Skies*, 232.

171 **her reproductive organs**: Raymond E. Fowler, *The Andreasson Affair: The True Story of a Close Encounter of the Fourth Kind* (Pompton Plains, NJ: Career Press, 2015).

172 **"as frightened as a baby"**: Whitley Strieber, *Communion* (New York: Avon Books, 1987), 101.

CHAPTER 19: HOST-PLANET REJECTION SYNDROME

174 **"like kids in snowsuits," he told Hopkins**: Budd Hopkins, "Sane Citizen Sees UFO in New Jersey," *Village Voice*, March 1, 1976, 12.

176 **"time-consuming process of hypnotic regression"**: Budd Hopkins, *Missing Time: A Documented Study of UFO Abductions* (New York: Richard Marek Publishers, 1981), 52.

177 **so they'd appear more "childlike"**: Ray Morton, *Close Encounters of the Third Kind: The Making of Stephen Spielberg's Classic Film* (New York: Applause Theatre and Cinema Books, 2007), 144.

177 **a global reveal of the truth of aliens**: John Lear, "The UFO Coverup," August 25, 1988, archived at www.sacred-texts.com/ufo/coverup.htm.

178 he dubbed "the Announcement": Stephen C Finley, "The Meaning of 'Mother' in Louis Farrakhan's 'Mother Wheel': Race, Gender, and Sexuality in the Cosmology of the Nation of Islam's UFO," *Journal of the American Academy of Religion* 80, no. 2 (June 2012).

179 "you got the information from me on the Wheel": Quoted in Finley, "The Meaning of 'Mother' in Louis Farrakhan's 'Mother Wheel,'" 445.

180 "feeling tired or irritable": Don Crosbie Donderi, *UFOs, ETs, and Alien Abductions: A Scientist Looks at the Evidence* (Charlottesville, VA: Hampton Roads, 2013), 127.

180 "'through the mill'": David Michael Jacobs, *Alien Encounters: Firsthand Accounts of UFO Abductions* (New York: Simon & Schuster, 1992), 212–13.

180 "tired and weak during the day": Alien Abduction Help Forum, alienabductionhelp.com/phpBB3/viewtopic.php?f=3&t=289&view=next.

181 "You have to fight to get": Joseph Dumit, "'Come on, people . . . we *are* the aliens. We seem to be suffering from Host-Planet Rejection Syndrome': Liminal Illnesses, Structural Damnation, and Social Creativity," in Deborah Battaglia, *E.T. Culture: Anthropology in Outerspaces* (Durham, NC: Duke University Press, 2005), 219.

181 "arguing with my wife": Kim Fortun, "Lone Gunmen: Legacies of the Gulf War, Illness, and Unseen Enemies," in *Paranoia Within Reason: A Casebook on Conspiracy as Explanation*, ed. George E. Marcus (Chicago: University of Chicago Press, 1999), 373.

182 "citizens of that other place": Susan Sontag, *Illness as Metaphor* and *AIDS and Its Metaphors* (New York: Picador USA, 1989), 3.

182 "host-planet rejection syndrome": Dumit, "'Come on, people . . . we *are* the aliens,'" 231.

PART IV: THE WORLD TURNED SOUR

FIELD NOTES: RACHEL, NEVADA

185 "assembled at Guam to assault Japan": John McPhee, *Basin and Range* (New York: Farrar, Straus and Giroux, 1982), 45.

186 "another look at Roswell.": Charles Berlitz and William L. Moore, *The Roswell Incident: The Most Important UFO Encounter of Our Century* (New York: MJF Books, 1980).

CHAPTER 20: THE DISINFORMATION GAME

189 Friedman, the evening's headliner: The events of that day are recounted in, among other places, Greg Bishop, *Project Beta: The Story of Paul Bennewitz, National Security, and the Creation of a Modern UFO Myth* (New York: Paraview,

2005), and Mark Pilkington, *Mirage Men: A Journey in Disinformation, Paranoia and UFOs* (London: Constable & Robinson, 2010).

192 **"but . . . but they're mad"**: Bishop, *Project Beta*, 18.

192 **"but it wasn't discussable"**: Bishop, *Project Beta*, 24.

192 **"then a quick good-bye"**: Bishop, *Project Beta*, 25.

193 **"Do not ground the auto"**: Bishop, *Project Beta*, 28.

194 **"serious security problem"**: Bishop, *Project Beta*, 33.

196 **"as he could possibly afford"**: Quoted in Aaron John Gulyas, *Conspiracy Theories: The Roots, Themes and Propagation of Paranoid Political and Cultural Narratives* (Jefferson, NC: McFarland & Company, 2016), 87.

196 **"under psychiatric care"**: Quoted in Jim Keith, *Mind Control and UFOs: Casebook on Alternative 3* (Kempton: Adventures Unlimited Press, 2005), 173.

197 **"their poisonous seeds will be done by others"**: Keith, *Mind Control and UFOs*.

197 **"is inflected by it afterward"**: Interview with Jason Brown, April 24, 2018.

197 **"as far as you want to go"**: Interview with Jason Brown, April 24, 2018.

CHAPTER 21: THE PILGRIM'S ROAD

199 **"things of alien origin flying in Nevada"**: George Knapp, *KLAS Evening News*, November 11, 1989, transcript archived at www.sacred-texts.com/ufo /area51.htm.

199 **"other than Earth"**: Knapp, *KLAS Evening News*.

200 **"Bible-thumping and conspiracy mongering"**: Dennis Stacy, "The Ultimate UFO Seminar," *MUFON UFO Journal*, June 1993, www.ufomind.com/area51 /articles/1993/mufon_9306/.

201 **"exactly what his problem is"**: "Owner Refuses to Leave Ranch on Missile Range," *New York Times,* October 15, 1982, A12.

202 **"the grass was knee high"**: "Owner Refuses to Leave Ranch on Missile Range."

202 **"remote and uninhabited"**: Kelsey D. Atherton, "Survivors of America's First Atomic Bomb Test Want Their Place in History," *Popular Science*, May 1, 2017, www.popsci.com/survivors-americas-first-atomic-test-want-their-place-in -history.

202 **"all TWA flights to the Coast stopped there"**: Leslie M. Groves, *Now It Can Be Told: The Story of the Manhattan Project* (Da Capo Press, 1983), 65.

203 **"bringing cancer, mutation, or death"**: Joseph Masco, *The Nuclear Borderlands: The Manhattan Project in Post–Cold War New Mexico* (Princeton: Princeton University Press, 2006), 28.

204 can no longer legally access it: Tyler Rogoway, "The Unlikely Struggle of the Family Whose Neighbor Is Area 51," *Jalopnik*, November 9, 2015, foxtrotalpha .jalopnik.com/the-unlikely-struggle-of-the-family-whose-neighbor-is -a-1741346156.

205 "a certain boundary into the installation": Lou Michel and Dan Herberck: *Timothy McVeigh and the Tragedy at Oklahoma City* (New York: Avon Books, 2002), 184.

205 *"No rent-a-cop can tell me that":* Michel and Herberck, *American Terrorist*, 185.

205 "in one fell swoop": Michel and Herberck, *American Terrorist*, 186.

CHAPTER 22: ALIENS ON THE LAND

207 "reports of cattle mutilations": Greg Valdez, *Dulce Base: The Truth and Evidence from the Case Files of Gabe Valdez* (Albuquerque, NM: Levi-Cash Publishing, 2013).

207 "what you might find when you arrived": Valdez, *Dulce Base*, 2

207 a strong "medicinal" smell: Blanche Hardin, "The Legend of Snippy Hollow," *Life*, March 22, 1968, R2.

208 "with a glow surrounding it": Michael J. Goleman, "Wave of Mutilation: The Cattle Mutilation Phenomenon of the 1970s," *Agricultural History* 85, no. 3 (Summer 2011): 402.

208 "a plain white spot on the side": Goleman, "Wave of Mutilation," 403.

209 "and other western states,": Goleman, "Wave of Mutilation," 399.

209 "before someone gets hurt": Goleman, "Wave of Mutilation," 405.

210 while grain continued to rise: Goleman, "Wave of Mutilation," 402.

211 a standard cattle mutilation: Goleman, "Wave of Mutilation," 410.

211 Pacific Northwest in 1954: Alan J. Stein, "Windshield Pitting Incidents in Washington Reach Fever Pitch on April 15, 1954," HistoryLink.org, January 1, 2003, www.historylink.org/File/5136.

212 "bureaucratically crippled in thought": Daniel Kagan and Ian Summers, *Mute Evidence* (Toronto: Bantam Books, 1984), 409.

213 "They know more about it than we do": David A. Neiwert, *In God's Country: The Patriot Movement and the Pacific Northwest* (Pullman: Washington State University Press, 1999), 84.

214 "but no one knows what": Susan Lepselter, *The Resonance of Unseen Things: Poetics, Power, Captivity, and UFOs in the American Uncanny* (Ann Arbor: University of Michigan Press, 2016), 43.

214 people actually lived here—Sioux, maybe: Lepselter, *The Resonance of Unseen Things*, 108.

214 **"absolute liberty coexisted with the absolute":** Philip J. Deloria, *Playing Indian* (New Haven: Yale University Press, 1998), 185.

215 **"enjoying absolute, anarchic freedom":** Deloria, *Playing Indian*, 186.

215 *you've been abducted by aliens:* Lepselter, *The Resonance of Unseen Things*, 78.

CHAPTER 23: A HORSEMAN

216 **inside knowledge about the attacks:** Chapman University, "Survey on American Fears 2018," www.chapman.edu/wilkinson/research-centers/babbie-center/_files /fear-2018/fear-V-methodology-report-ssrs.pdf.

217 **9/11, but with aliens:** For a full biography of Cooper's life, see Mark Jacobson, *Pale Horse Rider: William Cooper, the Rise of Conspiracy, and the Fall of Trust in America* (New York: Blue Rider Press, 2018).

217 **"almost every UFOlogist in the field":** Don Ecker, "Who Is Milton William Cooper?," World of the Strange, www.worldofthestrange.com/index.html?doc _whomiltonwilliamcooper.htm.

217 **"and get violent":** Ecker, "Who Is Milton William Cooper?"

218 **"It will fulfill prophecy":** Milton William Cooper, *Behold a Pale Horse* (Flagstaff, AZ: Light Technology Press, 1991), 72.

219 **"who's fucking you":** Quoted in Jacobson, *Pale Horse Rider*, 19.

219 **"this scenario as being probable":** Cooper, *Behold a Pale Horse*, 234.

220 **"all those CAPITAL LETTERS":** Jacobson, *Pale Horse Rider*, 98.

221 **"New World Order conspiracy into UFO beliefs":** Michael Barkun, *A Culture of Conspiracy: Apocalyptic Visions in Contemporary America* (Berkeley: University of California Press, 2003), 178.

222 **"another Ruby Ridge":** Mark Shaffer, "McVeigh Listened to Militia-Inspired Arizona Broadcaster," *Arizona Republic,* May 6, 2001, archived at culteducation .com/group/1051-militias-or-private-armies-and-extremist-groups/13497 -mcveigh-listened-to-militia-inspired-arizona-broadcaster.html.

CHAPTER 24: THE SUBURBAN UNCANNY

223 **for use as a "processing" building:** *America Under Siege*, video, directed by Linda Thompson (American Justice Federation, 1994).

224 **"violent attacks upon the social order":** "US Department of the Army Civil Disturbance Plan 'GARDEN PLOT,'" Department of the Army, September 10, 1968, www.governmentattic.org/2docs/DA-CivilDisturbPlanGardenPlot_1968 .pdf.

225 **"local overpricing practices":** "US Department of the Army Civil Disturbance Plan 'GARDEN PLOT.'"

225 **currently had only three hundred prisoners:** William R. Pabst, *Concentration Camp Plans for U.S. Citizens*, 9.

226 **"ignorance of their true purpose":** Michael Barkun, *A Culture of Conspiracy: Apocalyptic Visions in Contemporary America* (Berkeley: University of California Press, 2003), 74.

226 **"decide to declare Martial law":** Quoted in Kenneth S. Stern, *A Force Upon the Plain: The American Militia Movement and the Politics of Hate* (Norman: University of Oklahoma Press, 1997), 73.

227 **an abuse of power:** Giorgio Agamben, *State of Exception*, trans. Kevin Attell (Chicago: University of Chicago Press, 2005).

229 **"now THAT is worrisome":** ThisSheetB4RealYo, "Closed Walmart FEMA camp San Jose Sept 2017 footage," September 20, 2017, www.youtube.com /watch?v=USTQE3PaIC4&list=PL6nsQ805w_9v-LEUtxz39mO3yiYbnjTSs &index=3&t=114s.

230 **"their appearance or their vacancy":** Julia Christensen, *Big Box Reuse* (Cambridge: MIT Press, 2008), 118.

PART V: THE POSTAPOCALYPTIC HANGOVER

CHAPTER 25: THE COMFORTS OF LEMURIA

233 **"The End of UFOs":** Mark Jacobson, "The End of UFOs," *New York Magazine*, August 9, 2014, nymag.com/intelligencer/2014/08/end-of-ufos.html.

237 **"mountains across the world":** "Aliens and Mysterious Mountains," *Ancient Aliens*, History Channel, December 13, 2013.

237 **"local Native American" beliefs:** "Aliens and Mysterious Mountains."

238 **Make America Great Again:** Interview with David S. Anderson, August 21, 2018.

239 **"how to make flexible watches":** John Napier, *Bigfoot: The Yeti and Sasquatch in Myth and Reality* (New York: E. P. Dutton, 1973), 28.

239 **"searching for extraterrestrial life":** N.a. *The Search for Alien Life: Who Shaped Our World?* (New York: Time, Inc. Books, 2018), 47.

239 **"The real truth is we don't know":** Steven Kurutz, "Suspicious Minds: Mingling with Wariness and Wonder at a Conference Devoted to 'Ancient Aliens,'" *New York Times*, July 21, 2018, ST1.

240 **legal sovereignty over him:** Ashley Powers, "How Sovereign Citizens Helped Swindle $1 Billion from the Government They Disavow," *New York Times*, March 29, 2019, BU1.

241 **the history of Sclater's Lemuria:** William DeLong, "Lemuria: The Fabled Lost Continent That Turned Out to Be Real—Almost," AllThatsInteresting.com, April 15, 2018, allthatsinteresting.com/lemuria-continent.

CHAPTER 26: UNDER THE SIGN OF THE COELACANTH

244 **"lost their chance at scientific acclaim":** Wayne Soini, *Gloucester's Sea Serpent* (Charleston, SC: The History Press, 2010), 13.

248 **Native American accounts he'd come across:** David Sands, "Michigan Dogman, Mysterious Upright Canine Creature, Haunts State's Backwoods," *Huffington Post*, October 26, 2012, www.huffpost.com/entry/michigan-dogman-upright -canine_n_2019442.

249 **"it sounded more like 'Yyyyhhh'":** "Broome County, NY Encounter," dogmanencounters.com/broome-county-ny-encounter/.

249 **"basically what Dogman seems to be":** Interview with Blake Smith, April 18, 2019.

250 **"seems to me singularly harmless":** Henry A. Bauer, *The Enigma of Loch Ness: Making Sense of a Mystery* (Urbana, IL: University of Chicago Press, 1988), 146.

251 **"it causes AIDS":** Quoted in Seth C. Kalichman, *Denying AIDS: Conspiracy Theories, Pseudoscience, and Human Tragedy* (New York: Copernicus Books, 2009), 71.

251 **"reach a reasonable judgment":** Bauer, *The Enigma of Loch Ness*, 28.

251 **"not incontrovertibly related":** Bauer, *The Enigma of Loch Ness*, 43.

CHAPTER 27: ELEGIES

256 **"people like that are easy to fool":** *Mirage Men*, directed by John Lundberg, Ronald Denning, and Kypros Kyprianou (Perception Management Productions, June 13, 2013).

256 **currently living among us:** Ragnar Larsen, "6 Alien Species Currently Fighting for Control Over Earth," www.locklip.com/the-6-alien-species-currently -fighting-for-control-over-earth. For a mirror site, see: https://www.lipstickalley .com/threads/the-6-alien-species-currently-fighting-for-control-over -earth.892724.

CHAPTER 28: CREATIVE MYTHOLOGY

261 **than VHS scan lines:** Allan J. Hynek, Philip J. Imbrogno, and Bob Pratt, *Night Siege: The Hudson Valley UFO Sightings* (New York: Ballantine Books, 1987).

261 **"I'm sure of that":** Hynek, Imbrogno, and Pratt, *Night Siege*, 22.

261 **"becoming local history":** Hynek, Imbrogno, and Pratt, *Night Siege*, 13.

262 **something new and disturbing:** Ellen Crystall, *Silent Invasion: The Courageous True Story of One Woman's Encounters with Aliens* (New York: St. Martin's Press, 1986).

CHAPTER 29: A PHILOSOPHY OF NON-FACTS

267 his chase to investigate: Curtis Peebles, *Watch the Skies: A Chronicle of the Flying Saucer Myth* (Washington, DC: Smithsonian Institution Press, 1994), 148–53.

271 "a philosophy of non-facts": Jacques Vallee, *Passport to Magonia: From Folklore to Flying Saucers* (Brisbane: Daily Grail Publishing, 2014), 11.

271 "dwarfish races haunting the land": Vallee, *Passport to Magonia*, 57.

271 "effect on humans are constant": Vallee, *Passport to Magonia*, 152.

272 "confusing appearance as reality": Vallee, *Passport to Magonia*, 152.

272 "into which they are projected": Vallee, *Passport to Magonia*, 152.

272 "the gondola-heads, or whatever": Interview with Ken Layne, March 18, 2018.

274 "pretty weirded out": Helene Cooper, Ralph Blumenthal, and Leslie Kean, "2 Navy Airmen and an Object That 'Accelerated Like Nothing I've Ever Seen,'" *New York Times,* December 17, 2017, A27.

274 "in my congressional service": Helene Cooper, Ralph Blumenthal, and Leslie Kean, "Glowing Auras and 'Black Money': The Pentagon's Mysterious U.F.O. Program," *New York Times,* December 16, 2017, A1.